China and the WTO

Global Trade Law Series

VOLUME 23

KLUWER LAW INTERNATIONAL

China and the WTO

A Long March towards the Rule of Law

Esther Lam

Wolters Kluwer
Law & Business

AUSTIN BOSTON CHICAGO NEW YORK THE NETHERLANDS

Published by:
Kluwer Law International
PO Box 316
2400 AH Alphen aan den Rijn
The Netherlands
Website: www.kluwerlaw.com

Sold and distributed in North, Central and South America by:
Aspen Publishers, Inc.
7201 McKinney Circle
Frederick, MD 21704
United States of America
Email: customer.service@aspenpublishers.com

Sold and distributed in all other countries by:
Turpin Distribution Services Ltd.
Stratton Business Park
Pegasus Drive, Biggleswade
Bedfordshire SG18 8TQ
United Kingdom
Email: kluwerlaw@turpin-distribution.com

Printed on acid-free paper.

ISBN 978-90-411-3144-7

Printed in Great Britain.

Dedicated to my dear grandma Poi Poi *(1915–2008)*

Table of Contents

List of Abbreviations

Administrative Licensing Law, PRC	ALL
Asian Development Bank	ADB
Association of South East Asian Nations	ASEAN
Bureau of Fair Trade, PRC	BOFT
Bureau of National Affairs	BNA
Central Commission for Discipline Inspection, CPC	CCDI
Communist Party of China	CPC
Convention against Torture, and Other Forms of Cruel, Inhuman and Degrading and Treatment	CAT
Convention on the Rights of the Child	CRC
Department of Commerce, the United States	DOC
Foreign Direct Investment	FDI
Foreign Trade Law, PRC	FTL
General Agreement on Tariffs and Trade	GATT
Gross Domestic Product	GDP
International Covenant on Civil and Political Rights	ICCPR
International Covenant on Economic, Social and Cultural Rights	ICESCR
International Convention on the Elimination of All Forms of Racial Discrimination	ICERD
International Monetary Fund	IMF
International Trade Commission, the United States	ITC
Investigation Bureau for Industry Injury, PRC	IBII
Kuomintang (Nationalist Party)	KMT
Least-Developed Country	LDC
Ministry of Commerce, PRC	MOFCOM
Ministry of Foreign Trade and Economic Cooperation, PRC	MOFTEC
Most-Favoured-Nation	MFN

Multi-fibre Arrangement	MFA
National Development and Reform Commission, PRC	NDRC
National People's Congress, PRC	NPC
People's Liberation Army, PRC	PLA
People's Republic of China	PRC
Renminbi (Chinese Yuan)	CNY
Republic of China	ROC
Special Economic Zones	SEZs
Standing Committee of the Communist Party of China	SCCPC
Standing Committee of the National People's Congress, PRC	NPCSC
State Development and Planning Commission, PRC	SDPC
State Economic and Trade Commission, PRC	SETC
State-Owned Enterprises	SOEs
Supreme People's Court	SPC
Supreme People's Procuratorate	SPP
Trade Policy Review Mechanism	TPRM
Transitional Review Mechanism	TRM
Universal Declaration of Human Rights	UDHR
United Nations Conference on Trade and Development	UNCTAD
US Trade Representative	USTR
World Trade Organization	WTO
WTO Agreement on Implementation of Article VI of the GATT 1994 (Antidumping Agreement)	ADA
WTO Agreement on Trade-Related Aspects of Investment Measures	TRIMS
WTO Agreement on Government Procurement	GPA
WTO Agreement on Trade-Related Intellectual Property Rights	TRIPS
WTO Dispute Settlement Body	DSB
WTO General Agreement on Trade in Services	GATS
WTO Trade Policy Review Body	TPRB
WTO Understanding on Rules and Procedures Governing the Settlement of Disputes	DSU

Foreword by WTO Director-General Pascal Lamy

There can be little doubt that joining the WTO in 2001 has been a major contributor to China's economic success. Little discussed in relation to this success story is how much of China's economic growth has been propelled by the reforms brought to its legal system. This book fills in this gap, examining the role that China's WTO accession has played in bringing vital changes to China's legal system, leading to its improvement and reform.

The book assesses the implications of WTO membership for the Chinese legal framework from a holistic perspective, covering the entire history of the Chinese legal system, starting with a description of the country's vast legal heritage. It then delves into China's arduous and protracted WTO-accession negotiation, describing in the process an unprecedented level of courage and political determination to adapt China's legal system to WTO requirements. In short, it is the story of China's entry into a broader community of nations.

The author argues that China's accession to the rules-based multilateral trading system has led to the incorporation of basic legal principles into China's legal code; such as those of transparency, non-discrimination and due process. She demonstrates that China has used WTO accession to push forward domestic reform in a comprehensive and unprecedented manner. In sum, China's WTO accession was a win-win game for both China and the international community.

Through this work, Esther Lam succeeds in demonstrating how WTO membership can benefit both the acceding country and the wider WTO family of nations. I trust this important work will provide valuable insight to all other countries currently negotiating their terms of entry to the WTO.

Acknowledgements

My thanks go to Ambassador Pierre-Louis Girard, who served as Chairman of the WTO China Working Party for Accession from 1987 to 2001, for generously giving me access to his materials and files on the fifteen years of accession negotiations; to WTO Director-General Pascal Lamy for providing a foreword to this book; to Professor Jean-Michel Jacquet and Professor Joost Pauwelyn of the Graduate Institute of International and Development Studies in Geneva, Professor Zhang Yuejiao of the WTO Appellate Body, and Daniel Pruzin for reviewing and commenting on an earlier draft, and to all the interviewees for their time and invaluable insights. The views expressed in this book are mine and do not represent those of the United Nations, where I am currently employed. Lastly, my deepest appreciation goes to Grace Lam for always being there for me; to Markus Schmidt for his love and support throughout the process of research, writing and beyond, and to our daughter Ines who is a constant source of joy.

Introduction

Two basic hypotheses underpin the present study. Firstly, joining the World Trade Organization (WTO) enables China to reform its legal order and to move towards a system incorporating major principles of the rule of law. Secondly, the WTO serves as an external impetus that guides contemporary Chinese legal reform and orients it in ways that domestic forces alone could not achieve and sustain. In other words, the hypotheses postulate that without the external WTO requirements and surveillance, as well as China's constant interaction with other WTO members, it would be far more difficult, if not impossible, for several important elements that make up the rule of law to take root and be institutionalized in China. WTO-induced reform measures also put in place a framework within which the Chinese legal system further develops in convergence with international legal standards and practices. It also results in elevating the role of law in Chinese society and the importance of law in governance in the People's Republic of China (PRC).

Much discussion on the WTO and the Chinese legal system has focused on the issue of compliance – whether the Chinese legal system has the capacity to fulfil China's WTO accession commitments.[1] The focus of the present research is less concerned with compliance issues in relation to substantive trade commitments, but rather with the extent to which the WTO's requirements vis-à-vis China actually affect the Chinese legal system. The fine difference between the two approaches lies in the fact that efforts by the Chinese government to meet its WTO obligations necessarily impact upon the Chinese legal order and its way of functioning, even if their end results may or may not be considered to be in full compliance with its WTO commitments and obligations.

In order to answer the hypotheses, this book first examines the core norms of the traditional Chinese legal culture and the salient features of the Chinese legal

---

1. See, for example, C. Duncan, 'Out of Conformity: China's Capacity to Implement World Trade Organization Dispute Settlement Body Decisions after Accession', *American University International Law Review* 18 (2002): 399–477; and D.C. Clarke, 'China's Legal System and the WTO: Prospect for Compliance', *Global Studies Law Review* 2 (2003): 97–120.

system before the country's accession to the WTO. Changes in China do not happen overnight. In its fifteen-year-long negotiations to join the global trade body, the Chinese government introduced laws, for example, in the area of commercial laws and intellectual property rights, as required by China's economic developments and simultaneously seeking to be compatible with the WTO system. Upon joining the WTO in December 2001, the Chinese government became legally bound by the WTO Agreement, its Accession Protocol, and Working Party Report, through which systemic requirements for improving the Chinese legal system are entrenched in an international agreement. It also formally started a process for WTO members to review regularly and annually, until 2010,[2] the changing Chinese legal regime and China's compliance with its WTO commitments.

Part II of the book examines the strategic and policy considerations, many of them not strictly related to trade, of the Chinese leadership in its determination to pursue a WTO membership for the fast reforming country. These considerations help explain why, despite the unusual treatment and harsh conditions China faced throughout the fifteen-year-long accession process, the Chinese government was determined to complete the negotiations and join the WTO. More importantly, analyses on these non-trade motivations for China's WTO accession provide insights into the long-term impact of the WTO system on the Chinese legal system and the role of law in Chinese society. Put succinctly, many of the systemic legal requirements from the WTO coincide with the bottleneck areas of China's economic and legal reforms since 1978. Therefore, external pressure and impetus from the WTO would help orient Chinese reforms in the future and overcome reform constraints. China's WTO membership poses a wide range of challenges to its legal system. Four major areas of systemic legal requirements stand out, namely uniformity in the administration of China's legal regime, transparency and predictability, non-discrimination, and judicial review by an independent and impartial judiciary. This book argues that should China succeed in incorporating these principles into its legal order, it would be edging towards a system closer to the rule of law ideal.

The final part of the present study seeks to articulate, from a holistic point of view, systemic impacts of the WTO on the Chinese legal system beyond the sphere of economic and trade law. Legislative efforts alone, however, are insufficient to demonstrate whether these key legal principles are taking root and being implemented in China. The book examines the changing role of law in China from the perspective where law is considered a continuum or a process.[3] It analyses, for

---

2. Through a WTO transitional review mechanism specifically designed to monitor China's compliance after its accession to the WTO.
3. Law, whether it is at the international or national level, is not a set of static rules, but a dynamic process capable of responding to the changing needs and norms of the society and the international community. Likewise, law does not stay on paper alone. It is a continuous process involving legislation, adjudication, and implementation. See, for example, R. Higgins, *Problems & Process, International Law and How We Use It* (Oxford: Clarendon Press, 1998); and N. MacCormick, 'Institutional Normative Order: A Conception of Law', *Cornell Law Review* 82 (1997): 1051–1070.

example, China's administrative law and the intellectual property rights legal regimes, and examines the extent to which these principles are respected in the legislative, judicial, and enforcement processes. It also sheds light on the possibility that large-scale legal reform required by the WTO would eventually lead to a 'spill-over effect'[4] in other areas of Chinese law. WTO-induced systemic improvements do not only affect trade and economic laws, but they also impact a much wider scope of laws and the Chinese legal system as a whole.

China is a special case indeed, and not only because the Chinese legal system traditionally differed greatly from the WTO rules-based system both in form and in substance. Systemic legal requirements and a post-accession monitoring mechanism, entitled 'Transitional Review Mechanism (TRM),' were designed especially for China and had never been imposed on other WTO members before. Other former Communist countries that recently joined or are negotiating to accede to the WTO after the accession of China, such as Vietnam and Russia, are not required to accept regular monitoring under the TRM. Such an international-institution-driven model of domestic legal reform, which in effect globalizes the WTO system initially designed primarily by Western countries, has resulted in a harmonization of certain areas of trade-related laws in different national legal systems. It is because for some WTO areas, such as intellectual property rights and trade remedy laws[5] as in the case of China, member states tend to directly transplant WTO rules into their domestic laws. In addition to its impact on substantive trade laws, perhaps more importantly, the WTO also globalizes its standards of governance, often expressed through some basic rule of law principles according to which the global trading system functions. It is argued that these principles, including due process and procedural fairness, transparency, equality, and justiciability of government action, as they are taken on board by the Chinese government and becoming generally acceptable and normative in Chinese society, have profound impact on the development of the rule of law in China. Despite some potential risks, such as the uncertain status of the Communist Party of China (CPC) in the Chinese legal system, weak implementation of laws, and growing income disparity and social conflicts, China's WTO membership has afforded the world's most populous country better opportunities for success as it continues its three-decade-long legal reform. Partly due to China's WTO accession, to rule the country according to the principles of the rule of law, as a stated goal of the Chinese leadership, stands a better chance of becoming a reality.

On the scope and methodology of the present research, it focuses on the impact of China's WTO membership on the Chinese legal system. It is, therefore, a study about the influence of an international organization, the WTO, on its member state's legal order. Although relevant political, economic and social factors are addressed as necessary in the analysis of the legal implications of China's WTO

---

4. In the context of the current study, spill-over effect means that changes, whether in the form of substantive laws or principles governing the functioning of the legal system, introduced to fulfil WTO requirements are affecting areas beyond trade and economic laws.
5. Such as anti-dumping and safeguard measures for protecting domestic industries.

membership, the impacts of WTO accession on the Chinese economy and political reform are beyond the scope of the present research. Also, the research will examine concrete examples in the course of investigating the systemic impact the WTO brings to the transformation of the Chinese legal system. It does not purport to provide an exhaustive account of measures the Chinese government has taken to fulfil its obligations as a WTO member.

Drawing on existing literature on the Chinese legal system and the WTO, this study primarily involves examining the *travaux préparatoires* of China's accession agreement, and interviewing key officials and players taking part in the WTO accession negotiations and the ongoing reform process in China. Another main source of information comes from my firsthand observation and interaction with sources in Geneva as a journalist writing about the WTO, from early 2001 to the end of 2006. My work as a Geneva-based correspondent has provided me access to important information, most of which was not readily available in the public domain, during the final stage of China's WTO accession process and first five years of China in the WTO as a new member.

Many Chinese laws are not available in English and there is not yet an up-to-date gazette of all new laws[6] in China. Where it is possible, this book uses English translation of Chinese laws by official sources, such as from websites of relevant Chinese authorities including that of the National People's Congress (NPC), the State Council, and the Ministry of Commerce. Another source of English translation of Chinese laws cited in this study comes from the private sector, such as academic publishers and legal search engines, newsletters, and websites of law firms. Access to judicial decisions in China is more complicated. Many Chinese courts do not post their judgments on their websites. For those which do, only selected decisions are posted online and often not up-to-date.[7] Many court cases come to light first and only through media reports. Efforts are made to cite original court decisions when they are available. Otherwise, reports from official Chinese media[8] are used.

---

6. One of the comprehensive sources of all new Chinese laws, decisions by the State Council, and judicial interpretations by the Supreme People's Court used in this study is a website entitled 法律图书馆 'Chinese Law Library' <www.law-lib.com>, which delivers via email to subscribers all new Chinese laws, in Chinese language, as they are issued by the relevant authorities.
7. As of March 2009, selected judgments posted on websites of Chinese courts are often those until 2006.
8. It is an established practice by the Chinese government to make its positions public through its two main official newspapers: The *China Daily* (published in English), the *People's Daily* (published in Chinese). While many newspapers and electronic media in China are governmental, the *China Daily* and the *People's Daily* are recognized as the two official newspapers representing the views of the government, and hence often used, by both Chinese and foreign researchers, as one of the important sources of information to ascertain the official positions of the Chinese government and the CPC. Hence the two newspapers are often cited in the present study either to complement other sources of information or to ascertain the official positions when primary materials, such as draft laws, court judgments, or official documents, are not available. Another source used often in this study is the official Chinese news agency *Xinhua*, which often posts the full text of official reports online.

Part I

Understanding the Chinese Legal Order

To appreciate fully the impact of China's WTO membership on the Chinese legal system, we must seek to understand the role of law in the long Chinese history, core features of the traditional Chinese legal system, the significant changes it underwent, and key lessons learned in China's past legal reforms. Considering that efforts to draft and adopt modern civil and criminal law codes in China did not start until the early twentieth century, detailed textual analysis of ancient Chinese laws, except when it reflects the underlying and long-lasting features of Chinese perception of law which are still relevant today, would not enhance our understanding of law and Chinese society today. This part of the book, therefore, first highlights the fundamental features of the ancient Chinese legal system; many of which continue to be prevalent in the Chinese people's perception of law in the twenty-first century. It then provides a more detailed analysis on the legal system of the pre-WTO China between 1949, when the PRC was established, and the end of 2001, when China became a WTO member.

Special focus is given to the economic and legal reforms under *Deng Xiaoping*'s rule since 1978. Reforms and their constraints during this important period of contemporary China are directly related to China's strategic and policy motivations in seeking to join the WTO and to the special conditions WTO members imposed on China under the terms of the accession agreement. The notion of developing 'a socialist market economy with Chinese characteristics', for example, was a creation of *Deng* which continues to guide China's national policy today.

Chapter 1

Burden or Assets? Chinese Legal History at a Glance

The Chinese perception of law and its role in society took a long time to develop. While the legal system of contemporary China differs significantly from that of the imperial period, the influence of both the Confucian School and the Legalist School are still perceptible in the Chinese people's perception of law today. This chapter highlights the core norms and origin of the Chinese legal system before turning to the modern legal regime put in place by the CPC in 1949.

I THE ANCIENT CHINESE LEGAL SYSTEM

Rituals and obligations enshrined in Confucianism have a long history of mingling with legal rules in China, dating back to the *Qin* (秦) and *Han* (汉) dynasties over 2,000 years ago when law – as described by the Legalist School of Thought, *Fa Jia* (法家) – was mostly an instrument for imperial rulers to control the people. This has long-lasting influence on the role of law in Chinese society. Some features concerning the Chinese perception of law were generated during the dynastic period of China, and they are still relevant in helping to explain the attitude of many Chinese vis-à-vis law. The prominence of morality, rather than law, in regulating ancient Chinese society, application of law as a mere instrument without an intrinsic value of its own, different treatment of individuals according to their social and family status, and the tendency to discourage and avoid litigation, for example, are still perceptible in contemporary Chinese society.

While there were legal reforms during imperial China, changes were made exclusively on substantive areas of law, such as taxation, military conscription, and distribution of farm lands, at the technical and operational level. These reforms did not touch on the underlying principles and fundamental features of the traditional Chinese legal system and the people's understanding of law. The first wave of challenges towards these standing features came only in the early twentieth century. Most of these challenges and pressures to introduce changes came from outside – the foreign powers which forced the much-weakened *Qing* (清) dynasty[1] to open China's door to the outside world. Through the so-called 'gun-boat diplomacy', foreign powers installed themselves in different areas of China, historically called a period of 'scramble for concessions', and asserted extra-territorial jurisdiction over Chinese territory. Claiming that the Chinese legal system was barbaric, the foreign powers enforced their own laws in the occupied Chinese territories. In these circumstances, for the first time, China sought to reform its legal system to the extent that the ancient features and perception of law were challenged and that Western concepts were incorporated. Resistance abounded; and the nascent legal reform was soon interrupted by the civil wars, first amongst warlords and then between the Nationalists and the Communists that swept through China.

A CORE NORMS AND ORIGINS: LEGALISM AND CONFUCIANISM

According to a classical study analyzing the main characteristics of traditional Chinese law from 202 BC (the beginning of the *Han* dynasty) to 1911 (the end of the *Qing* dynasty), 'the Confucianization of law' was the most significant development in the Chinese legal order.[2] It suggested that, in the course of the 2000-year-old history of ancient Chinese law, Legalism and Confucianism remained fundamental in shaping the characteristics of the Chinese legal system. Examining historical data, the study showed that the law codes of the *Qin* (221–207 BC) and early *Han* (202 BC–220 AD) dynasties were complied with by the Legalists, who considered law a key tool of control and power for rulers to maintain social order. Law, therefore, should apply equally to all. There should be a uniform standard of behaviour for all, and the most effective way of ensuring observance of such a standard was law enforcement and punishment. The Confucians, who also recognized law as a tool, though only supplementary to moral values and beneficial to social stability, quickly became influential in the imperial court and Confucianism was made the state ideology of *Han*. The Confucians sought to incorporate into the law elements of *Li* （礼）, literally translated as 'rituals' or 'a set of rites'. However, the terms 'rules of proper conduct' or 'proprieties' would be closer to the meaning of the Chinese word. *Li* is the basis of Confucianism, which emphasizes the concept of family and the stratification of

1. The *Qing* Dynasty (1644–1911) was the last ruling dynasty in Chinese history.
2. 瞿同祖, 中國法律與中國社會, 北京, 中华書局, 2003年 T. Ju, *Law and Society in Traditional China* (Beijing: Zhonghua Bookstore, 2003).

   The book was first published in Chinese in 1947 and its first English translation was published in 1961. Citations of the book hereafter are from its 1965 revised English edition: T. Ju (Ch'u T'sun-tsu), *Law and Society in Traditional China* (Paris, The Hague: Mouton, 1965).

society. Individuals should have different modes of proper behaviour, depending on their positions in the context of both family and social structures. The Confucians advocated that law should be applied differently to different people, depending on their social status.[3] The most thorough and long-lasting way of ensuring observance of *Li*, and thus ultimately achieving social order and harmony, was through moral influence and education.

The Legalists and the Confucians shared a common goal in their teachings – maintaining social order. In essence, they were both political ideologies seeking to offer rulers what they considered an ideal way of maintaining social order and the best way to govern. While sharing this common goal, they advocated different means to achieving this end.

B The Confucianization Process

In early *Han*, emperor *Wu*（武） (141–187 BC) eliminated all other schools of thought and made Confucianism the sole state ideology. But legal rules in place then had already been drafted by the Legalists who dominated the imperial court during the preceding *Qin* dynasty. As abandoning the existing rules was impractical, the Confucians instead started incorporating elements of *Li*, such as different rights and obligations according to individuals of different social and family status, into the legal system and using the Confucian doctrine to interpret and apply legal rules. This process, which *Ju Tongyu* termed 'the Confucianization of law', had a long-lasting impact on the Chinese legal system.

Ju's study, still an authority in the area of law and society in traditional China, concludes that:

> The most significant development in the legal system of China, prior to the 20th century modernization of Chinese law, was the Confucianization of law.... Confucianization was a gradual process, one which began in the *Han* dynasty and continued through the Southern and the Northern Dynasties. Such important laws as not permitting sons to live separately from their parents, *pa-i* (eight conditions for consideration), ten offences, punishment based on five degrees of mourning, criminals reprieved from execution in order to serve their aged parents, concealment, and *kuan-t'ang* (cancellation of punishment by surrendering one's official post) – all were introduced in this period, between the third and sixth centuries. By the time of the *Sui*[4]（隋, Cui） and the *T'ang*（唐, Tang）, the process of Confucianization was more or less completed. The *T'ang* law represented the fullest development of Confucianization. Confucian doctrines, especially the essential themes of *li*, then came to dominate the law.[5]

3. *Ibid.*, 10–12.
4. Ju's book uses Wade-Giles transliteration of Chinese terms. This book uses *Pinyin*, and when directly quoting passages with Wade-Giles, its *Pinyin* equivalence is included in a bracket.
5. Ju, *Law and Society in Traditional China* (Paris, The Hague: Mouton, 1965), 280.

C KEY CONFUCIAN TEACHINGS INCORPORATED INTO CHINESE LAW

Three intertwining themes in Confucian teachings were solidly embodied in both traditional Chinese legal rules and the spirit underlying the entire system. The overarching significance of Confucian influence for the traditional Chinese perception of law was that morality, rather than law, assumed the primary and most important function in shaping and maintaining social order. The threads through which morality kept the Chinese social fabrics tightly knitted were the deep-rooted kinship system and social hierarchy. With the Confucianization of law, the traditional Chinese legal system in many ways represented a codification of Confucian teachings, presented as law.

1 Family and Kinship System

In Confucian teachings, filial piety was always a guiding principle in governing an empire. This cardinal principle was present in many ancient Chinese legal rules, which fully recognized the parents' authority in controlling and chastising their children, who had no independent right to private property, to living separately from their parents, or to choose their spouse.[6] As a rule, killing a son who failed his filial obligations was exempted from punishment in the *Yuan* (元), *Ming* (明) and *Qing* dynasties. According to law, seniors and husbands enjoyed supremacy over junior relatives and wives. In cases of disputes between, as well as persecution of, family members, an individual's status in the kinship group was always a deciding factor in judgment and sentencing.

Confucius disapproved of a son's bearing witness against his father in such matters as sheep-stealing and developed the idea that 'a father should conceal the fault of a son and that a son should conceal the fault of a father'.[7] As an indication of the dominance of family ethics in Chinese law, the law of all dynasties recognized the principle of concealment among relatives. As early as 66 BC, it was permitted to conceal the crime of a close relative. Since the *Tang* dynasty, the right, in fact the obligation, to conceal was extended to other categories of relatives. It covered not only direct line blood relatives and spouses but also relatives living together, granddaughters-in-law, brothers-in-law, and sisters-in-law. A son who accused his parent acted not only contrary to the principle of concealment but in an unfilial manner.[8] Such behaviour was severely punished under the law of all Chinese dynasties. Since the law recognized the right of concealment and forbade relatives to accuse each other, a relative of an accused should not be asked to testify

---

6. See examples throughout the imperial period in Ju, *ibid.*, 72–73 and 280.
7. Ju, *ibid.*, 70, citing 'Lun-yu chu-su, I3, 4b', in J. Legge, *Chinese Classics I, Confucian Analects, the Great Learning, and the Doctrine of the Mean* (London: Legge, 1861), 134.
8. During the reign of Emperor *Wu* (武) (502–549) of *Liang* (梁) dynasty, a man was sentenced to banishment because he had testified against his mother who was a kidnapper. See Ju, *ibid.*, 280 for details.

against the defendant in court.[9] This is in sharp contrary to what happened during the period of *Mao Zedong*'s (毛泽东) Cultural Revolution, when children were turned into 'Red Guards' and induced to denounce their parents and seniors.

2 Social Hierarchy and Stratification

Social stratification was another major Confucian influence on traditional Chinese law.[10] *Ju* shows that there were sumptuary laws[11] regulating a person's mode of life according to his or her social and legal status. Officials, commoners and the 'mean' people remained the three major social classes throughout ancient China, with their status clearly defined by legal rules that also governed their right of consumption, marriages, legal privileges, or deprivation.[12] As Confucianism considered that people of different social status should have different sets of conduct, the law recognized and consolidated the different status of nobles, officials, commoners, and the 'mean' people: 'Above all, people of different status were not treated alike before the law. Nobles and officials enjoyed certain legal privileges, whereas the "mean" people were legally unprivileged.'[13]

Such differences were written into law and applied throughout the empire. Hence these differences became institutionalized and deep-rooted in the social esteem and class consciousness of people from different classes. For example, the merchant class, which depended on trade and was then considered an inferior occupation, was forbidden to enter officialdom as early as the *Han*. The same prohibition applied also to artisans, who were prevented from taking civil service examinations – the ultimate goal of all learned persons in ancient China – during the *Cui*, *Tang* and *Song* (宋) dynasties.[14] That 'corporal punishment should not be applied to government officials' (*Xin Bu San Da Fu*, 刑不上大夫) was a common legal doctrine in ancient China. It was firmly established in traditional Chinese law that officials enjoyed the privileges to redeem their crimes through payment and to be spared of criminal punishment by surrendering their official positions. The law of the *Ming* and *Qing* dynasties permitted fewer privileges of this kind than during the *Tang* and the *Song* dynasties. Officials then were punishable by penal servitude and banishment and were allowed to redeem themselves if only corporal punishment was in order.[15]

This unequal treatment concerning the differences between *Jun Zhi* (君子), gentlemen, and the *Xiao Ren* (小人), little men, was further developed and

9. *Ibid.*, 70–71.
10. See both Ju, *ibid.*, and 郭建, 姚荣濤, 王志強, 中國法制史, 上海人民出版社, 2000年 (Gao Jiang et al., *History of the Chinese Legal System* (Shanghai: The People's Publishing, 2000), esp. Ch. 2).
11. Sumptuary laws (from Latin *sumptuariae leges*) were laws that regulated and reinforced social hierarchies and morals through restrictions on clothing, food, and lifestyle.
12. Ju, *Law and Society in Traditional China* (Paris, The Hague: Mouton, 1965), 282.
13. *Ibid.*, 281.
14. *Ibid.*
15. *Ibid.*, 282.

elaborated by Confucius, Mencius （孟子）, and other scholars of the Confucian School. It played a dominant role in Chinese social stratification.[16] Both law and social norms recognized their difference in status – the officials being superior, the commoners inferior. Their respective lifestyles were clearly defined and distinguished. Officials enjoyed particular legal and political privileges, such as legal protection against assault by commoners, and officials of different ranks were assigned their respective costumes and accessories, with different degrees of superior legal treatments assigned to them accordingly. Officials and commoners were two distinct classes and there was little social communication between them. The superiority of the officials and nobles was acknowledged by both commoners and society at large.

The 'mean' people encompassed government and private slaves, prostitutes, entertainers, government runners such as messengers, horsemen, and doormen. Under the law, all those who had social and legal status inferior to that of the common people were considered 'mean' people. The law further stipulated that the 'mean' people and the commoners should keep social distance by, for example, prohibiting intermarriages between the two classes.[17] To prevent class mobility, the 'mean' people and their offspring were not allowed to take civil examinations, which in effect closed to them all channels for social mobility. Some argued that the 'mean' people category formed a caste more than a class:

> [I]t is most important to realize that the objective criteria of wealth and income, which are decisive factors in a capitalist society, did not play an equally decisive role in traditional Chinese society. A merchant might be wealthier than an official, but the social status of the latter was much higher.[18]

It was more by occupation and birth that people were categorized – a commoner would be degraded to the 'mean' people category if he/she became an entertainer. The discriminatory treatment to people of lower classes were prescribed and entrenched by law.

3 Law and Morality

The Confucianization of law gradually blurred the difference between law and morality. Behaviour considered immoral in Confucian teachings was also deemed illegal. Such categorization was either written in the law itself or read into it through adjudication and legal interpretation, making Confucian norms the most powerful tool of social control:

> We may say that originally *li* were enforced by social sanction, and later by legal sanction. A rule of behaviour enforced by social sanction is *li*; the same rule of behaviour is law when legal sanction is introduced. It is obvious that

16. See Ju, *ibid.*, Ch. VI, for details and examples.
17. *Ibid.*, 129–132.
18. *Ibid.*, 133.

> the same behaviour pattern may be subsumed under *li* and law at the same time. Thus the Confucianists used political and legal power to enforce their rules of behaviour, but these norms were still included in their books of *li*, and they still sought to enforce them by morality and education. *Li* and law, while separate entities, were supplementary to each other. As the norms were simultaneously sustained by both social and legal sanctions, they imposed a strong compulsion on the members of the society.[19]

Many examples in traditional Chinese law demonstrate that the family and the social stratification order were fundamental features of the traditional Chinese legal system and moral values. Not surprisingly, a legal system so closely woven into the social fabric of Chinese society remained relatively stable throughout ancient Chinese history. There were, of course, changes in the contents of law, which reflected policy changes. But the central spirit and underlying features of the ancient Chinese legal order remained unchanged. Therefore, *Ju* concluded that after Confucians crystallized the law with moral teachings, there were no fundamental changes in the underlying features of the traditional Chinese legal system, especially when family and social classes were concerned. Traditional Chinese law was dominated by *Li*, which considered status in the kinship system and in the stratification system the backbone of the social and political order.[20]

II BASIC FEATURES OF THE TRADITIONAL CHINESE LEGAL SYSTEM

As a result of the Confucianization of law in ancient China, the main characteristic of Chinese law was its 'emphasis on the status factor which found expression both in the kinship system and the system of stratification'.[21] These characteristics shaped the Chinese perception of law and the legal system itself. With the emphasis on the status factor in the old system, modern legal concepts such as equality before the law and equal protection of individual rights, though developed much later in Western societies, would take much longer and considerably more efforts to take root in modern China, because of its unique Confucianized legal and cultural heritage.

A A Secondary Role of Law in Society

As a result of the Confucianization of its law, ancient China 'failed to develop a body of rules independent of *li* and ethics'.[22] While legal developments in Western

19. *Ibid.*, 279.
20. *Ibid.*, 283.
21. *Ibid.*, 280.
22. *Ibid.*, 283–284.

societies also experienced phases during which law and morality were closely related, the separation of religion and politics and the increased awareness of individual rights meant that law and morality gradually developed and defined their own spaces of influence and roles. Such developments did not occur in China for 2000 years, largely due to the dominance of Confucianism in Chinese society and its impact on the role of law. When the first republic was established in China in 1911, law struggled to assume a distinct function and legal rules independent of Confucianism started to emerge. But this development did not take root in Chinese society for many more years to come.

According to *Ju,* it was due to the fact that law was essentially a penal code that mainly dealt with violations and their penalties throughout the history of imperial China. Matters such as those concerning family, marriage, adoption, inheritance, property and debts, which would be considered civil laws in modern concepts, were largely neglected by law and largely left to custom or *Li*. These two played a more important role than law in regulating social activities.[23] The lack of public reliance on law in their daily lives also helps explain why it was not until the early twentieth century that efforts to draft a civil code began in China. Another consequence of this tradition was that in ancient China, law remained inaccessible. The general public knew little about the legal system. There was no confidence in law because law was not a channel ordinary people would normally resort to when they were in disputes or when their rights were violated.

B LAW: MERELY A MEANS TO AN END

Given the limited role of law in ancient Chinese society, there was a long tradition of equating law with instrumentalism – it was used to achieve something, it was a means to an end but not an end in itself that should be respected. Law was an instrument for the emperor to control the people. The ruling class could and often did manipulate legal rules. Words and decrees from the imperial court could be applied as law and it was not for the people to challenge such a practice. In fact, the practice was fairly internalized in the mindset of the people, and they mostly complied with it. In feudal times, the law was an instrument for ruling the people, and the nobles did not fall under its jurisdiction. Even in modern day China, law was for a long subordinate to politics and secondary to economics. The incentive of legal reform in China since 1978 was to integrate with the global market, rather than to reform its legal system and to introduce the rule of law as an end in itself. Legal reform by and large remains a means to an end.

---

23. *Ibid.*, 284. With the exception of some rules concerning civil matters starting from the *Tang* dynasty, see 張晉藩, 法史鑑略, 北京, 群眾出版社, 1988年 (J. Zhang, *A Brief Review of Chinese Legal History* (Beijing: Qun Zhong Press, 1988)).

C INEQUALITY BEFORE THE LAW

Unlike the approach first advocated by the Legalists, the universal application of law failed to take root in the traditional Chinese legal system. In line with Confucian teachings that *Li* was not designed for the commoners and punishment was not applicable to officials, law in ancient China was never meant to apply equally to all. Particularism was given primacy over universality. This was one of the key contentions between the nobles and Legalists. The nobles sought to keep the law secret and to maintain themselves above the law, while the Legalists tried to make the law accessible and applicable to everyone. Moreover, the Legalists wanted all law to be written down as well as made known to the public. *Han Feizhi* (韩非子), a leading figure of the Legalist School, advocated that the law 'must be put down in written documents, kept in the government offices, and announced to the people', so that they would be 'sure about the punishment', and know what was legal and what illegal.[24] Such was one of the earliest calls for legal transparency in China. However, as noted, the Legalists soon lost their influence, and their ideal of transparent and equal application of law did not materialize.

On the contrary, Confucianism's emphasis on status resulted in a substantive part of ancient Chinese rules being specific to and tailored for persons of different family and social status. When it came to adjudication, this part of the law was always given first and primary consideration. Only when law specific to status with detailed provisions failed to apply could the general laws – that is, those not tailored to status-related issues – be invoked.[25] The status of the parties involved was the main consideration in the administration of justice. There was no absolute standard applicable to all with regard to right or wrong. Everything was relative to one's status, which corresponded to the Confucian principle of 'rectification of names' (*zheng min* 正名) – a person must act in accordance with one's socially and family-defined status.[26]

D INSIGNIFICANT INDIVIDUAL RIGHTS

Universal application of law and unalienable and equal individual rights, which were incompatible with particularism, did not develop in ancient China. Traditional Chinese law focused primarily on particular status, relationships, and the corresponding obligations. It paid little attention to the equality of individual rights or universal standards. The emphasis on particularism has arguably prevented the Chinese legal culture from developing abstract legal principles and universally applicable set of rules. This also resulted in a theoretical deficit in Chinese law which would hinder the development of legal theories in China. The Confucian concept of law has long regarded it as an instrument to implement *Li*. Law was

24. *Ibid.*, 171.
25. See Gao et al., Ch. 2.
26. Ju, *Law and Society in Traditional China* (Paris, The Hague: Mouton, 1965), 284.

seen 'as more or less identical to punishment, which was invoked whenever *li* or moral principles were violated'.[27] This also partly explains why the areas of civil law and administrative law developed much slower in China than in Western societies. Wang Zhenmin, Dean at the Tsinghua University Law School of Law, told the following story:

> When I was a student at law school, a professor once asked my class to list things that we associated with the law. Most students came up with concepts such as jail, execution, death penalty, police, army, and criminal tribunal. No one mentioned civil rights or supervision of government. For a long time, it was difficult to see the law in terms of rights or justice in China. Today, as a law professor, I raise this very same question in my first-year classes and receive very different answers. Students of this generation are beginning to associate the law with ideas such as protection of civil rights, dispute resolution, equity and justice. This reflects the progress that has been made in the attitude of the Chinese towards the law and the rule of law.[28]

Wang's observation is typical in China. For a long time, the role of law in Chinese society was perceived as having to do with criminals, and ordinary citizens were better off not to have anything to do with law. In the traditional Chinese perception of law, individual rights or due procedures to guarantee the respect for these rights were not emphasized.

E A Non-litigious Society

Traditionally, the role of law was basically punitive and a tool of social control. People were often treated in a humiliating manner in the courts in ancient China. So it was considered a disgrace to be involved in a legal dispute. Litigation was also costly, as the parties were usually subject to extortion by clerks and runners. China was essentially a non-litigious society. People were encouraged to avoid litigation and settle their disputes outside the court. Very often disputes were resolved within the family or *tsu*, the village or the guild, with elders or local leaders acting as mediators.[29] Litigation also was seen as an assault to the harmonious relationships people from all walks of life were taught to maintain within their social circles, as Confucianism emphasized. With the society's general disapproval of litigation and a lack of knowledge and confidence in the legal system, most people were also unwilling to become involved in others' litigation, such as through appearing in court as witnesses. The tendency to avoid litigation in order to preserve harmony in Chinese legal culture also has implications for the development of legal institutions in modern China. Stanley Lubman suggested traditional

---

27. *Ibid.*, 283.
28. Z. Wang, 'The Developing Rule of Law in China', *Harvard Asia Quarterly* (Autumn, 2000), <www.fas.harvard.edu/~asiactr/haq/200004/0004a007.htm>, 3 Nov. 2005.
29. Ju, *Law and Society in Traditional China* (Paris, The Hague: Mouton, 1965), 284–285.

Chinese attitudes towards law 'have caused the populace to avoid and fear involvement with formal legal institutions'.[30]

F NO SEPARATION OF POWERS

The concept of separation of powers between the legislative, executive, and judicial authorities is alien to the Chinese traditional legal system. An independent judiciary that provides checks and balances of state power did not exist in feudal China. Throughout the history of imperial China, executive officials also performed the role of judges. The highest official in a province also presided over legal disputes brought to the same provincial court. No separate institutions or positions were deemed necessary to perform these two different functions. The notion that a separate organ should be established and entrusted with the sole authority to deal with judicial matters did not take root in China before the early twentieth century, when the *Qing* dynasty was under intense pressure from foreign occupied powers to establish an independent judiciary.[31] The lack of independent legal institutions in the traditional Chinese legal system was also reflected by the fact that the emperor enjoyed absolute power and had final authority to decide on cases involving capital punishment. Sanctions and coercions were used at times to ensure compliance by the people, who were habitually obedient to the ruler and his absolute power.

III THE LEGAL REFORMS OF THE EARLY TWENTIETH CENTURY

Given the aforementioned core features of the ancient Chinese legal system – albeit elaborate and rich in details – the rule of law is not a product of Chinese legal culture, and legal traditions of ancient China could not offer much help to develop the rule of law in contemporary China. The rule of man – the emperor – in ancient China soon found its way to modern China, especially after the establishment of the PRC under *Mao*, and it reached its peak during the Cultural Revolution (1966–1976).

The Chinese value system, reinforced both by *Li* and legal rules, remained basically unchanged throughout the Chinese dynastic period. Short-lived legal

---

30. S. Lubman, 'Bird in a Cage: Chinese Law Reform after Twenty Years', *Journal of International Law and Business* 20 (2000): 383–413, 393; see also Z. Liang, 'Explicating Law: A Comparative Perspective of Chinese and Western Legal Culture', *Journal of Chinese Law* 13 (1989): 55–91, and Y. Shen, 'Conceptions and Receptions of Legality: Understanding the Complexity of Law Reform in Modern China', in *The Limits of the Rule of Law in China*, eds Karen G. Turner, James V. Feinerman & R. Kent Guy (Seattle: University of Washington Press, 1999).
31. 張恆山等,法治與黨的執政方式研究,北京,法律出版社2004年,223 (In Chinese) (Hengshan Zhang et al., *A Study on the Rule of Law and the Ruling Model of the Communist Party of China* (Beijing: Law Press China, 2004)).

reform introduced late during the *Qing* dynasty, and which continued in a piecemeal and fragmented manner during the civil war and Japanese invasion, did not succeed in taking root before the CPC took power in 1949. However, the motivations for these legal reforms revealed the instrumental approach the Chinese adopted when confronted with changes. This was compatible with the traditional Chinese perception of law, where law was a means to an end and not an end in itself. The same approach would resurface again when legal reform was introduced under *Deng Xiaoping*'s rule.[32]

A LATE *QING* REFORM MEASURES

The experience during the late *Qing* period and after the establishment of the republic in 1911 illustrated the strength of traditional forces that resisted the modernization of the Chinese legal system, as well as the continued influence of Confucianism in the Chinese legal order even after the end of the dynastic era. The arguments advanced by the Legalist and Confucian schools 2000 years ago resurfaced in the early twentieth century.

In the early 1900s, *Shen Jiaben* (沈家本),[33] a renowned legal scholar and government official and who later was called the 'father of modern Chinese law', was appointed Legal Commissioner to steer legal reform throughout the empire, including the drafting of modern legal codes. The project, however, did not result from the late *Qing* imperial court's realization that the legal regime of China required modernization. It was mostly a response to new challenges posed by external factors, namely forceful demands from Western powers that their nationals in China should be exempted from Chinese law; and the humiliating defeat to its much smaller neighbour in the Sino-Japanese war. The *Qing* imperial court and many government officials clearly stated that the purpose of formulating a penal code basically similar to that of the West was to urge the Western powers and Japan to renounce their extraterritoriality rights. When Western powers occupied several Chinese coastal cities after the Opium War of 1839–1842, they simultaneously demanded extra-territorial judicial power. Lawsuits involving foreign nationals did not fall under Chinese jurisdiction and were judged according to the laws of the occupying powers. The latter dismissed Chinese law as something barbaric. And even for genuine believers in the necessity of modernization of Chinese law (such as *Shen Jiaben*), they also conveniently cited this external factor as a reason to push ahead with reform measures against stiff domestic resistance.

As pointed out by an informed observer, the Western powers' criticisms of the Chinese legal system reflected their lack of understanding of China's socio-juridical background. Nor did they understand the relatively limited role law

32. See Part I, Ch. 2 Section II.
33. 李贵连, 沈家本传, 北京, 法律出版社, 2000年 (G. Li, *Bibliography of Shen Jiaben* (Beijing: Law Press China, 2000)).

played in Chinese society, and its interaction with Confucianism and social norms:

> It did not occur to these intruders to reflect on the comparative novelty of the legal systems they were introducing. Modern legal institutions were introduced in the West only one or two centuries ago, the separation of criminal law from civil law dates only from the eighteenth century; the old English law knew no distinction between them, and in the old Germanic law inhuman punishments, including the cutting off of hands, were common. Up till the end of the eighteenth century, 'quartering', cutting off the tongue, banishment and other extreme punishments were part of French law... China began to introduce modern Western legal institutions a century after they appeared in the West – a process that suffered a severe setback from *Mao*'s imposition of lawless arbitrary rule in the middle of the twentieth century.[34]

B Towards Criminal and Civil Law Codes

The drafting of a criminal law code and civil law code, and, more importantly, the conflicts and debates accompanying the exercise, provide ample insights into the relation between law and society, in particular the resistance from the ruling elites and the lack of public confidence vis-à-vis thorough legal reform in early twentieth century China. A bibliography of *Shen Jiaben*[35] details the debates between late *Qing* officials about the drafting of new criminal and civil law codes, which reflected the deep-rooted conflicts and tensions between traditional and modern forces. Politically, this first effort of modernizing the Chinese legal system came at a time when imperial rule was seriously weakened and China experienced the 'scramble for concessions' by foreign powers. Socially, China then remained an agrarian society, and the vast majority of the Chinese population were rural farmers and agriculture their mainstay. The main incentive for the late *Qing* legal modernization project was to reclaim from foreign powers the legal sovereignty over occupied territories. The conflicts and debates surrounding the project has been termed the 'Conflict between Traditional Ethics (*Li*) and Law' in Chinese legal history, focusing on whether Confucian teachings or Western legal doctrines and procedures should be the future of Chinese law.

Under *Shen* and with his Japanese and German legal advisors, the drafts of criminal and civil law borrowed primarily from European and Japanese laws and they brought about radical changes. Thus, the draft *Criminal Code* of 1907 contained very few specific clauses dealing with family and social status as well as their corresponding privileges, except for a few articles covering injury or murder

34. L. Ladany, *Law and Legality in China: The Testament of a China-Watcher* (Honolulu: University of Hawaii Press, 1992), 3–4.
35. Li.

of parents and grandparents.[36] The draft introduced a basic change in the Chinese legal doctrine's understanding of the social structure, even though society was not ready for such a paradigm shift. The value system that shaped the traditional legal codes in the first place remained largely unchanged. With respect to kinship and family structure, for instance, the draft code erroneously assumed that patriarchy would be weakened, and that a husband's authority over his wife would diminish. With regard to class hierarchy, the draft code included no specific legal privilege granted to nobles and officials; nor were there specific clauses regulating the lower strata of commoners and 'mean' people.[37] The draft, therefore, in effect put an end to 2000 years of legal recognition of class differences in Chinese society. Compared with traditional Chinese law, the draft *Criminal Code* projected a different world view and legal doctrine – particularism had to give way to universalism, and law should be applicable equally to all regardless of family position and class status.

The draft *Civil Code* of 1911, with three sections on some general principles, the law of debts and obligations, and the law of properties, was mainly complied by a Japanese jurist (松冈义正). However, the 1911 revolution swept through China and eventually overthrew the *Qing* rule before the draft code was officially adopted and could be implemented. Two other draft sections of the code, on family and successions respectively, were not even presented to the emperor for approval.[38] Continuous political turmoil in China meant that its first civil law code was not promulgated until the late 1920s. As a reflection of the difficulties involved in formulating modern legal rules relating to family and social structures, a law dealing with inheritance and a family law were promulgated only in 1930.[39]

C RESISTANCE TO LEGAL REFORM

The conflict between traditional Chinese values and modern legal concepts, as embodied in the draft criminal code, drew vehement protests from Confucian scholars and officials among the ruling elites, notably *Zhang Zhi-tong* (张芝桐) and *Lao Naixuan* (劳乃宣).[40] The submissions *Zhang* and *Lao* filed in opposition to the draft code were full of citations from Confucian teachings and classics. They argued that the application of Western legal concepts to Chinese society ran counter to the existing social values and teachings of ancient Confucian scholars. They submitted that for new situations not specifically covered by existing Chinese law, traditional teachings and *Li* should be interpreted into the law for purposes of adjudication, and therefore an overhaul of the traditional legal system was not only

36. *Ibid.*, 300–355, and see Ju, *Law and Society in Traditional China* (Paris, The Hague: Mouton, 1965), 285.
37. See Li., Ch. 11 and Ju, *ibid.*, 286.
38. Ju, *ibid.*, 288 and Li, 291–292.
39. Ju, *ibid.*, 288.
40. See Ju, *ibid.*, 286, Ladany, 47–51 and Li, 297.

unnecessary but also counterproductive.[41] In response, the reformers argued that morality and traditional ethics should be separated from the law, and the development of the law should not be held back by traditional ethics.[42]

So strong was the resistance that the draft code, as it stood in 1907, was never fully implemented. Several amendments were made to the draft, for example, to reinstate traditional restrictions of the legal rights of juniors in a family and criminal punishment of those having sexual relations with unmarried women.[43] Traditional forces remained very strong for decades and the draft, later promulgated by the government of the Republic of China (ROC) in 1911, was further amended in 1914. The amendments provided for a parent to request the court to hold a child in detention for up to six months, and a family elder could escape punishment if he only slightly injured a junior. Further efforts to restore traditional legal rules continued through 1935, when a new *Criminal Code* was promulgated.[44] All this shows that even after the end of imperial rule and the establishment of the republic, traditional forces were strong enough to rein in China's first ever modern legal reform.

D Lessons from the Reform Efforts

Law and society are closely linked, and very often the latter shapes the former, and when the respect for law has reached a mature level in societies, law in turn can affect the functioning of a society as well. Even when the Chinese political system underwent drastic changes – from over 2000 years of absolute monarchy to the establishment of the republic in 1911 – Chinese society of the time and its value system remained by and large unchanged. The 1911 revolution did not bring about the necessary changes in social norms and people's value system, and the short-lived and fragmented legal reform measures, the ensuing decades-long civil war, and the lawlessness that further deteriorated under *Mao Zedong*'s rule are historical testimony to this conclusion.

With the civil war and Japanese invasion soon after the promulgation of modern laws in China, political instability and social turmoil prevented the new laws from taking root before the Communists took power in 1949, when laws inspired by the Soviet model were introduced to replace the only recently adopted laws. The ten years of the Cultural Revolution, which sought to break Chinese society away from both Confucian values and the existing legal system, left China with a legal vacuum. Only when *Deng Xiaoping* resumed power and pursued an open-door policy in 1978 did economic and legal reforms begin afresh.

Before 1949, traditional moral values and the basic social structure remained by and large the same. Significant social changes which would support an overhaul

41. For excerpts of their submissions, see Li, 300–320.
42. For some of the reformers' responses, see Li, 323–329.
43. See Ju, *ibid.*, 287 and Li, 321–356.
44. Ju, *ibid.*, 278–287.

of the Chinese legal system had yet to emerge. Only after the CPC took power in 1949, together with the spread of Communism, *Mao*'s 'Great Leap Forward' policy, and, above all, the Cultural Revolution, did drastic changes to traditional social and family values take hold in China. Confucianism itself was criticized and children were encouraged to denounce their parents and teachers. Law was criticized as a tool of 'capitalist oppression of the mass', and China experienced a decade of lawlessness, with political struggles within the CPC leadership causing upheaval of society. This drastic break from the traditional values and legal system, to a certain extent, enabled *Deng Xiaoping*'s reform process to begin.

E THE THEORETICAL DEFICIT OF CHINESE LAW

The Chinese legal tradition is rich in details reflecting moral teachings, rituals, and ethics; but it is arguably poor when it comes to legal theories. It is clear from the above discussion that before 1949, home-grown legal theory was almost non-existent except for the Legalist School, which briefly exerted influence some 2000 years ago, during the *Han* dynasty. Legal scholars or theorists were rare in ancient China. There was no lack of government officials and Confucian scholars who excelled in interpreting and applying legal rules with traditional teachings, but ancient China suffered from a lack of jurists, legal scholars or philosophers who managed to develop their own theory of law, like the early founders of the Legalist School *Han Feizhi* and *Guan Zhi* (管子) 2000 years ago.

Chinese legal theory did not exist per se; at best there were works[45] explaining Chinese law in the light of its influence under Confucianism or its characteristics in certain dynasties. Unlike in the Western legal development, the natural law tradition, for example, provided a theoretical basis for the growth of human rights law. The paucity of the theoretical basis for legal development in China continues to hamper its ability to find its own way of legal development/model while integrating with the global market. There is a risk simply to repeat the type of legal modernization imperial China underwent, which was motivated by instrumentalism, and where the modalities of reform were more of an imitation of Western concepts.

Such a theoretical deficit in traditional Chinese legal history can be explained by the fact that law never acquired a primary role in ancient Chinese society, nor did law per se manage to establish an identity of its own, independent of Confucianism as a subject, or a discipline of its own. Incentives for Chinese scholars under the imperial system to study or specialize in law were limited

---

45. See, for example, 林端, 儒家理論與法律文化 – 社會學觀點的探索, 台灣, 巨流圖書公司, 1994年 (D. Lin, *Confucian Ethic and Legal Culture – A Sociological Analysis* (Taiwan: Ju Liu Publishing, 1994)); 金勇義, 中國與西方的法律觀念, 瀋陽, 遼寧人民出版社, 1989年 (H.I. Kim, *Fundamental Legal Concepts of China and the West, Shenyang*, trans. Chen Guangping (Shenyang: Liaoning People's Publishing, 1989)); 黃仁宇, 萬歷十五年, 北京, 三聯書店, 2002年11月第12版 (R. Huang, *1587 – A Year of No Significance* (New Haven: Yale University, 1981); and 黃仁宇, 黃河青山 – 黃仁宇回憶錄, 台灣, 聯經出版, 2001年 (R. Huang, *Yellow River and Blue Mountains – Memoir* (Taiwan: Taiwan Linking Publishing, 2001)).

indeed. The only road to officialdom in dynastic China was to study Confucian classics and succeeded in civil service examinations. To excel in law would not reap rewards in material terms or government positions. As litigation was discouraged, involvement in legal proceedings and acting as legal counsel was not a respectable vocation. As a result, there was hardly any Chinese legal theory or theoretical *raison d'être* for traditional Chinese law, but merely a set of Confucian values interwoven with legal rules.

IV CONCLUDING REMARKS

The close relationship between law and morality is not unique to ancient Chinese legal tradition. The Justinian codification of Roman law in the sixth century, which became the foundation of all subsequent European laws, for example, was deeply influenced by Christian concepts of justice and equity. The concept of equity, as well as the principle of equity in the common law tradition, was also informed by the link between morality and law.[46] The concept of natural law and natural law principles, even though their influence was overshadowed by the positivists' conception of law, were instrumental in the development of human rights law and principles. While the Reformation and the Enlightenment gradually led to the separation of law and morality in the West, in Chinese legal history such a separation was achieved through far more destructive activities and at high cost.

When the PRC introduced its own legal system in 1949, the existing paucity of legal theory meant that legal principles borrowed from the Soviet Union took prominence. This, together with drastic changes in both the political and economic spheres, paved the way for a radical change in social values at the end of the Maoist era. The edifice of the traditional Chinese social fabrics and the legal system shaped by Confucianism was shaken. Ironically, this same period prompted *Deng Xiaoping* to push ahead with drastic reforms in 1978. The soil for such reforms was fertile enough for a modern economic model as well as a legal system to begin to take root and eventually bear fruits towards the end of the twentieth century. The theoretical deficit in the Chinese legal culture has hampered modern China's ability to adapt the legal system to its changing needs. From 1978 onwards, China sought to converge with the globalized market economy while simultaneously trying to orient its legal development in a way that would be conducive to its own special needs. Its legal reform was stalled by institutional constraints and reform bottlenecks. It was the systemic legal requirements from the WTO throughout China's fifteen years of accession negotiations that finally provided a much-needed sense of orientation and an external push to bolster China's legal reform.

46. Ladany, 34.

Chapter 2
The Pre-WTO Chinese Legal System after 1949

The Chinese legal system before China's accession to the WTO, that is, from 1949 to 2001, can be divided into two major phases. The first phase, from 1949 to 1978, started by incorporating the Soviet legal model and jargon, but mostly in a superficial manner, and soon Soviet legality in China gave way to complete lawlessness during the decade-long Cultural Revolution. The second phase ran from 1978, when *Deng Xiaoping* returned to power and initiated his open-door policy, to the end of 2001 when China became a WTO member. This period witnessed rapid economic reform and many activities in introducing new laws and regulations, seeking to catch up with the changing regulatory needs of a quickly transforming Chinese economy. Towards the end of this period, constraints and bottlenecks in both economic and legal reforms became evident. It was clear to the Chinese leadership that in order to sustain the momentum of over two decades of reform and to gain additional impetus to overcome these bottlenecks, China needed an external push.

The WTO's rules-based system, with its emphasis on trade and economics and less on politics, became an ideal candidate for providing the much-needed external impetus. Joining the WTO would require long-term commitments as well as legal and systemic changes. Lessons learned from both *Mao*'s rule and the economic and legal reforms under *Deng Xiaoping* provided the foundation upon which the Chinese government identified China's accession to the WTO as a national policy. It is crucial to understand the Chinese legal system and reform efforts during this period to appreciate fully the significance of WTO membership to Chinese legal reform.

I COMMUNIST INFLUENCE: *MAO* AND CULTURAL REVOLUTION

In 1949, *Mao* made it clear in his *On the People's Democratic Dictatorship* that a legal system, as understood in the context of Marxism, was part of a superstructure where '[t]he State apparatus, including the army, the police and the courts, is the instrument by which one class oppresses another … .'[1] He added that in Communist China, law should be a weapon of class struggle by the proletariat against the capitalist: 'The law must be observed and the revolutionary legal system must not be undermined. Laws form part of the superstructure. Our laws are made by the working people themselves … . Counter-revolutionaries must be eliminated',[2] *Mao* said. The destruction of the Chinese social structure, traditional morality, and legal system under *Mao*'s rule was total and its result disastrous. Ironically, *Mao*'s rule also succeeded in dismantling social and ideological resistance to changes, which the short-lived reforms from 1911 to 1949 had not succeeded in doing. *Mao* died on 9 September 1976. A well documented book that appeared four years later illustrates the first thirty-year legal history in Communist China under *Mao*'s rule.[3]

A An Overview of the Law under *Mao*

In the early years (1949–1957) of the PRC, efforts on the legal front focused on abolishing existing laws put in place by the Nationalist government and enacting new laws to reflect the Communist rule of China. In February 1949, the CPC annulled all laws adopted during the Nationalist government and abolished the old judiciary to ensure that no checks and balances could restrain its supremacy and absolute power. In September 1949, a so-called 'Common Programme' was promulgated to serve as a provisional constitution, while courts staffed by revolutionaries were set up. In 1950, a marriage law, a trade union law, and a land reform law were adopted, followed by regulations on the suppression of counter-revolutionaries and on 'corrective labour' in 1951 and 1952 respectively. The first PRC State Constitution came into force in 1954 with organic laws regulating state organs and the judiciary. Its Preamble stated that China was a republic under 'the People's Democratic Dictatorship' led by the CPC and headed by *Mao*. During this period, the Party announced regulations governing arrest and detention, military service, and the introduction of an 'education through labour' (*Lao Gai* 劳改) programme, which allowed for prolonged detention without trial.

It is clear that for the PRC under *Mao*'s rule, only a short period of efforts were made to introduce legality, which was modelled mostly after the Soviet regime and Marxism. This came to an end by the time *Mao* launched his 'Great Leap Forward' (1958–1966) campaign, when rules and legal procedures were ignored and party decrees replaced them for political expediency. During the 'Great Leap Forward', a total of 420 decrees were published. The NPC published

1. Ladany, 53, citing 'Report on an Investigation of the Peasant Movement in Hunan', in *Selected Works of Mao Tse-tung*, ed. English (Peking, 1961–1976), IV, 411–424, 418.
2. 27 Jan. 1957, *Mao* addressing a conference of provincial Party committees as recorded in Ladany, 53.
3. Lan Chuan-pu (ed.), *Survey of 30 Years' Development of Laws and Regulations in our Country* (Beijing: Peking, 1980), cited in Ladany, 54–55.

an *Outline for Twelve Years' Development of Agriculture*. Constantly changing policies, arbitrary party decisions, and political campaigns threw the whole country into chaos. Party members who defended legality were labelled 'rightists' and accused of trying to tie the hands of the leaders through laws. The era of the Cultural Revolution and the reign of the 'Gang of Four'[4] (1966–1976) followed, subjecting China to a decade of total anarchy and a legal vacuum. It ended when *Deng Xiaoping* toppled the 'Gang of Four' and returned to power. *Deng* soon embarked upon a course designed to restore a sense of legality.[5]

For the courts and judges, an *Instruction on Legal Work* was issued by the Cabinet in 1950, which explicitly stated that '[l]aw is a tool for the oppression of one class by another.'[6] Legal professionals still using legal concepts were branded as counter-revolutionaries. Party cadres and military personnel were nominated to serve as judges to enforce Soviet legality, where 'the people' and the 'class enemies' were treated differently in legal proceedings.[7] Internal circulars, executive orders, and party policies and decisions were enforced as law and soon the line between legal rules and propaganda became so blurred that the people no longer knew which legal codes actually still applied.

B THE SIGNIFICANCE OF *MAO*'S RULE TO CHINA'S LEGAL DEVELOPMENT

The significance of *Mao*'s rule – in particular the Cultural Revolution and its aftermath – on the legal development of China is two-fold. Firstly, the long legal vacuum and its consequences deeply and negatively affected the Chinese people's perception of law. People simply did not believe in law anymore. The traditional influence of social hierarchy and family structure on the law was also shaken. During and after the Cultural Revolution, politics and changing Communist Party policies were firmly established to be above the law.

Secondly and more positively, the painful experience largely wiped out the 2,000-year-long Confucian influence in Chinese law. This made the challenge of legal reform under *Deng Xiaoping* less formidable, and hence allowed legal reform to start taking root in China. Put differently, the disastrous experience of *Mao*'s era acted as a vivid psychological deterrent in the collective mind of the Chinese, to such an extent that no one wanted to let China lapse into a state of lawlessness again. The lawlessness during the Cultural Revolution also left a mark on future Chinese ruling elites. This partly explains why the successive Chinese leaderships, from *Deng Xiaoping, Jiang Zemin*, to *Hu Jintao*, all emphasized the importance of law in nation-building.

4. Four members of the central leadership working closely with *Mao* during the last stage of his rule, led by *Mao*'s second wife *Jiang Qing*.
5. Lan Chuan-pu (ed.), cited in Ladany, 54–55.
6. Ladany, 61.
7. *Ibid.*, 61–65.

This state of affairs was even registered in CPC's rhetoric and a 'legal construction project' was launched in the early 1980s. Summing up the lessons learned from the Cultural Revolution, the third plenary session of the eleventh Central Committee of the CPC convened in 1978 concluded: 'To guarantee the people's democracy, it is necessary to strengthen the socialist legal system, and institutionalize and legalize the democratic system, to ensure the stability, continuity, and maximum authority of this system as well as the laws.'[8] It further stated that such a system of laws should not be affected by a change in leadership.

A Chinese jurist thus sums up the lessons learned, and his perception is widely shared by the generation that lived through the Cultural Revolution:

> No natural or man-made disaster could rival the damage suffered by China from the Great Leap Forward and the Cultural Revolution.... The costs of the Cultural Revolution were not purely monetary. It is impossible to quantify its devastation of China's scientific progress and cultural heritage, not to mention the untold suffering of its citizens and the permanent scars left on the collective consciousness. While we may not be able to prevent natural disasters like floods and earthquakes, we can and should prevent socio-political disasters such as the Cultural Revolution. The key to achieving this is the rule of law.[9]

When *Deng* returned to power and began to reform the Chinese economy in 1978, the rebuilding of a functioning legal system – though not a priority in itself – became a necessity. With the Chinese legal system shattered and the legal profession destroyed, the type of economic reconstruction envisaged by *Deng* would not be considered viable without reinstating a basic legal structure and introducing some economic rules under which transactions should take place. It was on this primitive foundation with a prudent goal of facilitating economic activities that the second attempt of Chinese legal reform in the twentieth century began.

II ECONOMIC AND LEGAL REFORM UNDER *DENG XIAOPING*'s RULE

Not unlike the series of legal reform measures of the early 1900s, legal reform introduced under *Deng Xiaoping*'s rule was not prompted by ideals of the rule of law or the law itself but instead was driven by realistic concerns and necessities. Legal reform measures were initiated in the early 1980s because they were necessary to re-establish order after the chaos of the Cultural Revolution.[10] The role of law, then, in relation to China's economic order, was to regulate a state planned economy and to direct state-owned enterprises (SOEs). Meanwhile,

8. Z. Wang, 'The Developing Rule of Law in China', *Harvard Asia Quarterly* (Autumn 2000), <www.fas.harvard.edu/~asiactr/haq/200004/0004a007.htm>, 3 Nov. 2005.
9. *Ibid.*
10. See, for example, S. Lubman, *Bird in a Cage: Legal Reform in China after Mao* (Stanford: Stanford University Press, 1999), for an overview of legal reform efforts after *Mao*'s rule.

Deng's open-door policy and economic reform also required economic law and functional administrative and judicial procedures for China to trade with the outside world.

A THE CHANGING ROLE OF LAW

Legal reconstruction proved to be a formidable and long process. Upon returning to power, *Deng* immediately made the reform of the shattered Chinese economy a top priority. Work on new laws started officially in June 1981, when the Standing Committee of the National People's Congress (NPCSC) decided that legal interpretations should be left to the courts, and that the NPCSC would have ultimate authority to interpret laws. It further recommended 'model cases' be formulated for the public to learn about law, but soon it was obvious that the endeavour was difficult to implement.

A report presented to the 1984 annual session of the NPC stated that '[t]o many people the notion of acting according to the law is new, unfamiliar, not something they are used to.'[11] In 1986, the State Economic Commission and the Ministry of Justice announced that over 300 laws and regulations had already been published concerning the economy, but equally noted that 'their non-observance is quite universal'. This was because the heads of the enterprises had no notion of law, and there were no legal experts to advise them, nor was there any machinery to control the implementation of laws and regulations.[12] Similar difficulties existed with regard to enforcement of court decisions, as indicated in a lead article of the government-controlled newspaper, *People's Daily*, 'The Verdicts and Decisions of the Court Must Be Carried Out'.[13]

This situation is not surprising. With trained lawyers and judges persecuted and stripped of their jobs during the Cultural Revolution, the courts were filled with politically reliable but legally ignorant military personnel and party cadres. Corruption became daily routine. A long-time China observer summarized the situation as follows:

> [T]he relaxation of the economic system, the erosion of Party discipline and the official encouragement given to people to make money through their own efforts – to which the Party cadres took no exception – made the implementation of the regulations almost impossible. The fundamental difficulty lay in the dissolution of the traditional Chinese moral texture.... During the 30 years of Mao's rule, the moral texture of the nation was torn to shreds. The younger generation has hardly heard of traditional morality. The endless political

11. Ladany, 95–96.
12. *Ibid.*, 96 citing the *People's Daily*, 7 Oct. 1986.
13. *Ibid.*

> campaigns, campaigns of class hatred, blew through society like a hot sirocco, creating a vast desert.[14]

It was upon such a basis China started to rebuild its legal infrastructure. The twenty years of efforts yielded some results by 2001. They were, however, not enough to allow China to be fully convergent with international standards and the ways of functioning that governed the world economy.

B THE LEGAL REGIME OF PRE-WTO CHINA

Understanding the different roles of law and politics in China is essential to appreciate the significance of the rules of the game which the WTO regime brings the country. Legal authority has yet to acquire a superior status in China. The desire of the political leadership to develop 'a socialist market economy' has been a major force and incentive for the PRC to reform its traditional 'rule by man' system. Besides, several features make the Chinese legal regime quite distinct from the legal systems of other WTO members. For example, the Chinese state structure reflects the unity of legislative and executive power, meaning that there is no effective separation of powers nor checks and balances between legislative, executive, and judicial branches. In addition, the CPC enjoys unique status, not only because it is the ruling party of China's one-party rule system but also because of its precarious status in the Chinese legal system. While CPC organs exist alongside most government organs at the central and local levels, the CPC is not mentioned in the Chinese Constitution except in the Preamble.

1 The CPC and the Government under Chinese Law

Especially during the early stage of this reform period, the CPC and the government were not fully subject to law, while law, to a large extent, was merely an instrument for governing the country. The PRC Constitution stipulates the principle of equality of all before the law and that no one is beyond the law.[15] However, it also asserts the absolute leadership of the CPC as a fundamental principle in the Preamble.[16]

The NPC is nominally the highest legislative body in the PRC. It has the highest unitary legislative power over the nation. The NPC has absolute power to enact laws, and there is no constitutional review.[17] The NPC is simultaneously a political

---

14. Ladany, 98.
15. Article 5, the PRC Constitution.
16. See Preamble of the PRC Constitution.
17. The PRC Constitution, promulgated in 1982 and subsequently amended in 1988, 1993, 1999, 2004, and 2007, is considered vague and having no directly applicable effects. To review legislature and government practice on the basis of constitutionality has been politically and legally problematic. See also C. Wang & X. Zhang (eds), *Introduction to Chinese Law* (Hog Kong: Sweet and Maxwell Asia, 1997).

organ subordinated to the CPC. Law is always secondary and subject to the authority to the supremacy of the political power enjoyed by the CPC. The executive and judicial branches are accountable to the NPC and its Standing Committee, NPCSC, under a system of 'unity of legislative and executive power'.[18] Immediately subordinate to the NPC and NPCSC are the highest judicial organ, the Supreme People's Court (SPC), the executive branch, the State Council (i.e., the Central People's Government of the PRC), the Supreme People's Procuratorate (SPP), and the Central Military Commission. There is clearly a division of labour, but equally clearly that there is no separation of powers.

Notwithstanding the formal structure of state organs, the CPC, with its Politburo of the Central Committee, is the body that exercises supreme power. CPC organizations exist parallel to state organs at all levels, as an institutional guarantee and for party guidance – thus, the mayor of a Chinese city is simultaneously the deputy secretary of the parallel party organ of that city. While as a government official, the mayor's authority of office is defined by law, in the CPC hierarchy, the mayor is accountable to the party secretary of the city, whose power is in turn governed by the CPC and its party discipline, policed by the CPC's Central Commission for Discipline Inspection (CCDI), not by law.

2 'A Socialist Market Economy'

The concept was first brought into the Chinese context by *Deng Xiaoping* in 1985. It was fine-tuned in 1992 during his famous 'tour to the south', which marked a watershed of economic reform efforts undertaken by the PRC since the early 1980s. The fourteenth General Assembly of the CPC that same year formally incorporated the concept of 'a socialist market economy' into China's national policy. The essence of *Deng*'s speeches was to adopt a flexible approach in interpreting ideologies to further the pragmatic ends of enhancing Chinese productivity and economic development:

> Socialism and market economy are not contradictory to each other. The question is how we can enhance social productivity in a more effective manner. Should there be more (state) planning or more market? This is not the fundamental distinction between socialism and capitalism. Planning does not mean socialism, whereas there is planning in a market economy as well. Market does not mean capitalism, and market can exist in socialism too. Both planning and market are merely economic instruments.[19]

18. See 張鋆, 中國法律, 中文大學出版社, 1994年 (H. Chang, *The Chinese Legal System Explained* (Hong Kong: The Chinese University of Hong Kong, 1994), 46 and 263–264); C. Wang & X. Zhang (eds), 17, 43 and 53; and A. Chen, *An Introduction to the Legal System of the People's Republic of China* (Hong Kong: LexisNexis Butterworths, 2004).
19. Speeches by *Deng Xiaoping* in 1985 and 1992 (In Chinese, English translation by the author), *People's Daily*, available at <www.people.com.cn/GB/shizheng/252/5303/5304/20010627/498360.html>, 23 Mar. 2009, see also the resolution by the 14th General Assembly of the CPC.

The significance of *Deng*'s speeches has to be seen in the context in which they were made. Economic reforms in China were not free of political opposition. In the aftermath of the Cultural Revolution, during the last phase of *Mao*'s era, there was much debate about socialism and capitalism, which manifested itself in the political struggles within the top Chinese leadership. Discarding this ideological hindrance, *Deng* once stated that 'it doesn't matter whether a cat is white or black; it's a good cat as long as it catches mice'.[20] Symbolically, catching mice refers to favouring economic reforms because they are likely to bring about a stronger country and a better livelihood to Chinese citizens.

This author's interviews with sources from the State Council, the Ministry of Commerce (MOFCOM), the legal profession, and academia in China all confirm that there is no official or legal definition of 'a socialist market economy with Chinese characteristics'. All interviewees indicated that the concept could only be fully appreciated by looking at the context of China's state ideology and reform process. In summary, the concept's main features include:

- First, the model of ownership. A socialist market economy means that despite other forms of ownership, such as private ownership and joint-venture – those prominent in a market economy, are accepted, state ownership should remain dominant and the majority, that is, 51% or above, of the Chinese economy. Currently, the notion of majority is no longer applied literally and rigidly. With the development of the Chinese economy and with WTO commitments, state ownership cannot remain the dominant model of the economy. In some sectors, already less than 51% of enterprises are state-owned.[21]
- Second, the word 'socialist', nevertheless, must remain in the formula that characterizes the country's reform towards a market economy, because the PRC officially remains a Communist state. It is not only a tradition but concerns the legitimacy of the CPC as the ruling party of China. In the past, that is, at the beginning of *Deng Xiaoping*'s open-door policy in the early 1980s, certain CPC factions argued that socialism and capitalism could not be integrated and that China had to choose between one and the other. It was, therefore, all the more important for *Deng* to emphasize that China could benefit most from a 'socialist' model of 'market economy' tailored to the level of development and the national realities of China – hence the term 'with Chinese characteristics'.
- Third, and in addition to the notion of state ownership, another main characteristic of the formula concerns the role of state planning. Contrary to a laissez-faire approach applicable in a market economy, macro-economic control measures were heavily used in the first decades of China's economic reform. They remain present in the areas of foreign

20. In Chinese, English translation by the author.
21. Interview with Professor Zhang Hengshan, Deputy Dean of Department of Politics and Law, Party School of the Central Committee of the Communist Party of China, Beijing, 10 Sep. 2004, Beijing.

> exchange and sensitive sectors such as transportation, telecommunication, energy, basic utilities, and banking.[22]

By 1992, *Deng's* reform efforts continued to be obstructed by political struggles within the CPC. The 1989 June Fourth Student Movement, which ended when the People's Liberation Army (PLA) cleared demonstrators from *Tiananmen* Square, marked the peak of such struggles. Thereafter, reactionary forces in the CPC became influential and further stalled the reform process. *Deng*'s 'tour to the south' in 1992 reaffirmed a determination from the top leadership that despite the political turmoil, economic reforms had to continue. The eighth session of the NPC in 1993 passed a constitutional amendment and the policy of running China as 'socialist market economy' was entrenched in the PRC Constitution.

Accession to the WTO is another milestone of China's reforms. It reaffirms that China must reform towards a 'socialist market economy' and take part in the global market. Chinese WTO membership means that the PRC's pursuit of 'a socialist market economy' cannot be reversed. This time the policy is not only backed by the top political leadership but also entrenched legally in an international agreement, the WTO accession agreement. On a theoretical note, former President *Jiang Zemin*'s 'Three Represents' theory[23] and his announcement in 2001 that he would welcome capitalists to join the CPC was further evidence of a parallel development that China undertakes to transform towards a 'socialist market economy'.

In sum, as reflected by the number of constitutional amendments over the years, the role of the private sector and private property have been gradually moving towards centre stage in China's long road toward economic reform. In 1988, the PRC Constitution stipulated that the state allows the private economy to exist and grow within the limits prescribed by law, as a 'complement' to the public economy. In 1993, the term 'socialist market economy' was added; and the role of the private sector was upgraded to make it an 'essential part' of the socialist market economy in another constitutional amendment in 1999. The 2004 amendment formally recognizes private property rights and their constitutional protection. This move set the stage for the drafting and the adoption of an epochal property law.

3 An Economics-Driven Legal Reform

During the fifteenth CPC Congress in 1997, *Jiang Zemin* endorsed the notion of 'rule by law' to be practised in China, by stating that:

> Rule by law means, under the people's leadership as entrusted to the Party, to rule the country according to the Constitution and legal rules…and to

22. Interview with Professor Wang Xixin, Associate Dean, Peking University Law School, and Research Consultant, the Standing Committee of National People's Congress of China, Beijing, 7 Sep. 2004, Beijing.
23. Speech by *Jiang Zemin* in a meeting for the 80th anniversary of the CPC, 1 Jul. 2001 (In Chinese, English translation by the author), available at <www.people.com.cn/GB/shizheng/16/20010702/501591.html>, 15 Mar. 2007.

> gradually implement a socialist democracy in a systemic and legalized way. Such a system and law would not change due to changes in political leadership, nor would it change because of the change of leaders' views or attention. 'Rule by law' is a fundamental policy that the Party has chosen to lead the country. It is also an objective imperative for developing a socialist market economy.[24]

At that point, 'rule by law' was as far as the CPC leadership was willing to go in the context of legal reform. *Jiang* was yet to proclaim 'the rule of law' as the next goal of China's legal reform. In September 1999, he also pledged to sustain the pace of reform and to have a full-fledged socialist market economy in place within a decade.[25] A constitutional amendment of the same year recognized the notion of 'rule by law' or 'rule according to law'.

C LEGAL REFORM

China's legal reform did not begin with WTO accession. Indeed, legal reform has been a continuous process since *Deng Xiaoping*'s rule. Chinese WTO accession in December 2001 is used here as a dividing point in the discussion of the salient features of the pre-WTO Chinese legal system and the constraints of the country's legal reform. As indicated, there were four constitutional amendments between 1982 and the end of 2001. Other important constitutional amendments, such as the inclusion of the term 'human rights' and the protection of private property rights, followed thereafter.

1 The CPC and the PRC Constitution

The CPC has a precarious position in the Chinese Constitution. While the Communist party does not appear in any substantive provisions of the PRC Constitution, the leadership of the CPC, however, is repeatedly affirmed in the Constitution's Preamble. Some argue that such political statements in the Preamble are not legally binding and by no means imply that the CPC is above and beyond the reach of law. But the pattern that developed since the adoption of the 1982 Constitution shows that no major constitutional amendments could be introduced to, and subsequently be passed by, the NPC, the highest state organ, before clearance by the highest body of the CPC – the Congress of the CPC, held every five years.[26]

---

24. 江泽民在中国共产党第十五次全国代表大会上的报告, 1997, 年9月12日 (Jiang Zemin's Report to the 15th CPC Congress, 12 Sep. 1997, available at the website of *People's Daily*, <cpc.people.com.cn/GB/64162/64168/64568/65445/4526285.html>, 22 Aug. 2007, in Chinese, English translation by the author.
25. '2010 Deadline to Build Market Economy: Jiang', *South China Morning Post*, 8 Sep. 1999.
26. The last one took place in October 2007.

The following sequence of events illustrates CPC supremacy over key constitutional issues. The controversial subject of providing legal protection to private property is a case in point. In 1987, the thirteenth CPC Congress first recognized the private sector as a necessary supplement to the state sector, which was followed by a constitutional amendment during the annual NPC session in 1988 that acknowledged the private sector as a complement to the socialist public economy (Article 11). The fourteenth CPC Congress in October 1992 endorsed the establishment of a 'socialist market economy' as a national reform policy. During its annual session the following year, the NPC amended the Constitution to include that '[T]he state has put into practice a socialist market economy. The State strengthens formulating economic laws, improves macro adjustment and control and forbids according to law any units or individuals from interfering with the social economic order (Article 15).'

At the fifteenth CPC Congress in 1997, *Jiang* put forward the notion that China should practise 'rule by law'. In 1999, the NPC amended the Constitution to strengthen the role of law as a means of governing the country; '[t]he People's Republic of China practices ruling the country in accordance with the law and building a socialist country of law (Article 5).' The term '*Deng Xiaoping* Theory' was incorporated into the Preamble of the Constitution as one of the guiding principles, together with 'the leadership of the CPC, the 'guidance of Marxism-Leninism', and '*Mao Zedong*'s Thought' to run the country, and to 'develop a socialist market economy'.

In 2002, the sixteenth CPC Congress incorporated into its party charter the so-called 'Three Represents' put forward by *Jiang*, with the ground-breaking concept that the CPC should welcome capitalists to become members, affirming that the party must always represent 'the development trend of China's advanced productive forces, the orientation of China's advanced culture and the fundamental interests of the overwhelming majority of the Chinese people'.[27] The CPC then engineered constitutional amendments to include the 'Three Represents', and in line with the theory the protection of private property, in the Constitution. The 2004 NPC annual session further amended the Constitution, adding 'the important thought of "Three Represents" as a guidance of the country (Preamble). The concept of inviolable private property rights was recognized and protected against state expropriation without compensation: "Citizens" lawful private property is inviolable' and '[t]he State, in accordance with law, protects the rights of citizens to private property and to its inheritance' and '[t]he State may, in the public interest and in accordance with law, expropriate or requisition private property for its use and shall make compensation for the private property expropriated or requisitioned' (Article 13). In addition and importantly, the term 'human rights' was for the first time written into the PRC Constitution (Article 33).

Despite the unclear status of the CPC in the PRC Constitution, the chronology above clearly demonstrates that since 1982, no major constitutional amendments

---

27. 'Constitution Amendments to Have Far-reaching Influence', *China Daily*, 28 Dec. 2003.

could be introduced without prior clearance by the highest body of the CPC. The CPC continues to have the final say over Chinese national policies, and the pace and orientation of its economic, legal, and political reforms.

2 Legislative Aspect

The initial phase of China's modern economic reform came together with a phase of legislative fervour, during which new laws and regulations were introduced simultaneously throughout the country in order to speed up economic reform and to create a legal framework that would promote and regulate foreign investment in the economy. An *Accounting Law* was promulgated as early as 1985; it was amended in 1993 and 1999. The *General Principles of Civil Law* was passed in 1986, the *Company Law* in 1993, the *Guaranty Law* and the *Insurance Law* in 1995, the *Law on Partnership Enterprises* in 1997, the *Securities Law* in 1998, and the *Contract Law* in 1999. A flurry of new laws was put into place at the regional and local levels, very often without any accompanying systemic elements and well-suited institutional infrastructure for their enforcement. Numerous bodies were given the authority to legislate, and very often priority was given to quantity over quality.

Both the NPC and its standing organ, the NPCSC, can enact and amend national laws, while the State Council, the highest executive body, has authority to enact administrative regulations and orders applicable nationwide. Meanwhile, People's Congresses at provincial levels and in large cities, as well as their standing committees, can adopt local legislations. Local organs of the State Council, governments at the provincial, municipal, and local levels, as well as governments of autonomous regions and special economic regions, are all authorized to issue their own rules and regulations. NPC statistics indicate that from the early 1980s to the beginning of 2001, over 7,000 laws were enacted by local People's Congresses and their standing committees, compared to about 200 enacted by the NPC and the NPCSC over the same period. For those local laws, over one half were regulations and rules addressing economic activities.[28]

Beijing advanced the notion of 'Administration in accordance with Law' (*Yifa Xingzheng*, 依法行政) in November 1999, when the State Council adopted a decision calling for all government organs and officials to conduct administration according to law. A series of administrative law was promulgated during the first two decades of China's reform and open-door policy, including the *Administrative Litigation Law* which entered into force in 1990, the *State Compensation Law* in 1994, the *Administrative Punishment Law* in 1996, the *Administrative Redress Law* in 1999, and the *Law on Legislation*,[29] which regulates legislative activities and clarifies the authority of different sources of law, in 2000.

---

28. '地方人大20年来的立法工作', 中国人大新闻, 2001年1月3日, 1–5 in 1–20 ('Legislative Work of Local People's Congresses in the Past 20 Years', *News of the National People's Congress*, 3 Jan. 2001; 1–5 in 1–20, <www.npcnews.com.cn/gb/paper12/1/class001200001/hwz64637.htm>, 17 Feb. 2006.

29. 立法法, effective 1 Jul. 2000, Chinese version available at <www.law-lib.com/>.

More administrative laws were enacted after China's accession to the WTO. Figures from 2004 indicate that from the early 1980s onwards, the State Council issued over 650 administrative regulations, while over 50,000 administrative rules were issued by regional bodies and the local governments.[30] The most ground-breaking administrative law is the 2004 *Administrative Licensing Law* (ALL), which is discussed further in Part III.

3 Judicial Aspect

In the Chinese state structure, the SPC is the highest judicial organ, and it is directly subordinate to the NPC. Subordinate to the SPC are three levels of regional and local courts, including:

- the higher courts at the provincial levels, in autonomous regions and municipalities under the central government;
- the Higher People's Courts; the intermediate courts at the level of prefectures, provincial capitals, and big cities;
- the Intermediate People's Courts; and the basic courts at the level of counties, and the Grassroots People's Courts.

While the PRC legal system is closer to the civil law tradition, it officially characterizes itself as a system of socialist legality. Unlike in the common law system, judicial precedents are of no formal authority in the Chinese legal system. It is, however, a common practice for lower court judges to seek advice from higher level courts or even executive and party organs before adjudicating important cases.

The Supreme People's Procuratorate, or Procuracy (SPP, *Zuigao Renmin Jianchayuan*, 最高人民检察院), the highest prosecutorial (specifically called 'procuratorial' in the Chinese state structure) organ under the NPC, also perform some supervisory functions over the courts. The procuratorate structure and its functions to ensure legal supervision, investigate, and prosecute corruption and other offences were reinstated in 1978 after the Cultural Revolution. Procurators at different levels can file protests in relation to judicial proceedings before courts and launch investigations into criminal cases. The procurators sometimes issue comments and decisions on whether the courts have handled cases before them properly and refer judgments considered erroneous back to the court. Unlike in an adversarial system, the main judicial function of procurators is not to act as an impartial adjudicator in the resolution of disputes.

In the PRC, both the courts and procurators are meant to work in tandem in an inquisitorial system, to combat crimes and uphold 'legality'. Unlike under the common law tradition, the authority to interpret laws does not lie with the courts or ultimately the SPC, but is the exclusive domain of the NPC and NPCSC. The SPC, however, can issue 'interpretations' with effects similar to supplementary

---

30. '当代中国的法治改革与发展', 中国人大网, 2005年12月8日, 1–7 ('Legal Reform and Development in Modern China, *the NPC Website*', 8 Dec. 2005, 1–7, <cms.npc.gov.cn:87/servlet/PagePreviewServlet?siteid=1&nodeid=221&articleid=343175&type=1>, 17 Feb. 2006).

legislation. The State Council has the authority to amend, correct, and repeal rules and regulations issued by regional and local authorities.

Systematic and reliable data on China's judiciary are hard to obtain.[31] According to the SPC's annual report to the 2002 NPC session, the SPC adjudicated 3,047 cases and issued thirty-four judicial interpretations in 2001. At the levels of local and specialized courts, close to 6 millions cases (5,927,660) were dealt with in the same period, 12.31% of which were criminal cases, 85.64% civil cases, and 2.05% administrative cases.[32] But the report does not mention the number of judges, the judicial personnel, or the number of Chinese courts in 2001. An article[33] in the NPC website posted in 2005, however, indicated that by 2004, there were 3548 courts, 190,627 judges, 3,626 procuratorates, and 142,614 prosecutors throughout China, without, however, citing the sources of these figures.

In 1999, the SPC issued a *Five-Year Reform Plan of the People's Courts*[34] calling for some thirty-nine reform measures to be implemented, which included items such as holding public trials, combating judicial corruption, reforming the judicial supervisory system, and improving the management of judicial personnel. Statistics posted on the NPC website[35] indicate that for the period 1998–2002, the SPC adjudicated 20,293 cases, thus registering a 46% caseload increase compared to the previous five-year period. Local courts at different levels and specialized courts saw an increase of 22% in their caseload during the same period of time, among which 26,399 cases involved foreign entities – an annual increase of 4%. Remarkably, from 1998 to 2002, 464,689 administrative cases were adjudicated, a 65% jump compared to the total number of the previous five years. A *Second Five-Year Reform Plan of the People's Courts* for the period 2006–2010[36] was issued in 2006.

Contrary to expectations of some China observers, especially those looking at the Chinese court system from a common law perspective, Chinese courts have not played an independent role. Normally courts are not allowed to challenge the legality of laws by way of judicial review, as in common law jurisdictions. Often, judges do not enjoy institutional guarantees such as security of tenure. The importance placed on judicial review mechanisms by WTO members during China's accession negotiations perhaps reflects their misplaced expectations on Chinese courts, though there is hope that the continued judicial reform will result in empowering the Chinese courts to assume a more proactive role in shaping the Chinese legal system.

---

31. D.C. Clarke, 'Empirical Research into the Chinese Judicial System', in *Beyond Common Knowledge: Empirical Approaches to the Rule of Law*, eds E.G. Jensen & T.C. Heller (Stanford: Stanford University Press, 2003), 164–192.
32. Annual Report of the Supreme People's Court 2002, 1, available at <www.npc.gov.cn>.
33. See 'Legal Reform and Development in Modern China'.
34. 人民法院五年改革纲要 (1999–2003), issued by the Supreme People's Court, 22 Oct. 1999, <www.dffy.com/faguixiazai/xf/200511/20051128111114.htm>, 3 Mar. 2006.
35. See 'Legal Reform and Development in Modern China'.
36. 人民法院第二个五年改革纲要 (2004–2008), issued by the Supreme People's Court, 26 Oct. 2005, <www.law-lib.com/law/law_view.asp?id=120832>, 3 Mar. 2006.

4 Law Enforcement

Law enforcement remains the weakest link in the Chinese legal reform. Law enforcement, broadly defined, refers not only to the implementation of judicial decisions, but also to the extent to which laws and regulations are enforced by government agents, such as the police, customs officials, officials handling administrative matters, and, in the case of China, public security offices and procuratorates. The different functions of the procuratorates and the public security forces are not clearly defined, though the procuratorates deal mainly, but not exclusively, with offences involving government officials. The *People's Daily*, for example, declared in an article[37] that the SPP and procuratorates at various levels focused their investigation and prosecution on four categories of cases:

- the misuse of administrative power, including the abuse of power by officials above the county level;
- the practice of favouritism, perverting the law, extorting confessions by torture, and unlawful detention by judicial officers;
- irregularities committed by law enforcement authorities, especially those responsible for economic order and security; and
- so-called 'the violation of legal and democratic rights and interests of citizens'.

In line with the PRC's national economic policy to reform SOEs, the SPP announced that its special focus would be to crack down on 'cases that are harmful to reforms in state-owned enterprises', to 'help build a diligent and clean government', and to 'promote the development of a market economy with socialist characteristics'.[38]

Performance indicators of law enforcement agencies are hard to obtain in China, but sporadic figures are cited in official sources about widespread deficiencies in the enforcement of judicial decisions and arbitrations. In a rule of law system, law enforcement agents are bound by law and are expected to perform their duties solely in accordance with the law. In China, in addition to law, CPC orders and instructions of government officials often also serve as a basis and justification for the actions of law enforcement agents. Official figures show that in 1998, the authorities corrected 11,600 court judgments considered to be erroneous and prosecuted about 7,000 judicial officers and law enforcement agents for bribery and abuse of power. In addition, 130,000 police officers were found to have broken the law and 850,000 court rulings involving a total of CNY 31 billion (*Yuan Renminbi*) (about USD 2.8 billion) had not been implemented.[39]

---

37. 'Chinese Procuratorate to Target Misuse of Administrative Power', *People's Daily*, 28 Apr. 2000.
38. *Ibid.*
39. Figures quoted from a report in *Xinhua*, the state news agency. It was not explained why and how those judgments were characterized as 'wrong'. 'War on Law Abuse Nets Thousands', *South China Morning Post*, 14 Apr. 1999.

According to a report by *Xinhua* news agency, citing 2004 petitions figures from the State Letters and Complaints Bureau, over 30% of petitions received that year concerned complaints relating to laws and legal procedures.[40] The report concluded that '[s]uch phenomena as "the case closes, but the dispute remains unresolved" and "placing greater trust in petitions than in procedural laws" are causing people to lose faith in the judicial system.'

D CONSTRAINTS IN LEGAL REFORM

Shortcomings of the Chinese legal system and constraints faced by China's legal reform are closely related. As to shortcomings of the legal system itself, some are attributable to the design of the PRC's state structure and its political system, which is not on the Chinese leadership's reform agenda. The constraints in China's legal reform, however, refer to areas the Chinese leadership is willing to reform except that several factors made such changes difficult. Constraints in the context of the present study refer to factors which prevent reform efforts from producing results.

Some constraints stem from weak institutions and historical deficits in the respect for law and the paucity of the legal culture, while others are, ironically, the result of China's economic development since 1978. Modern China's legal reform has been primarily driven by economic considerations. Sources from the NPC indicate that as of 2001, over half of the local regulations focused on economic rules.[41] The pace of legal reform, while commendable, still lags behind the growth of the economy, and those who benefit from legal loopholes seek to maintain their vested interests and are reluctant to submit themselves to legal discipline.

Chinese economic reform has resulted in an increasingly unequal distribution of wealth and economic power. The early stages of reform proceeded in an improvised manner. *Deng*'s approach to reform is illustrated by one of his famous adages: 'crossing the river while feeling out for the boulders'. It can be interpreted as a spontaneous approach to the process of bringing about a more open and market-driven economy – shedding the ideological burden, moving ahead, remaining flexible but cautious. Contrary to the ideal of Communism, *Deng* also postulated that in the process of developing a socialist market economy, a small fraction of China's population had to become rich first. As a result, both at the central and local levels, a few elites, mostly party cadres, influential personalities in the PLA, and those well-connected to powerful political figures, took advantage of loopholes in the legal system. Those were in the best position to reap the benefits of an opening and growing economy.

As economic reform edges on and legal reform tries to catch up, such developments naturally threaten the vested interests of those who went into the reform

40. He Dawei, '30 Percent of Petitions Stem from Loss of Popular Faith in Legal Justice', 29 Nov. 2005, *China Comment*, <news.xinhuanet.com>.
41. 'Legislative Work of Local People's Congresses in the Past 20 Years'.

process with a head start. From the perspective of law, to adapt legal reform to the pace of economic change means a change of paradigm in the game-play. With both substantive and procedural laws introduced to govern economic and administrative activities, legal reform implies that the re-distribution of wealth and economic opportunities should be rules and rights based, instead of power and connection based, as tended to be the case. Legislative aspect of Chinese legal reform redefines the rules of the game, judicial reform is designed to empower the courts to act impartially and as the referees of the game, and the enforcement aspect – the weakest link in legal reform – serves to implement the new rules and erodes vested interests. With this in mind, we obtain additional tools to analyse the constraints of China's legal reform.

1 Regionalism

Regionalism has been a recurrent obstacle in the way of China's reform efforts. One of the major complaints of foreign investors in China concerns widespread protectionism at the local level. The phenomenon is commonly known as '*Shang You Zheng Ce, Xia You Dui Ce*'(上有政策, 下有对策) in Chinese, meaning that no matter what policies the central government in Beijing may adopt, local authorities have their ways of circumventing them to serve their own interests. There is a category of 'law' in the PRC, dubbed 'documents in red letterhead', that is, instructions and rules written on paper with official letterhead in red colour, that local government or party officials arbitrarily issue and seek to enforce as law. Such 'documents in red letterhead' can be found in the thirty-one Chinese provinces, though often they are arbitrarily drafted and enforced, resulting in inconsistent rule enforcement from one province to another and conflicts with national laws issued by the central authorities.

As these local regulations are issued by local people's congresses and government departments, they often are tailored to protect local interests. Price control by local authorities, for example, became a sticking point in the final stages of the WTO accession negotiations, and the central authorities repeatedly urged local governments to abandon price control, although national legislation had been amended to this effect in preparation for China's WTO accession. When accession negotiations were close to an end in July 2001, Beijing announced that from August 2001, items subject to state price control would be reduced to only thirteen categories of commodities and services. Yet soon afterwards, Beijing had to issue another decree whereby local governments were ordered to abandon price controls.[42] A central government official in charge of price control policy admitted in a television interview[43] that price control at local levels remained confusing.

---

42. 林美茵, 中国入世面对的法律挑战, 信报, 2001年7月30–31日 (Esther Lam, 'WTO Legal Challenges to China', *Hong Kong Economic Journal*, 30–31 Jul. 2001).
43. *Ibid.*, citing the Central Chinese Television, 17 Jul. 2001.

An interview[44] with a NPC official reveals that several years before China joined the WTO, the NPC had been seeking the cooperation of regional and local people's congresses to 'clean up' local laws and administrative regulations which were inconsistent with central laws but which had met with limited success. Discrepancies remained both in regulations and practices throughout the country. One month before China joined the WTO, the CPC central leadership ordered local laws to be 'cleaned up' and promptly brought in line with WTO rules. The State Council adopted an executive order requesting all local NPCs to cooperate with the central government in preparing for the WTO accession.

Within a year, several hundreds of regional and local rules and 'documents in red letterhead' incompatible with WTO rules were thus 'cleaned up'. This shows that not only were there widespread inconsistencies in regulations between the central government and regional authorities, but also that regional authorities widely resisted compliance, and that the NPC was not as effective as party and executive orders when it came to putting order into local legislative affairs.

Regionalism does not only manifest itself in the legislative realm but also in judicial practices and law enforcement. An overwhelming percentage of these local regulations concerned the collection of fees, licensing rules, fines, and the examination and inspection rules, while very few imposed procedures and restrictions on the administrative power of local authorities, and even less provided for legal protection of the rights of enterprises and citizens.[45] There have been growing signs of protectionism and regionalism since the start of economic reform. The CPC controls the courts through various levels of political legal committees parallel to the judicial structure. Local CPC units, acting through local government and the people's congress, determine the remuneration of judges and make personnel decisions. Even if they do not take bribes, judges are pressured to rule in favour of local litigants.

Local protectionism has triggered widespread non-compliance with court judgments. According to SPC senior judge and vice-president *Wan Exiang*, Chinese courts deal with some 6 million commercial and civil disputes per year, but over half of the civil and trade-related judgments require coercive enforcement procedures for implementation.[46] One of the major reasons cited by *Wan* was the multi-level administrative structure for enforcement of judgments, which makes it hard to resist local protectionism. In other words, enforcement of judgments requires the cooperation of administrative officials from different local authorities, who are subject to the influence of local interests adversely affected by such judgments.

---

44. Author's interview with a Chinese official on 21 Aug. 2005; interviewee requested to remain anonymous.
45. *Ibid.*
46. A speech by Wan Exiang in the Tenth National Committee session of the Chinese People's Political Consultative Conference, quoted in '多半民商事判决需强制执行民革中央建议司法改革', 新华网, 2005年07月07日 ('Over Half Civil Judgments Require Coercive Enforcement, Judicial Reform Urged', *Xinhua Net*, 7 Jul. 2005, available at <lawprofessors.typepad.com/china_law_prof_blog/2005/07/wan_exiang_over.html>; 15 Mar. 2006).

Wan did not elaborate on what types of coercive enforcement procedures are required for the implementation of judgments, nor were there data about the effectiveness of such procedures. Some cases in Shanxi province documented by the newspaper *Legal Daily* are typical examples of how local protectionism can turn judgments into empty words. *Feng Yongan*, chief of the Court Enforcement Bureau in the low income Yanchuan county of Shaanxi province, told the press that '[i]t's not entirely the court's fault that some rulings have become meaningless words'.[47]

2 Arbitrary Administrative Power

While, ideologically, the PRC is run by the CPC as a socialist country, many observers argue that in practice, China functions in an 'administrative-led' manner. It refers to the lack of checks and balances or judicial recourse, which results in administrative officials enjoying wide discretion in the discharge of their daily duties.

Several factors further aggravate this situation. While economic and legal reforms prompted numerous new laws and regulations, they are generally vague and badly drafted and therefore subject to wide administrative discretion and interpretation when it comes to implementation. Secondly, there was no law providing redress against administrative abuse of power until 1990, when the *Administrative Litigation Law* entered into force. The law, however, only allows the courts to

47. Zhang Yirong, 'Courts Not Entirely At Fault When Rulings Become Empty Words', *Legal Daily*, 2 Dec. 2005. Feng mentioned three cases he dealt with, none of which resulted in the court judgments being enforced. Case 1: Liang managed the county's limited liability farm machinery company, which was a SOE before being restructured into a private enterprise. When it was still state-owned, the firm mortgaged its office buildings to secure two loans worth CNY 700,000 (about USD 90,000) from the county bank. After the restructuring, the obligation to repay the loan was transferred to Liang's company. In 2003, the county government dismantled the mortgaged buildings in order to construct a plaza. The court ruled that Liang's company had to repay the loan, but since the local government had not compensated him for the dismantled buildings, he had no money to repay the loan and the judgment could not be enforced.

Case 2: Wang Jianhua ran a cigarette and liquor store, where leaders from two township governments frequently shopped. But the local leaders never paid cash and only bought on credit. The governments each owed Wang more than CNY 10,000. Wang went to the township leaders to collect payment but was refused. He then won his case in court. The two governments both acknowledged that the court ruling ordering the township governments to pay Wang Jianhua was just, but still there has been no compliance, citing lack of fund as the reason. The court proceeded to freeze their bank accounts, but the county leaders immediately called the court, questioning how it could freeze the township governments' accounts, as this would result in difficulties in paying the township officials' salaries. The court was then ordered to rescind the freeze of the accounts immediately.

Case 3: The forestry department's driver in Shanxi province caused a traffic incident, and the court ruled that the department and driver were jointly liable. However, the unit assisting with enforcement of the judgment – the county accounting settlement centre – refused to comply, and the centre's most senior official asked why the driver's employer had to pay the fine imposed on the driver. The judge explained that this was a case of joint liability, to which the official replied that he did not understand and refused to enforce the ruling.

review administrative decisions themselves, but not the rules or laws on which such decisions are based. The *Administrative Litigation Law* specifically states that the courts shall not accept lawsuits against 'administrative rules and regulations, regulations, or decisions and orders with general binding force formulated and announced by administrative organs (Article 12(2))'. It also prohibits the courts from adjudicating cases that concern 'specific administrative acts that shall, as provided for by law, be finally decided by an administrative organ (Article 12(4))'. Third, a combination of weak courts, powerful executive authorities, and local interests implies that even where administrative decisions are revoked by the courts, there is no guarantee that the judgments are eventually enforced.[48] An article published in late 2005 quoted *Xi Xiaoming*, deputy president of the SPC, as saying that since the promulgation of the *Administrative Litigation Law,* courts at different levels had heard over 1 million first-instance administrative cases. Among the cases that had been resolved, the plaintiffs had won in about 30%.[49] The article, however, did not mention the percentage of final resolution of the overall total, nor the extent to which the 30% of judgments in favour of plaintiffs had been enforced. *Xi* also noted that the various forms of illegal interference by the administrative departments varied in severity, without giving further details.

In addition to the deficiencies of the *Administrative Litigation Law*, there was no mechanism to enforce constitutional provisions. The PRC Constitution contains several provisions stipulating that government organs and officials should function in accordance with the law. All these, however, remain largely rhetorical because there is no constitutional review mechanism which would enable the courts to invoke constitutional provisions to correct administrative mistakes.

3 Weak Law Enforcement and Institutions

The relationship between local protectionism, excessive administrative power, a weak judiciary, and inadequate enforcement of law and of judgments begs a 'chicken and egg' question. All these factors reinforce each other and lead to a vicious cycle that makes enforcement the weakest link the Chinese legal system. Weak law enforcement manifests itself in different aspects: lack of professionalism and corruption of law enforcement officials, while the lack of an independent monitoring authority results in arbitrary enforcement of laws, abuse of power; high non-compliance with judgments, and a general lack of trust of the people vis-à-vis law enforcement agencies.[50] According to the NPC, from 1998 to 2002, a total of 207,103 cases of corruption and abuse of power were investigated, among them

48. See, for example, J.A. Cohen, 'Reforming China's Civil Procedure: Judging the Courts', *American Journal of Comparative Law* 45 (1997): 793–801, and F. Shen, 'Are You Prepared for This Legal Maze? How to Serve Legal Documents, Obtain Evidence and Enforce Judgements in China', *University of Missouri at Kansas City Law Review* 72 (2003): 215–240.
49. Li Weiwei, 'Of the over One Million Lawsuits Filed against Government Departments, 30 Percent are Won by Plaintiffs', *Beijing News*, 29 Nov. 2005.
50. In Beijing, 66% of respondents in an online survey expressed dissatisfaction with the police, while only 2% approved of the work of judicial departments. 'Poll Shows Overwhelming Numbers of

24,886 cases involving abuse of power and corruption by law enforcement officials.[51] In 2003, violations of the law by officials reportedly caused financial losses exceeding CNY 650 million and the death of 460 individuals.[52]

Problems in the area of Chinese intellectual property rights have drawn much criticism, particularly with regard to law enforcement. When China joined the WTO, legislation required by the WTO's Agreement on Trade-Related Intellectual Property Rights (TRIPS) was already in place. During the WTO accession negotiations, the TRIPS Agreement was one of the few areas covered by the WTO system which the Chinese government agreed to implement promptly after accession, without transitional implementation periods as in other services sectors, and the gradual reduction of tariffs in goods and farm products. Even though laws compatible with the TRIPS Agreement were in place by late 2001, weak or lack of effective law enforcement in this area has not ceased to be a major complaint by foreign traders.[53]

Problems in law enforcement underscore that China still has a long way to go in building up and strengthening institutions essential for the effective functioning of the Chinese legal system. Institution-building also lags behind the pace of economic reform and development. Needs in the economic sphere require the promulgation of new Chinese laws, and new institutions must be set up to implement these laws. Such a process, however, often results in the overlap of old and new institutions. Thus, SOEs used to be run by entities associated with the CPC, such as workers' congresses, and party leaders' committees at different levels. Economic reform requires these enterprises to be governed by a board of directors and chief executive officers, instead of party organs. Sometimes the reform process only involves a change of title and the same personnel remains, while in other cases there is overlap of leadership. And confusions over authorities entrusted to the old and new entities abound. These new institutions, some of them nominally independent governmental or statutory bodies, nevertheless remain under the influence of powerful vested interests and party officials.

Beijingers Dissatisfied with Government', *Agence France-Presse*, 21 Nov. 2003, quoted in the US Congressional-Executive Commission on China's 2004 Annual Report, 1–168, 16.

51. 'Legislative Work of Local People's Congresses in the Past 20 Years', and according to the Supreme People's Procuratorate Work Report to the NPC's 2004 session, 18,515 cases of corruption, embezzlement of funds, and bribery were investigated in 2003. There were 9,720 administrative law enforcement and judicial personnel and 14,844 employees of SOE investigated for alleged corruption. There were 1,408 state employees investigated for abuses of power such as torture, illegal extended detention, and interfering in elections, and there were 7,160 state employees investigated for abandonment of duty and abuse of power that resulted in safety related incidents.

52. See also '行政执法人员犯罪造成 6.5亿多元损失，460死亡'，新华社，2003年10月10日 ('Violations of Law by Administrative Law Enforcement Officials Result in More Than 650 Million Yuan in Losses and 460 Deaths', *Xinhua*, 10 Oct. 2003).

53. The relation between the WTO's TRIPS agreement and the Chinese legal system is discussed further in Part III, Ch. 6 Section II.C.

4 Lack of Transparency and Predictability

In many instances, the existence of laws is unknown to the Chinese population, let alone to foreign investors, unless and until these laws effectively are invoked. This phenomenon, combined with weak law enforcement, makes Chinese laws rather unpredictable. The multiple legislative bodies and diversified sources of law also mean that there are frequent conflicts of law. An independent and competent judicial system, through the interpretation of law in adjudication and judicial reviews, would normally resolve such inconsistencies, but the Chinese courts are ill-equipped to perform this function.

Conflicts of law, both vertically – at different levels ranging from municipal, provincial to the central levels – and horizontally – among different Chinese regions and provinces – remain an obstacle to legal reform efforts seeking to establish a more unified and predictable legal system. As part of efforts to ensure consistency in Chinese law and to comply with the WTO requirement of uniformity in the administration of the Chinese trading regime, the NPCSC had to revise its *Working Procedures for Filing and Reviewing Administrative Rules and Regulations, Local Regulations, Autonomous Regulations and Specific Regulations, and Special Economic Zone Regulations* and passed the *Working Procedures for Filing and Reviewing Judicial Interpretations* in 2005. Their impact on rectifying widespread inconsistencies in Chinese laws is discussed in Part II and Part III.

5 Corruption and Weak Due Process

The respect of due process still has to take root in Chinese legal culture. Avoidance of perceived conflicts of interest, statutory limitation on the duration of detention pending charges and trial, the presumption of innocence, public trials, and the principle of equality before the law may well appear in government rhetoric or even laws, but weak law enforcement means there is no guarantee that these principles are adhered to. Compounding the problem are weak public institutions, a weak civil society, and corruption.

Most Chinese government officials and judicial officers are badly paid. Taking the Chinese judiciary as an example, deep-rooted problems with the PRC's judicial personnel policy explain the prevalence of corruption, irregular practices, and the low professional qualifications of most Chinese judges. This was especially true for the lower courts, where officers discharged from the PLA or persons with good personal relations could be appointed as judges. It was estimated in 2002 that among the 260,000 Chinese judges, about one fourth have been transferred from the PLA.[54] The overdue reform of judicial personnel policy would necessarily affect the interests of those in power and prompts resistance, especially at local levels. The central government was able to implement an amendment to

54. 缪美香, '入世与中国司法制度', 信报月刊, 第300期, 2002年3月 (Figures from Liu Mei Hseung, 'Incompatibilities between the Chinese Judiciary and the WTO Standards', *Hong Kong Economic Journal Monthly*, March 2002, Issue 300).

the *Law of Judges* short after it joined the WTO, which introduced a national judicial examination for recruitment of judges based on uniform criteria.[55]

6 Blurred Party and Government Power

The PRC, under the single-party rule of the CPC, has parallel party organs and cadres who operate parallel to almost every governmental body and position, to buttress the CPC's influence both at policy formulation and implementation levels. Also, party policy announcements and decisions are considered 'soft law'. The peculiar status of the CPC's organs and senior officials in China's constitutional and legal regime makes it impossible to legally challenge and redress various abuses of power committed by CPC officials.

In the Chinese legal system, CPC organs are not recognized as government bodies, and therefore their acts not governed by law as official acts, as they would otherwise be subject to administrative or judicial review if considered *ultra vires*. Party documents, internal circulars and guidelines, and decisions of the CPC Central Committee, including those on the strengthening of economic activity, are binding on the internal operation of the CPC and for non-party and governmental organizations. But the legality of such party decisions and instructions is not clearly defined either in the Constitution or in law. Theoretically, even assuming that the legal system can provide some sorts of checks and balances to guarantee that government departments and officials act according to the law, acts by party cadres remain effectively out of reach of the courts and are not subject to legal challenges. The only way to challenge abusive acts of CPC officials is through the internal party discipline mechanism of the CPC, which is not governed by procedures compatible with due process and transparency.

Since the establishment of the PRC, the political power of the CPC has not been clearly separated from authority exercised by government organs and officials. Only in the most recent past has the CPC begun to commission studies on how it could be made to govern in accordance to the law. A study published in 2004 has to identify the role of the CPC in the functioning of the NPC, the state council, and the judiciary.[56]

III CONCLUDING REMARKS

The first part of this book traces the core norms and salient features of the traditional legal cultures, which are deeply rooted in the Chinese people's perception of law. Legal reform efforts in China and their failure in the early twentieth century have demonstrated the strength of this particular legal cultural heritage in resisting change. Ironically, the second series of Chinese legal reform under *Deng*'s rule benefited from the sweeping devastation *Mao*'s policies brought to

55. See Part II, Ch. 5 of for details.
56. Zhang Hengshan, more details on the study in Part III, Ch. 8 Section I.B.

Chinese society, which destroyed its traditional values, its economy, and its legal system. This part also examined over two decade-long efforts of Chinese legal modernization under two major perspectives. First and foremost, the role of law remained secondary in Chinese society. Legal reform was introduced as a necessary tool to support China's economic reform. There was no blueprint for the long-term development of the Chinese legal system or parallel changes in the PRC state structure to ensure the effective and coherent functioning of the legal system across the country. Secondly, and largely due to a piecemeal approach to legal reform measures, a number of bottleneck areas emerged by 2001, which not only have prevented legal reform from moving forward but which also risk making further economic reform unsustainable.

It was under such domestic circumstances that the Chinese government grew determined to complete its accession to the WTO during the final three years of fifteen years of difficult negotiations. This part serves as a starting reference point against which the impact of China's WTO membership on the Chinese legal system can be assessed. It also provides the context and perspectives necessary to comprehend both the economic and non-trade considerations of the Chinese government in pursuing WTO membership. An understanding of this background also helps explain the unusual treatment WTO members accorded to China, the extraordinarily stringent systemic demands on the Chinese legal system, and the unique post-accession monitoring mechanism on China's compliance with its WTO commitments.

Part II

China's Long March to the WTO: Motivations, Process and Challenges

The 15-year negotiation is indeed a long process. However, it is only a blink of eyes comparing with the 5,000-year history of China.[1]

Long Yongtu

The Chinese economy was blooming prior to China's accession to the WTO. From the perspective of the Chinese leadership, there had to be considerations in addition to foreign trade alone for the government to be so determined to join the global trade body. The government's persistence in the negotiations demonstrated that accession to the WTO entailed a holistic set of policy considerations which did include trade and economic concerns. Yet non-trade concerns also played a significant role in China's determination to join the WTO.

Indeed, to be a WTO member offers China protection from arbitrary or discriminatory treatment in international trade and opportunities to take part in negotiating and shaping WTO rules. But some unequal and discriminatory treatment, tailored to China and applicable to China alone, was also institutionalized during the accession process.[2] When China joined the WTO, it agreed to limit its agricultural subsidies to a level lower than that normally allowed for developing countries. It thereby reduced its own policy margin for manoeuvre in addressing the widening poverty gap between rural and urban populations. China also agreed

1. Statement by Long Yongtu, Head of the Chinese Delegation, to the WTO's Working Party on China, on the completion of China's accession negotiations, Geneva, 17 Sep. 2001; document on file with the author.
2. Among the current 153 members of the WTO, the majority (128) were signatories of GATT and automatically became WTO members on 1 Jan. 1995. Any state or customs territory with full autonomy in the conduct of its trade policies may join the WTO through accession negotiations. See section 'WTO Accession Mechanism' for further details.

to accept a clause on transitional safeguards applicable to its textile and clothing exports,[3] as well as a special safeguards mechanism for restricting other exports. China agreed to be treated as a non-market economy in anti-dumping investigations, which in effect meant that a complainant could use third country reference prices when determining whether China exports its products at below market prices (dumping) for fifteen years after its accession.

Concessions made by the Chinese government on the sensitive issue of farm subsidies, for example, are illustrative of Beijing's determination to join the global trade body. In May 2001, the multilateral phase of the accession negotiations was in a stalemate when the United States insisted that China should not be allowed to subsidize its farmers more than 5% of its total annual agricultural production, even though China would join the WTO as a developing country. According to Article 6 of the WTO's Agreement on Agriculture, developing countries can provide domestic support to farmers in an amount equivalent to 10% of total annual agricultural production without making any commitment to reduce such subsidies. For developed countries, the cap is set at 5%. For the Chinese leadership, concessions on this issue were particularly sensitive because it involved the interest of China's 900 million-strong rural population, who would be hardest hit by China's WTO accession. Because joining the WTO would entail a lowering of farm tariffs and the removal of trade barriers, Chinese farmers with already scarce resources were being put in direct competition with heavily subsidized farm products flooding the Chinese market from Europe and the United States.

WTO members demanded such exceptional concessions from China in an attempt to contain highly competitive Chinese exports and to protect their domestic industries from competing with Chinese ones at the same level according to the WTO's principle of non-discrimination. Any government aiming to join the WTO for trade considerations alone would not accept such concessions designed to contain its export strength.

---

3. China agreed to include in its WTO accession agreement a special safeguard mechanism to limit its textile export growth, which in effect deprived its textile exporters of the full benefits from the end of the global quota regime until the end of 2008. Both the United States and the European Union started using this safeguard mechanism to curb imports of Chinese textiles in 2005, when the textile quota system ended after a ten-year phase out period. See also Daniel Pruzin, 'China Warns Countermeasures Possible against "Discriminatory" Interim Safeguards', *WTO Reporter, Bureau of National Affairs* (BNA), 6 Apr. 2005, and Esther Lam, 'No Material Gain in Textile Row', *South China Morning Post*, 1 Jun. 2005.

Chapter 3
Motivations

When China joined the WTO, it registered the strongest economic growth rate in the world. Traders worldwide were eager to do business with China for a number of reasons, regardless of whether the world's biggest emerging market remained outside the WTO system. From the perspectives of China's trading partners, it was in their interest to subject China trade to WTO rules. While a blooming Chinese economy provided ample business opportunities, China also represented an unpredictable business environment with limited transparency and many uncertainties. To bring China into the WTO was one way to ensure that trade with China would be conducted within the parameters of the WTO's rules-based system, with possible recourse to its strong dispute settlement system to ensure compliance.

When China started economic reform under *Deng Xiaoping*, China's exports in merchandise goods accounted for only 0.8% (USD 9.955 billion) of total world trade. By 1998, China had become the tenth largest trading nation worldwide, with exports and imports accounting for 3.3% (USD 183,712 billion) and 2.5% (USD 140,237 billion) respectively of total world trade.[1] Foreign investment in China also flourished in the 1990s. In 1998, China was the world's second largest beneficiary of foreign direct investment (FDI).[2] Just before joining the WTO in 2001, China exported USD 266.098 billion worth of goods, accounting for 4.31% of the world total.[3]

1. Statistical Database, World Trade Organization, <www.wto.org/english/res_e/statis_e/statis_e.htm>; additional data provided by the WTO via email 8 May 2006.
2. Minutes of the WTO's General Council meeting, 9–11 and 18 Dec. 1998, 40, WT/GC/M/32.
3. Trade Statistics Online Database, United Nations Conference on Trade and Development (UNCTAD), <stats.unctad.org/Handbook/>, and WTO data.

I TRADE AND ECONOMIC CONSIDERATIONS

Evidence of further economic growth during the first five years following China's WTO accession helps illustrate that there was a strong trade and economic case for China to join the global trade body. Despite some of the discriminatory conditions China accepted as part of the bargain, WTO membership means that China no longer has to negotiate annually with the United States over its trade status. Equally, WTO members, over 140 by 2001, can no longer impose trade sanctions or retaliatory measures against China without justifying themselves under WTO rules and, if they fail, face the consequences of a dispute settlement. In addition, China can for the first time participate in shaping the global trade rules through participation in the Doha Round of trade negotiations; and meanwhile, Chinese exports and investments enjoy a more predictable market access environment.

According to statistics which the Chinese government provided to the WTO in 2006[4] in the context of its first trade policy review, China's gross domestic product (GDP) rose from CNY 10,965.5 billion (about USD 1,324.8 billion) in 2001 to CNY 18,232.1 billion (USD 2,225.7 billion) in 2005, thus averaging an annual average growth rate of 9.5% for five consecutive years after its WTO accession. The per capita income during the same period has passed USD 1,000 to reach USD 1,702 in 2005. Import and export trade and inflow of FDI also registered rapid expansion during the same period. Total value of imports and exports rose from USD 509.6 billion in 2001 to USD 1,422.1 billion in 2005, putting China in third place among the world's biggest traders, after the European Union and the United States.

Market access commitments made by China as part of the WTO accession package, including the opening up of the domestic market, especially in the services sector, give foreign investors a more predictable and rules-governed business environment. By the end of 2005, a total of 552,942 foreign investment enterprises, with a total contractual value of USD 1,285,673 million, had been established in China. The increased presence of FDI and foreign corporations offers not only foreign capital but also allows domestic Chinese industries to reap more advanced technological and managerial experience and increases research and development resources and job opportunities domestically.

Although China experiences a widening poverty gap, the rapid economic growth has improved living standards of the people as a whole. According to official data, the annual per capita disposable income of urban residents reached CNY 10,493 in 2005, which is equivalent to a 58.3% increase compared to that of 2000 in real terms and which represents an annual growth of 9.6%. Though less well-off, the rural population's annual per capita income reached CNY 3,255 in 2005, an increase by 29.2% in real terms compared to 2000, with the annual growth rate averaging about 5.3%.

---

4. Government report by the People's Report of China, WTO Trade Policy Review Body, 17 Mar. 2006, WTO Document: WT/TPR/G/161, 5–6, paras 1–5.

II NON-TRADE CONSIDERATIONS

Each time the accession negotiations ran into difficulties,[5] the Chinese leadership emphasized that to join the WTO represented China's fundamental national policy, and that this policy would not be deterred by unreasonable demands made by some WTO members. In May 2001, *Long Yongtu*, China's chief negotiator and Vice-Minister of Trade, reiterated China's commitment to the WTO bid, saying 'this is an important strategic decision which will not be affected by some incidents ... . Our stance has been very clear. It's beneficial to both China and the whole world for China to join the WTO. Open reform policy in China is not going to change, and China's commitment to join to the WTO is not going to change.'[6] *Long*'s statement makes it clear that WTO membership was a strategic decision about the orientation of China's national policy, and China would persist even when faced with difficulties with other WTO members.

Why was the Chinese leadership so determined to join the WTO, to the extent that it made numerous the so-called 'WTO-plus' commitments (concessions beyond those normally required by the WTO agreements) and accepted 'WTO-minus' treatment (forgoing some benefits and rights conferred by the WTO agreements) as a virtual 'entrance fee'? The following reasons, not necessarily trade-related, were not set out clearly when China requested to return to the General Agreement on Tariffs and Trade (GATT) in 1986. However, during the accession process, it gradually became clear that reform measures, motivated by and entrenched in an external institutional mechanism – the WTO rules-based system – would reap considerable benefits for Chinese development and reform.

A Regaining Central Control

A principal but not obvious motivation of the Chinese leadership to bring China into the WTO was that it would help the central government regain control over the country. Economic reforms since 1978 have intensified regionalism in China. During the first decade of reform, disparate regional developments were encouraged under the open-up policy. Central control was loosened in a planned and incremental approach, and SEZs, such as, Shenzhen, Zhuhai and Shantou in Guangdong province, Xiamen in Fujian province, the province of Hainan, the Pudong area of Shanghai, and the city of Dalian, were created to promote faster economic development and attract FDI. *Deng* had said in 1985, '[o]f course, some

---

5. The deadlock in negotiations over farm subsidies, for example, coincided with a period during which comments by the Bush Administration over issues of missile defence and arm sales to Taiwan held up China's WTO accession talks. Beijing later reached a deal with Washington, agreeing to an 8.5% cap on domestic farm subsidies – less than the 10% enjoyed by developing countries, but better than the 5% cap on which Washington had initially insisted.
6. Author's interview with Long Yongtu, 21 May 2001, Geneva, partly published in Esther Lam, 'Long Eager on Talks Resumption', *South China Morning Post*, 23 May 2001.

regions and some people may prosper before others do, and then they can help other regions and people to gradually do the same.'[7] Some regions indeed prospered faster than others, though increased protectionism rather than inter-regional assistance was the result.

Efforts to reform China from a strictly centrally planned economy during *Mao*'s time to a 'socialist market economy' went hand in hand with an inevitable decentralization process, through which local governments gained more power in areas such as taxation, legislative and administrative authority, as well as fiscal and personnel policies. Regionalism gradually fuelled increased local protectionism and barriers to internal trade, which the WTO has described as 'a key feature of the Chinese economy' and which resulted in 'further distortions in the economy'.[8] During the reform period, according to the WTO, 'there appears to have been a rise in inter-regional trade barriers and therefore that, while the Chinese economy has gradually opened up internationally, internal markets may have become more fragmented'.[9]

During the 1990s, Chinese economy faced bottlenecks, and the grievances of those who had not benefited from economic development continued to grow and threaten social stability and the rule of the CPC. The potential threats of regionalism to the central government and the Communist leadership, whereby regional and provincial authorities subtly or openly defied Beijing's instructions and policies in pursuit of their own local interests, lie beyond the trade and economic realms. Adding to the problems is corruption among and abuse of power by local officials, which provoked numerous cases of social unrest and violent clashes with law enforcement agents in recent years. The CPC no longer exercises a firm grasp on the discipline of local party officials; and the central government finds it increasingly difficult to secure the local implementation of its instruction.[10]

---

7. 'There is No Fundamental Difference between Socialism and Market Economy', 23 Oct. 1985, in *Selected Works of Deng Xiaoping*, vol. III (1982–1992), *People's Daily*, <english.peopledaily.com.cn/>.
8. Trade Policy Review, Report by the WTO Secretariat, People's Republic of China, 28 Feb. 2006, WT/TPR/S/161, 41.
9. *Ibid.*, 41, citing Young &Alwyn, 'The Razor's Edge: Distortions and Incremental Reform in the People's Republic of China', *Quarterly Journal of Economics* 115, no. 4 (2000): 1091–1135.
10. Cases of social unrest have involved villagers dissatisfied with compensation for land confiscation, migrant workers petitioning for back pay and basic social welfare, and laid-off workers at SOE. In October 2004, thousands of laid-off workers from a large state-owned textile factory in Bengbu city, Anhui, blocked the streets demanding better pensions; in another incident, a car accident in Chongqing, Sichuan province, set off a riot involving 10,000 people after one of the parties involved falsely claimed to be a government official and attempted to bully the other driver, hence provoking public outcry over abuse of power; in April 2005, about 1,500 police officers and government officials faced up to 30,000 villagers angered by appropriation of their land for factories in the Zhejiang village of Huaxi; in December 2005, police shot dead at least three protesters in riots linked to a land dispute in Shanwei; Guangdong, in March 2006, dozens of villagers were injured and a 15-year-old girl killed during clashes with police over a land dispute in Zhongshan, Guangdong. See 'Recent China Protests a Possible Sign of Growing Unrest', *Chicago Tribune*, 9 Nov. 2004, Josephine Ma, 'Riots Provide Bleak Picture of Society's Ills', *South China Morning Post*, 4 Nov. 2004, Irene Wang, 'Police Official Denies

In a keynote address before the January 2006 meeting of the CCDI of the CPC, *Hu Jintao*, Secretary-General of the CPC, called on the party's top anti-graft body specifically to target areas where corruption and collusion with businessmen had sparked a wave of riots and protests over the past few years, including, in his words:

The widespread misappropriation of funds for education, the spread of bribery in the health system, illicit confiscation of farming land for urban development, failure to pay migrant labourers, random and illicit fees imposed on farmers, and official negligence and corruption that lead to deadly industrial disasters.[11]

The central leadership has consistently endeavoured to maintain law and order and social stability, fearing that nationwide social unrest would shake the core of the Communist rule. Efforts to regain central control since mid 1990s have met with limited success. Local authorities have harnessed both political power[12] and material resources that enable them to bargain over and resist Beijing's policies, especially when their vested interests are affected. Regional interests remain diverse, as the coastal and more developed regions seek to protect existing privileges, whereas the less developed regions of central and western China demand a more equitable distribution of the country's newly acquired wealth and development opportunities. These factional groups compete for resources and material benefits, which further aggravate official corruption at the lower levels. At higher levels, factionalism has resulted in the growing inclusion of bureaucratic interests and other policy issues on factional agendas.[13]

Within the WTO system, however, the central government alone represents China and is the sole interlocutor on trade issues for other WTO members. This helps the government's effort to unify the diversified trade regimes, customs and licensing mechanisms in place in the different provinces. In fact, the WTO explicitly requires every Member State to administer a unified trade regime throughout its territory. This requirement therefore serves as a further external impetus for Beijing to regain and reaffirm control over local authorities and vested interests. The central government's strategic position between domestic forces and international negotiating counterparts affords it considerable power. It can, for example, stage-manage the process by projecting its own policy priorities as external demands from the WTO. The domestic and external dynamics involved in international organizations, such as the WTO, and their Member States is known as 'a two-level game'.[14]

Conflict with Farmers', *South China Morning Post*, 12 Apr. 2006, Shi Jiantao, 'Rein in State Power or Face a National Crisis, Says Professor', *South China Morning Post*, 4 Feb. 2006.

11. Wang Xiangwei, 'Leaders Need More Than Just Inspiring Words to Tackle Corruption', *South China Morning Post*, 9 Jan. 2006.
12. Factionalism in Chinese politics often manifests in divisions of gangs from different regions, most notably the so-called 'Shanghai gang', 'Beijing gang', 'Hunan gang' and 'Guangdong gang'.
13. L. Dittmer & Y. Wu, 'Leadership Coalitions and Economic Transformation in Reform China: Revisiting the Political Business Cycle', in *China's Deep Reform: Domestic Politics in Transition*, eds L. Dittmer & G. Liu (New York: Rowman & Littlefield Publishers, 2006).
14. C. E. Barfield, *Free Trade, Sovereignty, Democracy: The Future of the World Trade Organization* (Washington: The AEI Press, 2001), 9–11.

B CONSOLIDATING REFORM POLICY TOWARDS A MARKET ECONOMY

For China, accession to the WTO was a means to entrench the open trade and market economy reform policy. Throughout the reform period, there were many challenges to both the pace and the orientation of reform. In July 1986, when China first requested to resume its contracting-party status with the GATT, it explained that return to the GATT was in line with its 'basic national policy of opening up to the outside world and revitalizing the domestic economy'. It further reaffirmed 'the firm belief' of the Chinese government that 'the on-going process of economic reform will contribute to the expansion of economic and trade relations' with the contracting parties of the GATT.[15]

Beijing's decision to 'link' its reform policy to membership in an external/international entity, the GATT, must be viewed against the background of internal political dynamics in China. In October 1984, the third Plenum of the 12th CPC Central Committee adopted *A Decision on the Reform of the Economic Structure*, which launched the urban-industrial reform designed to overhaul the national economy. Politically, this marked the beginning of continuous factional rifts within the central Chinese leadership over both the extent of reform and the pace of growth. The reformers under the leadership of *Deng Xiaoping*, who represented the pro-growth faction, were challenged by the pro-stability group led by *Chen Yun*. When reform resulted in inflation and social tensions, the group around *Chen* asked that marketization be put on hold in order to maintain social and political stability. Research on the cycle of factional competition in the central Communist leadership during the reform period indicates that 'Chinese politics as a whole has been changing to reflect the economic shift from plan to market and form public to private ownership.'[16]

Throughout *Deng*'s era (1978–1993),[17] factional fights in Chinese politics were about economic policies. Reformers were most vulnerable, 'as the boom phase of the cycle tended to correlate with an increase in corruption, intellectual liberalism and dissent'.[18] The fall from power of top reformers *Hu Yaobang* in 1987 and *Zhao Ziyang* in 1989, whose reform and liberalization policies were considered to have triggered social unrest and political turbulences, are cases in point.

The *Tiananmen* Square events of 4 June 1989 marked a sharp turn of political dynamics within the CPC. Thereafter, reformers such as *Zhao Ziyang* were either placed under house arrest or lost their political influence. The dynamics of internal political struggles and their link to economic reform made the return to the GATT

15. 'China's Status as a Contracting Party, Communication from the People's Republic of China', GATT, L/6017, 14 Jul. 1986.
16. L. Dittmer & Y. Wu, 56.
17. *Deng* officially stepped down from his positions in both the CPC and the PRC by 1990, though he remained influential from behind the scenes until his death in February 1997. His famous 'Tour to the South' in 1992 revived the sluggish economic reform process since the *Tiananmen* Square events in 1989.
18. L. Dittmer & Y. Wu, 51.

or accession to the WTO particularly significant, as an important external impetus and undertaking to help 'lock in' and sustain difficult domestic reform.

The conservative climate remained prevalent until February 1992, when *Deng*'s 'Tour to the South' revived the reform momentum. *Deng* took the opportunity to revive his 'reform and open policy' and began a determined counter-attack against the conservatives, in order to shield reformers from the political stigma of being seen as 'capitalists':

> In the beginning opinions were divided about the reform and the open policy. That was normal.... At present, we are affected by both 'Right' and 'Left' tendencies. But it is the 'Left' tendencies that have the deepest roots. Some theorists and politicians try to intimidate people by pinning political labels on them.... In the history of the Party, those [Left] tendencies have led to dire consequences. Some fine things were destroyed overnight.... China should remain vigilant against the 'Right' but primarily against the 'Left'....The proportion of planning to market forces is not the essential difference between socialism and capitalism. A planned economy is not equivalent to socialism, because there is planning under capitalism too; a market economy is not capitalism, because there are markets under socialism too. Planning and market forces are both means of controlling economic activity.[19]

Deng clearly sought to discard the ideological rifts over socialism and capitalism so that China could move on with its momentarily disrupted economic reform. *Deng* also brought in *Zhu Rongji*, then the Shanghai Communist Party Secretary who later became known as the 'economic czar' of China, as Vice Prime Minister in charge of economic affairs. During *Jiang Zemin*'s era (1993–2003), *Zhu*, who later became Premier and completed China's long quest for WTO membership with his commitment to continuing reform.

C COUNTERING DOMESTIC POLITICAL OPPOSITION

The political economy in China and attitudes towards reform changed significantly after *Deng*'s 'Tour to the South.' Factional fights in the so-called 'Third Generation' Communist leadership were no longer about whether to reform or not, but about its pace and extent. Under *Zhu,* swift WTO accession was clearly recognized as a means of completing the continuous structural reform policy. The pro-reform forces identified WTO membership as China's long-term commitment to transit and reform towards a market-oriented economy.

Zhu was not immune from political pressures from the conservative bloc. The Politburo of the Communist Party of China, officially known as the Standing Committee of the Communist Party of China (SCCPC), consists of the seven

19. 'Excerpts from talks given in Wuchang, Shenzhen, Zhuhai and Shanghai', 18 Jan. to 21 Feb. 1992, in *Selected Works of Deng Xiaoping*, vol. III (1982–1992), *People's Daily*, <english.peopledaily.com.cn/>.

most powerful leaders of the CPC. Among them, *Zhu* was the only expert in economics, which was also his main portfolio in the SCCPC. During the WTO negotiations, the SCCPC as a whole never endorsed the importance of WTO accession as a group, nor did it play an active role in promoting or explaining China's WTO strategies. *Zhu* himself took the responsibility for and the political risk in pushing for WTO membership. *Jiang Zemin*'s deference to *Zhu* on economic affairs, and most symbolically on the WTO negotiations, was more of a political nature.

Jiang was keen to see China's WTO accession completed while he was in power, leaving his name in history as the third generation Communist leader who finally led China to the global trade body. But he was not prepared to pay for any backlashes if the terms of accession were criticized by the political elites or had adverse socio-economic consequences. Politically, the best he could hope for was to gain recognition and praise if China's WTO bid was successful.

Jiang adopted a similar approach with regard to China's economic reform. *Zhu* was the lead person in the push for China's WTO accession and for overcoming economic reform bottlenecks. This explains the comparatively low profile of *Jiang* vis-à-vis China's WTO bid. *Zhu*'s determination to reform of the SOEs, to curb corruption and to continue structural reform showed that he had both the will and courage to push the limits of political constraints. However, the reform of the SOEs threatened the vested interests of many high-ranking members of the CPC, and the rising unemployment rate that resulted from the layoff of SOE workers posed threats to social stability. *Zhu*'s reform efforts therefore faced strong resistance in these areas. He used China's WTO accession commitments, which also required significant structural changes, as an external help to overcome domestic resistance to these painful but necessary reforms.

The SCCPC has always been divided into two camps – the liberal reformers and the conservatives. On the WTO accession issue, the liberal camp favoured China's swift accession but the conservatives were concerned that further commitments to opening China's market to foreign corporations and investment would destroy uncompetitive domestic industries, in particular the SOEs.[20] The conservatives preferred to see China accede to the WTO later rather than sooner. If China joined sooner, it should do so with only minimum concessions, in contrast to what was demanded by its principal negotiating counterparts, the United States and the European Union.[21]

Zhu's political influence suffered a severe blow after his April 1999 visit to the United States, when Washington unilaterally disclosed the extensive concessions

---

20. For specific concerns, see Y. Li, *China's Accession to the WTO: Exaggerated Fears?* United Nations Conference on Trade and Development, November 2002.
21. For discussion on Chinese domestic politics concerning its WTO accession, see W. Yang, 'China's Stakes in WTO Accession: The Internal Decision-making Process', in *China's Accession to the World Trade Organization. National and International Perspectives*, eds H. Holbig & R. Ash (London, New York: RoutledgeCurzon, 2002), 20–42; and Y. Yang, 'China's WTO Accession – The Economics and Politics', *Journal of World Trade* 34 (2002): 77–94.

that *Zhu* was prepared to accept in the bilateral Sino-US negotiations over China's WTO accession. However, when he retired in 2003, *Zhu* was widely acclaimed, both domestically and abroad, for steering China through the Asian financial crisis in 1997 and for his determination to make China a WTO member.

D OVERCOMING REFORM BOTTLENECKS

In addition to its political significance, China's WTO membership also served as an important force breaking down domestic bureaucratic obstacles to reform. The WTO accession contributed to deepening and expediting China's domestic reform efforts, since the Chinese government is obliged, under WTO requirements, to address deep-rooted problems of the Chinese economy and legal system, as well as its weak institutions.

The reform of the SOEs provides an illustrative example. Problems for Chinese SOEs surfaced in the mid 1980s. Many of them suffered from low productivity and a bloated workforce, and to keep them in place was costing the government billions of CNY in subsidies. Bad loans to SOEs severely damaged China's then rudimentary banking system. The provincial governments of Shandong, Guangdong and Sichuan began experiments with the privatization of small SOEs in 1992. Three years later, the central government endorsed a policy for the reform of SOEs, under which large SOEs would be saved and reformed and smaller ones would be squeezed out of operation, a policy unevenly implemented in different regions. By the mid 1990s, at least half of all SOEs operated with losses, though more realistic figures suggested that this was the case for nearly two thirds of SOEs.[22]

Reform of large-sized SOEs also met with little success, and a researcher for the State Council reported in 2000 that '[i]t is sad to see that after so many years of reform on large SOEs, China went full circle and almost returned to where it started.'[23] 'Despite two decades of reform, the financial performance of SOEs continues to decline and is ultimately responsible for the financial sector's problem', the study continued.[24] Reforms relating to the price control and tax system, especially in areas where discrepancies and overlaps between central and local competencies had to be addressed, suffered from similar bottlenecks. It was for such areas of sluggish reform, taken together with difficulties in reforming the financial and banking sectors and domestic obstruction, that reformers like *Zhu*

22. S. Breslin, *Capitalism with Chinese Characteristics: The Public, the Private and the International*, Working Paper No. 104, Asia Research Centre, Murdoch University, 2004, 8–9.
23. Y. Qian & J. Wu, 'China's Transition to a Market Economy: How Far Across the River', paper given at the Conference on Policy Reform in China at the Center for Research on Economic Development and Policy Reform (CEDPR), Stanford University, 18–20 Nov. 1999, revised version May 2000, 23.
24. *Ibid.*, 30–32.

looked to an external catalyser – the WTO and its requirements, pressure from WTO members and foreign competition– to help China implement reforms.

For some, Chinese WTO accession was an ineffective 'shock therapy' to address its enormous problems, which would contribute to the country's 'coming collapse'.[25] For others, Chinese WTO membership provided the impetus which would help accelerate reforms of the SOEs, of the financial and banking sectors, and promote new private enterprises and establish the rule of law.[26]

E ADVANCING STALLED LEGAL REFORM

The incremental nature of China's reform course initiated under *Deng*, under which many measures were introduced in an ad hoc basis, might well be inevitable, given *Deng's* search for the development concept most suitable to China's development. The other side of the coin, however, is that reform measures and policies were arbitrary, neither based on rules nor legally defined, and lacking solid institutional back-up.

The process of WTO accession negotiations helped orient the Chinese economy towards a stronger emphasis on rules-based reform. This would necessarily affect the Chinese legal system, whose reform was foremost motivated by economic necessities. So as to be able to integrate the global market economy via the WTO's rules-based system, the Chinese government had to follow the rules of the game of the world trade body.

In 2002, *Jin Liqun*, China's Vice-Minister of Finance, characterized WTO membership in terms of 'destructive construction' after two decades of economic and legal reforms. 'China did not strive for WTO membership for membership's sake. Joining this multilateral trading system builds on [two-decade] reforms', he said, adding that 'the accession is the destructive force that smashes whatever is left in the old edifice of a more or less closed economy', and 'the constructive force is about building or strengthening institutional capability and achieving an overhaul of the existing system of economic management'.[27]

More importantly, *Jin* emphasized the importance of WTO membership for the strengthening of China's institutions, for changing the mindset of government officials, and for developing and cultivating a local culture of playing by the rules:

> The mindset of the civil servants, entrepreneurs, and the general public must be completely reconfigured to fit into the changed circumstances in the post-accession era. Governmental institutions, be they central or local, are given to understand that they need to play by the international rules, even if it means

25. G. Chang, *The Coming Collapse of China* (Random House, 2001), xxi and Ch. 9.
26. Y. Qian & J. Wu, 48.
27. L. Jin, *China: One Year Into the WTO Process*, Speech delivered at the World Bank, 22 Oct. 2002, <web.worldbank.org/>.

> that the new practice will inevitably make a dent in their power base...when the 'approval system' gives way. And the business firms cannot...by any means defy the market discipline that is applied across-the-board.[28]

Much of the WTO's impact on the Chinese legal system and institution building involves enhancing transparency, public participation, and due process, restricting arbitrary administrative power, strengthening law enforcement, and establishing mechanisms to ensure accountability for official decisions and actions. These challenges are examined in detail later.

F Foreign Policy and External Concerns

Foreign policy motives were also behind the Chinese leadership's determination to join the WTO. For the purposes of this study, it suffices to highlight Beijing's main foreign policy considerations in relation to the WTO.

Firstly, the rise of China's economic and military power has caused mounting concerns worldwide, in particular, from its neighbours in the Asia-Pacific region and the United States. China's decision to join the global trade club was seen as an assurance that China was committed to following the rules of the game set by the multilateral trading system. Immediately after China completed its accession process in later 2001, Chinese Premier *Zhu* paid official visits to South East Asian countries, reassuring their leaders that the rise of Chinese economic power would not be a threat to the region. On the contrary, *Zhu* emphasized China's cooperative approach by announcing that China intended to start negotiations to form a free trade region with the Association of South East Asian Nations (ASEAN) countries by 2015.

Secondly, China's accession to the WTO has significant foreign policy implications for Sino-US relations.[29] It would, inter alia, end the annual ritual of US Congressional examination of and debate over Most-Favoured-Nation (MFN) status granted to China. Primarily because of domestic political considerations, the US Congress often linked the MFN status to the situation of human rights in China. The debate has attracted ample media attention and exacerbated tensions between the two countries.[30]

Thirdly, China jealously guards its national sovereignty, in particular when it comes to the status of Taiwan, which seeks international recognition as an independent state while the PRC insists that it remains a province of China. As a result, China has consistently blocked Taiwan's bid to become a member of international

---

28. *Ibid.*
29. For further analysis, see R.D. Hormats, *Beginning the Journey, China, the United States, and the WTO*, Report of an Independent Task Force sponsored by the Council on Foreign Relations, 2001.
30. See, for example, T.N. Srinivasan, *Trade and Human Rights*, discussion paper no. 765, Economic Growth Center, Yale University, 1996, 1–40 <www.econ.yale.edu/growth_pdf/cdp765.pdf>, 31 Aug. 2007.

organizations and it objected to Taiwan's bid for observer status in the World Health Organization. However, due to diplomatic pressure from other WTO members and in the belief that bringing both China and Taiwan into the WTO might accelerate the so-called 'three links'[31] between the two entities, China did not object to Taiwan's accession to the WTO, in its capacity a separate customs territory named 'Chinese Taipei' or 'Taiwan, Penghu, Kinmen and Matsu'.[32] Unlike the United Nations, non-state entities with the status of separate customs territories can become full members of the WTO.

Officially, *Sha Zukang*, formerly Chinese Ambassador to the United Nations Office at Geneva, has outlined three new elements that China's accession to the WTO has brought to the country's foreign policy.[33] According to *Sha*, China's WTO membership further integrates the country's economic objectives with its foreign policy goals. WTO membership will increase the weight of China in trade and economic matters and give China better opportunities to manoeuvre in and to influence the multilateral trading system. For *Sha*, China's decision to join the WTO reaffirmed its national policy to participate further in the development of economic globalization, including in the fields of dispute settlement, rules and policy-making. He also underlined that WTO membership would enhance China's cooperation and exchange with other regions of the world.

A combination of the above factors made the Chinese government determined to pursue WTO membership. Not all of these factors were present or obvious when China first requested to resume its status to GATT in 1986. However, as China embarked on the journey and struggled through the accession negotiations, these underlying reasons for the Chinese WTO membership bid became more evident and made the Chinese government determined to join the WTO.

31. This involves the establishment of direct transport, postal and trade links between Mainland China and Taiwan.
32. *Report of the Working Party on the Accession of Chinese Taipei to the WTO Agreement*, WT/ACC/TPKM/18, 2001.
33. Author's interview with Chinese Ambassador Sha Zukang, published in 林美茵, 联合国大使沙祖康谈中国外交政策, 战国策, 2月号, 2002 (Esther Lam, 'Exclusive Interview with UN Chinese Ambassador Sha Zukang', *Strategic Business World Monthly*, February 2002, Hong Kong, 52–62).

Chapter 4

China's WTO Accession Process

Compared to other international institutions such as the World Bank, the International Monetary Fund (IMF) or the United Nations, the WTO has a far more complex accession mechanism. Its accession procedures require applicants to negotiate with every existing WTO member, which may request to negotiate with a specific applicant bilaterally concerning its terms of accession. These bilateral terms are then 'multilateralized' and made applicable to all WTO members once the accession process is completed. This dual-track approach can pose significant hurdles to newcomers seeking to join the WTO, and also, in effect, as shown by the different conditions and commitments that different acceding members have accepted, lead to different demands and treatments being accorded to different applicants.

Given these features of WTO accession procedures, WTO members could treat China differently, with specific and additional demands being made in relation to both the Chinese trading and legal systems. Notwithstanding, countries are keen to join the WTO as they benefit from gaining access to the WTO members' markets, protect themselves from discriminatory treatment, and utilize the WTO dispute settlement system to assert their rights.

I THE WTO ACCESSION MECHANISM

The WTO came into being on 1 January 1995, following the conclusion of the so-called 'Uruguay Round' of trade negotiations. The WTO is the only body to deal with a set of global trade rules that are binding on its currently 153 members. But the WTO is not only an institution. It is also a set of agreements in itself and operates as a system of trade rules, with an in-built mechanism to settle disputes among its members. Therefore, the WTO regime is known as the rules-based multilateral trading system, in contrast to other bilateral and regional trade arrangements.

The WTO's history goes back to 1947, when its predecessor, the GATT, started work. In the beginning, the GATT functioned as a de facto organization designed to reduce tariffs, remove trade barriers, and to facilitate trade in goods. Over the years, it evolved through eight rounds of multilateral trade negotiations, the last and most extensive one named the Uruguay Round (1986–1994) that finally established the WTO. The GATT ceased to exist as an organization and was incorporated into the WTO as the 'GATT 1994.'

Among the current 153 WTO members, 128 were signatories of the GATT and automatically became WTO members on 1 January 1995. Any state or customs territory with full autonomy in the conduct of its trade policies may join the WTO (Article 12 WTO Agreement) through accession negotiations. Working parties on accession are established under the auspices of the WTO General Council, mandated to deal with the accession process. Although every applicant follows the same accession procedures, the time necessary for completing this complex process varies. If a number of members are keen to secure market concessions from the applicant, then the bargaining and accession process is likely to be more intense and difficult, and hence, more lengthy. Unsurprisingly, the bigger the traders are, the longer it will take them to join the WTO. China took over fifteen years to complete its accession process and became a WTO member in December 2001. The Russian Federation applied to join in 1993, and negotiations are still ongoing. The shortest accession negotiation was that of Kyrgyzstan, which took only two years and ten months. The following diagram illustrates the WTO's accession process:

Kicking off the Accession Process

The accession process starts when a country applies to join the WTO. The General Council considers the application and establishes a working party. But an objection from one single member can block this process.

↓

Working Party and the Fact-Finding Process

The applicant then provides a 'Memorandum' which describes its foreign trade regime in detail. The Memorandum is examined by members of the working party. The working party consists of WTO delegates and there is no room for impartial experts. This process allows members pursuing their own commercial interest to act as judge and jury on the trade regime of acceding countries.

↓

Bilateral Negotiations

Members and the applicant start bilateral market access negotiations on goods, services, and intellectual property rights. The applicant has to reach an agreement with every member which has requested bilateral negotiations, before it can join the WTO. But this bilateral process is a defensive battle for the applicant, because it cannot make any specific demands of WTO members in return.

↓

Multilateral Negotiations, Report, Protocol of Accession and Entry Into Force

Results of the negotiations are translated into a draft report of the working party, decision and protocol of accession, together with the applicant schedules of commitments. The whole package is submitted to the WTO General Council or Ministerial Conference for approval. The protocol of accession then enters into force. The applicant ratifies the protocol and becomes a WTO member 30 days thereafter.

The above accession mechanism can make it difficult for newcomers to join the WTO. Key to these hurdles is a combination of bilateral and multilateral negotiating processes that give existing WTO members considerable bargaining leverage over applicants. A study published by the Commonwealth Secretariat poses the question of whether the WTO's accession mechanism is not 'inherently flawed'.[1] Acceding countries often face tough negotiations during the accession process because any applicant must come to an agreement with every other WTO member which has requested bilateral negotiations. This bilateral process is a defensive battle for the applicant since while existing WTO members can, and always do, request specific market concessions from the applicant, the latter is unable to place demands on WTO members in return.

During the Doha round of trade negotiations, recently acceded WTO members such as China, Croatia, and Georgia have argued that since they made many concessions and commitments during their respective accession negotiations, they should not be expected to make further major concessions in new multilateral trade negotiations. This reflects the fact that acceding members very often have to make WTO-plus commitments and accept WTO-minus treatment[2] as an 'entrance fee' for joining the WTO. For example, Cambodia, a least-developed country (LDC) which joined the WTO in 2004, urged trading partners not to impose membership demands that went beyond existing WTO rules. Algeria and the Russian Federation, both still in the process of accession negotiations, complained that

1. R. Grynberg, V. Ognivtsev & M. A. Razzaque, *Paying the Price for Joining the WTO: A Comparative Assessment of Services Sector Commitments by WTO Members and Acceding Countries* (London: Commonwealth Secretariat, 2002).
2. See Part II, Ch. 3, Section II for their meanings.

major trading partners were unfairly asking for WTO-plus concessions in energy pricing and export subsidies.[3]

Paul Hunt, former Special Rapporteur on the Right to Health of the United Nations Human Rights Council and former United Nations Commission on Human Rights, took issue with the WTO's accession process and expressed concern that 'pressure in trade negotiations, particularly when exercised by stronger trading partners over small acceding countries, might lead to unsustainable commitments to trade liberalization that, in practice, diminish states' capacity to realize the right to health'.[4] He pointed to so-called 'TRIPS-plus' situations, where acceding countries are required to implement not just TRIPS-consistent but more stringent intellectual property rights legislation at an earlier date than is required by the TRIPS Agreement itself, or to limit their flexibility in using generic drugs.

On trade in services, the Commonwealth study has concluded that 'the commitments made by acceding countries were far larger than those made by WTO Members'.[5] The study found that

> WTO Members in general, and the Quad [meaning the United States, the European Union, Canada and Japan] in particular, have used their unique negotiating position, by virtue of inherent flaws of the accession process ensuring the vulnerability of applicant countries, to unleash their considerable strategic privilege in acquiring ever greater concessions from the latter, irrespective of their size and economic significance.[6]

After overcoming the accession hurdles discussed earlier, new members are equally bound and protected by the WTO Agreement and its subsidiary rules. Two key principles of the WTO system are MFN treatment and national treatment. Both mean that trading must be done without discrimination between trading partners. MFN refers to non-discrimination among WTO members. If a WTO member grants trade-related favourable treatment to goods and services from another WTO member, it must extend the same treatment to all other WTO members, thereby treating all members as 'most-favoured' trading partners. The MFN principle runs across all the subject areas covered by the WTO. 'National treatment' refers to non-discrimination between a WTO member's own nationals and those of all other WTO members. This means treating imported and locally produced goods and

---

3. See, for example, Daniel Pruzin, 'Cambodia Pleads for Flexibility, No Demands in WTO Accession Talks', *WTO Reporter*, BNA, 15 Feb. 2002, 'Officials Cite Progress in Algeria WTO Talks On Accession; Services, Energy Still Problems', *WTO Reporter*, BNA, 2 Mar. 2005, 'Minister Blasts "WTO-Plus" Demands In Talks on Russia's Accession', *WTO Reporter*, BNA, 2 Nov. 2000, and 'Russia's Trading Partners Set Out "Bottom Line" on WTO Accession Terms', *WTO Reporter*, BNA, 31 Jan. 2005.
4. United Nations Commission on Human Rights, *The right of everyone to the enjoyment of the highest attainable standard of physical and mental health – Special Rapporteur on the Right to Health, Paul Hunt, Mission to the World Trade Organization*, E/CN.4/2004/49/Add.1, Mar. 2004, 19.
5. R. Grynberg, V. Ognivtsev & M. A. Razzaque, 8.
6. *Ibid.*, 34.

services equally. The same applies to intellectual property rights, such as trademarks, copyrights, and patents.

During the accession process, applicants are often required to demonstrate the predictability and transparency of their trade rules and practices. This allows countries to reduce trade barriers in the well-founded belief that their trading partners will not subsequently raise barriers and erode their export markets. The WTO seeks to ensure predictability through what are called 'bindings' – when WTO members agree to lower tariffs and remove trade barriers, they 'bind' their commitments by listing them in their so-called 'schedules' – tables with details on goods and services items. Applicants for WTO membership must bind their commitments and concessions by listing them in their schedules, which are part and parcel of their respective accession package. For goods, 'binding' takes the form of placing upper limits on tariff rates, whereby members are bound not to raise tariffs beyond these ceilings ('bound rates'). For services, policies to open up the services sector to foreign competition are 'locked' in a so-called 'schedule of commitments'.

The members' tariff concession schedules and services commitments form an integral part of the WTO Agreement. The WTO seeks to ensure transparency in trade and domestic rules that govern trade. In addition to the Trade Policy Review Mechanism (TPRM)[7] that regularly reviews individual members' trade practices and policies, most WTO agreements require members to notify the WTO of their trade-related measures.

When acceding to the WTO, members are automatically subject to the jurisdiction of the WTO's dispute settlement mechanism – a quasi-judicial system under which final decisions are enforceable through authorization of trade retaliation measures, or 'suspension of concessions', to use the WTO jargon. This particular enforcement mechanism of the WTO regime, though representing a last resort, remains unique among international tribunals and judicial bodies dealing with non-criminal matters. WTO agreements stipulate that each member shall ensure that its laws, regulations, and administrative procedures conform to its WTO obligations. The Trade Policy Review Body (TPRB), through regular review of the individual members' trade policies and practices, seeks to improve members' transparency in relation to trade policy matters and their adherence to WTO commitments.

As of April 2009, twenty-eight applications for WTO membership are pending, indicating that most of the countries remaining outside the WTO system have started the accession process but yet to complete their negotiations. As indicated earlier, for some countries, WTO membership also serves as an external impetus to push forward otherwise domestically difficult reforms.

The following section illustrates the ways in which China was treated as a special case during the accession negotiations and was sometimes required to make commitments and concessions incompatible with the WTO's key non-discrimination principle.

---

7. The frequency of reviews depends on a WTO member's trade volume. The bigger traders are reviewed more frequently, up to once every two years. See 'trade policy reviews' at the WTO website <www.wto.org/english/tratop_e/tpr_e/tpr_e.htm> for details.

II AN UNUSUAL JOURNEY: CHINA AS A SPECIAL CASE

The following chronology illustrates the long Chinese negotiations process towards WTO membership:

A ACCESSION CHRONOLOGY

Time	Major Progress
1948	China becomes a founding contracting party to GATT
1949	People's Republic of China established
1950	The Republic of China (the Chiang Kai-shek government in Taiwan) withdraws from GATT
1978	*Deng Xiaoping* launches open-door policy and economic reform
1986	China applies to join/resume its status as a contracting party to GATT
1987	China submits a memorandum on its foreign trade regime; China Working Party established under GATT
1988	First meeting of China Working Party
1989	Progress of GATT Working Party stalled after *Tiananmen* Square events
1992	China and the United States sign a memorandum of understanding on market access
1995	The World Trade Organization succeeds GATT
1996	Informal multilateral consultations over China's WTO accession
1999 Apr.	Chinese Premier *Zhu Rongji*'s US visit over WTO negotiations
1999 Nov.	China and the United States conclude bilateral WTO negotiations and sign bilateral agreement
2000 May	China and the European Union conclude their bilateral WTO accession negotiations
2001 Sept.	Last meeting of China Working Party at the WTO; multilateral negotiations concluded
2001 Nov.	WTO Ministerial Conference in Doha, Qatar, approves China's accession
2001 Dec.	China becomes the 143rd member of the WTO

B THE GATT STAGE

The ROC, under the rule of the Nationalist Party (also called *Kuomintang*, or KMT), signed the Treaty of Havana in 1948 and GATT's provisional protocol in April 1949. It became a founding contracting party to GATT in May 1949.[8] When the KMT lost control over mainland China and fled to Taiwan, the CPC took power and established the PRC on 1 October 1949. The ROC in Taiwan notified its withdrawal from the GATT effective 5 May 1950, and the PRC government had 'not yet defined its position' towards the GATT.[9] In 1965, the ROC government applied for observer status at the GATT and was accepted.[10]

After the PRC replaced the ROC in the United Nations in 1971, the GATT decided to withdraw Taiwan's observer status.[11] Throughout this period, the PRC government remained aloof from the GATT. It did not protest the ROC's decision to withdraw China from the GATT, nor did it apply to return to the GATT in 1971 when Taiwan's observer status was withdrawn. In 1981, the PRC applied for observer status with the Multi-Fibre Arrangement (MFA), a plurilateral agreement under the GATT,[12] and eventually acceded to the MFA in January 1984.[13] In October of the same year, the Beijing government formally requested observer status with the GATT, stressing that its request was '[w]ithout prejudice to the PRC's position with regard to its legal status vis-à-vis the GATT',[14] which meant that China was a GATT founding contracting party and therefore should not be obliged to go through the process of accession negotiations, should it decide to 'resume' its GATT status.

In July 1986, China formally requested to 'resume' its status as a contracting party to the GATT,[15] arguing that because of 'historical reasons', the formal relationship between China and the GATT had been suspended.[16] The GATT contracting parties agreed to establish a working party to examine China's request, though some of them, such as the United States, expressed reservations over Beijing's position regarding China's legal status vis-à-vis the GATT.[17] It was not surprising that China's request was resisted by some contracting parties, who were keen to extract further concessions from China during the long process of accession negotiations. If China was allowed simply to 'resume' its contracting-party

8. GATT Document GATT/TN.1/38, GATT/CP.3/92, Accession to the General Agreement, 5 Sep. 1949.
9. GATT Document GATT/CP.5/SR.6, Summary Record of the Sixth Meeting, 9 Nov. 1950.
10. GATT Document SR.22/3, Summary Record of the Third Meeting, 8 Mar. 1965.
11. GATT Document SR/27.1, Summary Record of the First Meeting, 19 Nov. 1971.
12. GATT Document COM.TEX/W/92, Communication Received from the Permanent Mission of the People's Republic of China, 28 Apr. 1981.
13. GATT Document COM.TEX/36, Report of the Committee Meeting Held 19–20 Jan. 1984, 2 Mar. 1984.
14. GATT Document L/5712, China – Request for Observer Status, 26 Oct. 1984.
15. GATT Document L/6017, China's Status as a Contracting Party – Communication from the People's Republic of China, 10 Jul. 1986.
16. GATT Document C/M/201, Minutes of Council Meeting Held on 15 Jul. 1986, 4 Aug. 1986.
17. *Ibid.*

status, it would be unlikely that China had to make many non-GATT and GATT-plus concessions. To Beijing's disappointment, these negotiations did not complete in time for China to become a founding member of the WTO in 1995.

C The WTO Stage

Compared to other WTO members' Accession Protocols, which are in a standard two-page format divided into three parts – General, Schedules, and Final Provisions,[18] China's Accession Protocol is exceptionally long. It runs to eleven pages with an addition of eighty-nine pages of annexes.

According to a Chinese official who took part in the accession negotiations, China's lengthy Accession Protocol was a result of demands made by the United States and the European Union. They insisted that issues such as the uniform administration of the Chinese trade regime, transparency, judicial review, the right to trade, a transitional product-specific safeguard mechanism, and a TRM should be included in the Accession Protocol, rather than simply enumerating them in the accession Working Party Report. Though both documents are considered to have equal legal standing, major trading partners wanted to ensure that these issues were solidly entrenched in the protocol itself, which they considered to have a better legal status, as a binding international treaty, compared to the Working Party Report.[19]

Another trade official who followed China's negotiations from the GATT to the WTO, however, suggests that the reason for China's longer Accession Protocol was that those involved in China's pre-WTO negotiation process did not want to discard their draft protocol from the time of the GATT, and hence the GATT draft protocol was incorporated into the WTO Accession Protocol. 'Therefore the whole process for China to become a WTO member was very unusual and very confused', this official added, as negotiators tried to lump the two processes together.[20]

To accede to the WTO, an applicant has to reach a bilateral agreement with each and every existing WTO member that has requested bilateral negotiations. In China's case, thirty-seven WTO members (with the European Union counting as one representing its then fifteen Member States) requested bilateral negotiations. The first to conclude a bilateral agreement with China was Hungary (May 1993) and the last was Mexico (September 2001).

---

18. See, for example, accession protocols of Croatia (WT/ACC/HRV/61) which acceded to the WTO in September 2000, of Chinese Taipei (WT/L/433), acceded in November 2001, of Cambodia (WT/MIN(03)/18), acceded in September 2003, and of Saudi Arabia (WT/L/627), acceded in November 2005.
19. Author's interview with a Chinese official who took part in the negotiations and spoke under condition of anonymity, 19 Jul. 2005, Geneva.
20. Author's interview with a trade official who spoke under condition of anonymity, 13 Jun. 2005, Geneva.

As expected, the most difficult and sustained bilateral negotiations were with key trading powers including the United States and the European Union, which concluded their bilateral negotiations with China on 15 November 1999 and 19 May 2000, respectively. As all bilateral agreements for accession are 'multilateralized' into the applicant's final Accession Protocol, the Working Party Report, as well as schedules of commitments, all the concessions China made in its bilateral agreements with the United States and the European Union are also applicable to all other WTO members. Early on 18 September 2001, the WTO China Accession Working Party approved the package deal, which was then transmitted to and approved by the WTO's Ministerial Conference in Doha, Qatar, on 11 November 2001.

III WHY DID IT TAKE SO LONG? MAJOR STUMBLING BLOCKS

China remains the country which took the longest to complete its WTO accession process. There are procedural and substantive reasons to explain this phenomenon. Procedurally, China and the then GATT contracting parties were deadlocked for a long time over China's status in the global trade body. At the centre of the dispute was whether China, a founding member of GATT, could simply apply to resume its status in GATT or whether it would have to go through the accession negotiations as if it were a newcomer.

Once all those concerned had agreed to disagree on the subject and to proceed to substantive negotiations, significant domestic political turmoil – notably the events of *Tiananmen* Square of 4 June 1989 – resulted in a de facto suspension of the accession negotiations and the increase in power of the anti-reform elements within China's top leadership. Negotiations over the substantive conditions on which China would become a member of the WTO were even more difficult than the procedural hurdles. By the end of 2001, when China joined the WTO, it had survived many tough bilateral negotiations with individual WTO members and multilateral bargaining.

A Uncertain Legal Status: Resumption of Membership or Accession?

A laconic note from the ROC of 6 March 1950 paved the way for China's road to the WTO: 'I have the honour to inform Your Excellency of the decision of the Government of the Republic of China to withdraw from the General Agreement on Tariffs and Trade signed on the 30th of October 1947.'[21] The ROC requested the United Nations to transmit this message to GATT, thus prompting uncertainties over China's legal status in the GATT when the PRC requested to return to it in 1986.

---

21. GATT document GATT/CP/54, Communication from the Secretary-General of the United Nations regarding China; document on file with the author.

China had already missed a golden opportunity to resume its status in the GATT in 1971, when the GATT withdrew Taiwan's observer status under United Nations Resolution 2758. According to China's chief trade negotiator from 1992 to 2002, Vice Trade Minister *Long Yongtu*, the then GATT Director-General invited the PRC to return to GATT after the expulsion of Taiwan; China declined. *Long Yongtu* said that if Beijing had been willing then, resumption of its status in GATT would have been 'a very simple matter'. He recalled that in 1971 and 1972, the Cultural Revolution was still under way, and because China perceived the GATT as 'a club of rich nations' dominated by developed countries, it refused to join.[22]

After China's request to 'resume' its status as a contracting party to GATT of 10 July 1986,[23] it took GATT members nearly a year to debate whether the request should be treated as a resumption of status or as an accession application. No agreement on the terms of reference of the Working Party was reached until May 1987, which prompted the GATT representative of the European Community to 'state publicly the embarrassment felt by the Community and its Member States over the length of the consultations which had been held to date'.[24] Even after reaching a compromise on the terms of reference,[25] differences on China's legal status in the GATT remained, and the debate continued into 1988. China's chief negotiator summarized Beijing's position vis-à-vis GATT delegates as follows:

> China's request for the resumption of its status as a contracting party to GATT is justifiable. It is a historical fact that China is one of the founding contracting parties to GATT. The founding of the People's Republic of China in 1949 did not alter China's status as a subject of international law. The withdrawal from GATT in 1950 by the deposed regime in Taiwan was illegal and invalid. The United Nations in a resolution adopted in 1971, decided to restore all its rights to the People's Republic of China in the United Nations and in all organizations related to it and [sic] recognize the representatives of the government of the People's Republic of China as the only legitimate

---

22. 胡舒立, '龙永图：谈判是这样完成的', 《财经》第47期, 2001年11月5日, 38–46, 39 (Hu Suli, 'Long Yongtu : Negotiations Completed This Way', *Caijing Magazine* 47 (5 Nov. 2001): 38–46).
23. China's Status as a Contracting Party – Communication from the People's Republic of China, GATT Document L/6017, 10 Jul. 1986.
24. GATT Document C/M209, Minutes of Council meeting 14 May 1987, 9.
25. GATT Document L/6191, Working Party on China's Status as a Contracting Party, 19 Jun. 1987; the terms of reference read: 'The People's Republic of China has submitted to the GATT Contracting Parties a request to resume its status as a Contracting Party (L/6017) and a Memorandum on the People's Republic of China's Foreign Trade Regime (L/6125). Taking note of the statements made in the Council of 4 Mar. 1987, a Working Party was established by the Council. This Working Party will examine the foreign trade regime of the People's Republic of China, develop a draft protocol setting out the respective rights and obligations, provide a forum for the negotiation of a schedule, address as appropriate other issues concerning the People's Republic of China and the GATT, including procedures for decision-making by the CONTRACTING PARTIES, and make recommendations to the Council.'

> representatives of China. On the understanding that the GATT follows decisions of the United Nations on essentially political matters, the Contracting Parties terminated the status of the observer from Taiwan. The IMF, World Bank and other intergovernmental organizations have all restored China's lawful rights in accordance with the above-mentioned United Nations General Assembly Resolution. Therefore, there is a sufficient political and legal basis for China's request for resumption of its status as a contracting party.[26]

The United States maintained that China's request should be viewed as an accession process: 'Concerning the issue of whether China is "acceding" to the GATT or "resuming" its previous membership, my Government views this process as the same as an accession process. We recognize that China views these negotiations as part of the "resumption" of GATT membership. Whatever the description of its form, the terms of China's GATT membership must be negotiated with the contracting parties',[27] a US official told GATT delegates.

Regardless of the rhetoric, China appeared to accept that substantive negotiations with the contracting parties were required before it could reintegrate the GATT: '[H]aving taken into account the contractual nature of the General Agreement, we agree to enter into substantive negotiations with contracting parties for the resumption of China's contracting-party status and set the rights and obligations',[28] a Chinese representative said in 1988. When the Chinese government accepted to enter into substantive negotiations then, little could it know that subsequent events would prolong the negotiations for another thirteen years.

B HIATUS AFTER THE *TIANANMEN* SQUARE EVENTS

The *Tiananmen* Square events in Beijing of June 1989 put on hold any real movement over China's accession negotiations for more than two years. 'As early as the spring of 1989, there were many who thought progress was such that the working party could move into relatively advanced stages of the negotiations. However, following the.... Tiananmen "incident" in June 1989, very little happened on either the bilateral or multilateral front for more than two-and-a-half years',[29] the

---

26. Statement by Shen Jueren, Vice-Minister of Foreign Economic Relations and Trade, Head of the Chinese delegation at the 3rd session of GATT's Working Party on China, 26 Apr. 1988, on file with the author. In an interview with the author in Doha, 9 Nov. 2001, Doha, Shen confirmed that the 'Taiwan' question had held back the initial negotiations process.
27. Statement by W. Douglas Newkirk, Assistant US Trade Representative for GATT Affairs, to the 2nd meeting of GATT's Working Party on China, 23 Feb. 1988; document on file with the author.
28. Statement by Shen Jueren, Vice-Minister of Foreign Economic Relations and Trade, Head of the Chinese delegation at the 3rd session of GATT's Working Party on China, 26 Apr. 1988; document on file with the author.
29. Speech by Jeffrey L. Gertler, WTO Senior Legal Counsel and Secretary of the China Working Party, *'The Process of China's Accession to the World Trade Organization'*, delivered at the

late Jeffrey Gertler, Secretary of the China Working Party noted in 1997. In fact, 'active discussions' only resumed in October 1992.

Long Yongtu acknowledged that the 'June 4th disturbance' (风波 *Feng Bo*) of 1989 not only held up the negotiations for two years but also added a political dimension to the accession process:

> A working party session was originally scheduled to take place in July 1989. After the June 4th disturbance, Western countries led by the United States interrupted their negotiations with China. Now we say China experienced 15 years of negotiations to join the WTO, but real negotiations in fact took about 13 years because the process was suspended for two years.... Afterwards, China considered the resumption of its GATT status not just as negotiations for resuming international diplomacy and economic status, but as an important political act to break western blockage and sanctions against China at that time.[30]

Ambassador Girard of Switzerland, chairman of the China Working Party recalled: 'We wondered what to do. Given the situation, I decided to focus strictly on GATT aspects, and sent a letter [to the Chinese negotiator], not wanting to mix the political situation and the negotiations; and the Chinese were smart enough to reply to say that they were not ready.'[31] The Working party resumed late 1990, but the chairman said that after the *Tiananmen* Square events, there was practically 'no movement' until 1992, when GATT members began to discuss possible elements to be included in China's Accession Protocol.

The first major breakthrough after 1989 was the result of an 'understanding' between China and GATT members, notably the United States, in the autumn of 1992 over Taiwan's request to join the GATT. GATT Council chairman B.K. Zutshi reported in September 1992 that after extensive consultations on the subject of establishing a working party to consider the possible accession of Chinese Taipei, known in the GATT as the Separate Customs Territory of Taiwan, Penghu, Kinmen and Matsu, he had concluded that there was consensus among contracting parties to establish a Working Party on Chinese Taipei. Under specific terms, the Council should examine the report of the China Working Party and adopt the protocol for China's accession *before* examining the report and adopting the protocol on Chinese Taipei's accession (hence dubbed the 'China to join before Chinese Taipei' arrangement). The two reports should be examined independently of each other; and 'as a part of the understanding, the representation of Chinese Taipei in GATT would be along the same lines as that of Hong Kong and Macau during the period of its status as an observer and subsequently as a 'contracting-party

---

Third Annual Conference of the Library of International Relations, Chicago-Kent College of Law, 6–7 Nov. 1997; document on file with the author.

30. Hu Suli, 39.
31. Author's interview with Ambassador Pierre-Louis Girard, who served as Chairman of the China Working Party for Accession from 1987 to 2001, 19 May 2005, Geneva.

delegation', and 'that the titles carried by its representative would not have any implication on the issue of sovereignty'.[32]

Chinese Taipei's accession negotiations to the WTO were by and large completed in 1998; but as required by the 'China to join before Chinese Taipei' understanding, its Accession Protocol was not adopted until November 2001 – a day after the Doha ministerial conference adopted China's Accession Protocol. The official denomination and title of Chinese Taipei's representation in the WTO, after both joined the organization, resurfaced as a bone of tension between both sides, a dispute that resulted in a two-year delay in updating the WTO's internal directory.[33]

With these delays in the negotiations, it was not possible for China to complete the accession negotiations before the conclusion of the Uruguay Round that established the WTO in 1995. In December 1995, GATT's China Working Party was converted into a WTO Working Party on the Accession of China,[34] with an expanded mandate to include the new regulations established under the WTO, such as new rules on agriculture, textiles, General Agreement on Trade in Services (GATS), intellectual property rights, and Trade-Related Aspects of Investment Measures (TRIMS).

The terms of reference of the WTO China Accession Party also changed to standard ones under WTO rules: 'To examine the application of the Government of the People's Republic of China to accede to the World Trade Organization under Article XII, and to submit to the General Council recommendations which may include a draft Protocol of Accession.'[35] By that time, over nine years after Beijing first requested to return to the GATT, it was clear that the final hurdle before the completion of negotiations to join the WTO was not in sight.

C TOUGH BILATERAL NEGOTIATIONS

As in all other WTO accession negotiations, the bilateral and multilateral accession processes proceed concurrently. China, as a rising big trader with a large potential market, faced tough bilateral negotiations with the United States and the European Union – the world's two largest traders. Competition between the latter two in gaining concessions from China further complicated the already formidable tasks confronting the Chinese trade negotiators. While bilateral agreements with individual WTO members had to be multilateralized to become applicable to all members, strong American and European business lobbies exerted pressure on

32. GATT Document C/M/259, Minutes of Council meeting 29 Sep.–1 Oct. 1992.
33. See, for example, Melody Chen, 'Ploy Won't Affect WTO Rights: Official; Name Game: China is Pressing to Have the Name of Taiwan's WTO Mission Downgraded in a New Directory', *Taipei Times* 18 Mar. 2005; 'Taiwan-China Fight Delays Update of WTO Directory', *Taipei Times* 3 Jun. 2004; and Laurence Eyton, 'Status Quo: Beijing, Taipei and the WTO', *Asia Times* 23 Jun. 2003.
34. WTO Document WT/ACC/CHN/1, Communication from China, 7 Dec. 1995.
35. *Ibid.*

their governments to obtain an advantage over their respective trans-Atlantic competitors in gaining access to the Chinese market.

1 The United States

China's negotiations with the United States were the most difficult. Chinese chief trade negotiator *Long Yongtu* put it thus: 'At the beginning of the negotiations, we did not negotiate on the so-called substantive issues, we were negotiating on the attitude of negotiations',[36] Washington was adamant and uncompromising at the beginning; and it took the United States '5 or 6 years to adjust to the Chinese demand that China needed to negotiate on an equal footing'.[37] As to substantive negotiations, *Long* said the United States 'was probably the one who made the most demands', partly because of its vast economic interests and power as well as the role the US played as a 'leading sheep' – as many other WTO members with smaller economies relied on the US to extract concessions on their behalf, since China's concessions and commitments laid down in the Sino-US bilateral WTO agreement would be incorporated into China's final accession package and made applicable to all WTO members equally.[38]

More specifically, the US first demanded what *Long* described as 'a comprehensive negotiation', manifesting its interest in all of China's exports, over 6,000 tariff lines, and demanding negotiations on each and every of the products concerned. *Long* noted that the first stage of negotiations with the United States was spent on 'breaking the US demand on comprehensive negotiations' and reduced the scope to about 4,000 tariff lines. In the area of trade in services, keen US interests in the banking, insurance, telecommunication, distribution, and legal services sectors also prolonged the negotiating process.[39]

Key US officials perceived it as Washington's role to 'lead' in China's WTO accession negotiations. Charlene Barshefsky, the US Trade Representative (USTR) who finally signed the Sino-US WTO bilateral agreement' told the US Senate Finance Committee in 1997:

> At President Clinton's direction, the United States led the world in setting tougher standards for trade with China. We have battled to open a highly protected market, still dominated in many areas by the central or provincial governments. We have negotiated landmark agreements to combat piracy and advance the interests of our copyright industries. We have also negotiated – and vigorously enforced – agreements on textile trade, designed to prevent transhipments. We have taken the lead in consulting with China on its WTO accession, and insisted that this accession occur on commercially meaningful terms.[40]

36. Hu Suli, 40–41.
37. *Ibid.*
38. *Ibid.*
39. *Ibid.*
40. Prepared statement of Charlene Barshefsky, USTR, to the US Finance Committee, Federal News Service, 29 Jan. 1997.

The Clinton administration's failure to finalize a deal on China's WTO accession by April 1999, and the reasons behind this widely perceived political 'misjudgment' by the US leadership, are most revealing of the difficulties underlying the Sino-US WTO negotiations. According to US Senator Kent Conrad:

> [O]ne of the things he said – the premier [*Zhu Rongji*] – during our discussion was [that] he has never encountered a tougher negotiator than [we] are.... He said to us that they've made concession after concession, and it's never enough for [us]; [we] always want more. And he said he believes that Congress has put too much pressure on you. As he said to us repeatedly, 'You've turned an economic issue into a political issue.' Now the fact is, there are a lot of irritants in our relationship. Some of them are more than irritating – espionage, human rights, the controversy over Taiwan, our disagreements over Kosovo, the trade imbalance itself. We have a $57 billion trade deficit with China.[41]

Conrad told USTR Barshefsky in a hearing before the Senate Finance Committee in April 1999, after the Clinton administration failed to come to an agreement with the Chinese during Premier *Zhu Rongji*'s US visit. The deal then was widely perceived by US corporations as very protective of and beneficial to US commercial interests.

In addition to the aforementioned non-trade 'irritants' in the Sino-US relationship, competing commercial interests between different US sectors and constituencies stood in the way of concluding an agreement with China. 'WTO-plus' demands from the US over textile quotas and a transitional safeguards mechanism specifically designed for Chinese exports are cases in point, as identified by Senator Phil Gramm during the same Finance Committee hearing:

> [T]o insist that China's textile quotas extend five years longer than any other member of the WTO, is not only outright discrimination,.... [t]o be talking about protecting Americans from cheap and good-quality textiles is outrageous.... [I]t is driven by domestic politics.... The second thing that I strongly object to is another....protectionist issue, which you're negotiating hard for, which would change our standards for engaging in protectionist practices, just with regard to China, from an industry being seriously injured, which is the current standard for everybody else in WTO, to market disruption. [T]he American consumer loses in both. We're going to lose more jobs by protecting non-competitive American industry than we're going to possibly gain in those areas where people have strong political ties but very weak positions in the marketplace.... Basically what the president has done is he's taken two domestic political issues – one is textiles and protectionism of textiles; the other is protectionist interest that would like to have lower standards, so that they can cheat the American consumer by getting protection from the

41. Transcript of hearing of the Senate Finance Committee on the status of China's application to join the World Trade Organization, organized by Senator William Roth, 13 Apr. 1999, Federal News Service.

> federal government – and let those two issues stop this whole deal from going through.... The idea that China would be asked to have a quota on textiles five years longer than any other member of WTO is outrageous and unreasonable, and it's there for one simple reason – domestic politics. And I think the idea that we're going to set a separate, lower standard so that we can engage in more protectionism is a movement in the wrong direction.[42]

While most US constituencies from the services sectors accepted the concessions China had made in opening its domestic market to foreign service operators in the final stage of the Sino-US negotiations, powerful US manufacturing lobbyists pushed for further safeguards against Chinese exports of industrial goods, textile and apparels in particular.

USTR Barshefsky admitted in November 1999 that these were '[t]wo of the most important unresolved issues'[43] – special rules to curb import surges and the application of a 'non-market economy' methodology in anti-dumping investigations against Chinese exports. In addition to specific market access issues, the negotiations also stumbled over some over-arching principles, such as China's status as a developing country and the treatment of China as a non-market economy. In the earlier stages of the negotiations, *Long Yongtu* had noted that a major difficulty was that China did not acknowledge it was reforming towards a market economy. Only after *Deng Xiaoping*'s 1992 'Tour to the South'[44] did a 'genuine dialogue' with foreign negotiators using a 'common language' begin.[45]

When China and the United States finally concluded their negotiations in late 1999, China accepted to be treated as a non-market economy in anti-dumping investigations (meaning that a complainant could use third country reference prices in deciding whether China exports products below market prices (dumping)) for fifteen years after accession. China also accepted a clause on transitional safeguards applicable to its textile and clothing exports for three additional years after the end of the WTO textile quota system in 2005, as well as special safeguards system for its other products twelve years after its accession.

2 The European Union

Contrary to expectations that Brussels would quickly conclude its agreement with China after Beijing and Washington completed their negotiations, it actually took another seven months before the European Union finalized its bilateral accession negotiations with Beijing. In addition to substantive issues that needed to be solved, a political perception prevalent among European diplomats and business sectors to the effect that the US deal was not and should not be seen as sufficiently representing EU commercial interests contributed to the delay in the conclusion of

42. *Ibid.*
43. Transcript of USTR Barshefsky's press remarks following negotiations with China on the WTO, American Embassy, Beijing, China, 15 Nov. 1999; on file with the author.
44. See Ch.3 Section II.B.C.
45. Hu Suli, 40.

the Sino-EU negotiations. '[N]o one party to the talks can determine the outcome on its own, and no bilateral agreement between China and a third country can be imposed on other members of the WTO as a basis for a final accession deal', the then Vice President of the European Commission and trade negotiator Leon Brittan stated.[46]

Long Yongtu confirmed that there was comparison, if not competition, between the European Union and the United States over their respective bilateral negotiations with China:

> After we signed an agreement with the United States, EU representatives told us that, to take hosting a dinner reception as a metaphor, you could not serve us the same menu as the one you served the United States, we have our own demands. Our negotiations with the European Union to a very large extent had to do will fulfilling the pride of the Europeans as a big economic entity.[47]

With respect to outstanding substantive issues, the European Union made specific requests, particularly in the area of trade in services. These included market opening commitments such as distribution, legal services, accountancy, banking, and insurance. Competition between European and US corporations over the right of branching (opening of local subsidiaries) of insurance companies in China, for example, resurfaced later in the accession negotiations, when trade officials tried to incorporate accession commitments made by Beijing in its bilateral agreements with different WTO members into the multilateral accession package.

D MULTILATERAL BARGAINING

While China was subjected to tough bilateral negotiations, the multilateral front was not smooth sailing, either. To begin with, when the accession process reached the stage of drafting the basic elements and framework of the Accession Protocol, China was faced with what Ambassador Girard characterized as the 'maximum' demands from members, which China had to 'negotiate down'. The chairman of the Chinese Working Party described demands China faced when the negotiations restarted in 1992:

> We started to speak about the protocol itself. Then we decided that each one would put forward what they considered the basic conditions for China to join in the multilateral protocol. What everyone did was to put forward elements they wanted to be in the protocol. Then I talked to *Long* [*Yongtu*] [saying], I have all the elements from all the members. It's going to be a very very ambitious protocol and you won't like it. Before going into this exercise, you have to tell me whether you are ready for this. It seems that you have to

46. China- Sir Leon Brittan on China's accession to WTO, China Business Information Network (CBNET), 8 Mar. 1999.
47. Hu Suli, 44.

negotiate down the obligations because really they are asking the maximum [of you].... We came out with a very GATT-plus protocol, which was a kind of synthesis taking the extreme requests in terms of the systematic aspects.[48]

1 Foreign Exchange and IMF Intervention

A telling example of the so-called GATT-plus or WTO-plus requests from members concerned China's foreign exchange system, which prompted the IMF to address a note to the WTO China Working Party in March 1996, expressing 'serious concerns'. The PRC had returned to the IMF in 1979, and the IMF took issue with three provisions in the then draft protocol:[49]

(1) China shall not use foreign exchange controls or restrictions to regulate the level or composition of trade in goods and services. China shall, by [x date], establish a unified foreign exchange market, remove all restrictions on access to this market and eliminate guidelines specifying the priority uses of foreign exchange.

(2) China shall, by [*x* date], bring its foreign exchange regime into conformity with obligations under Article VIII of the IMF. Individual requests of foreign exchange for current account transactions shall not be subject to any form of approval, and the issuance of a letter of credit or a bank guarantee upon presentation of an invoice shall not be subject to any form of government restriction.

(3) China shall not resort to laws, regulations or other measures, including requirements with respect to contractual terms, which have as their object or effect to influence foreign exchange earnings or expenditure.

The requests formulated by members on China's foreign exchange system, as written into the February 1996 draft protocol, were so restrictive that not only no other WTO member was subject to the same restrictions; they also had no legal basis in the WTO Agreement itself. Furthermore, according to the IMF, 'these provisions risk inconsistency with Article XV of GATT (1994), Article XI of the GATS, and the principles set out in the Declaration on the Relationship of the World Trade Organization with the Fund'.[50] Specifically, Article XV(9)(a) stipulates that nothing in GATT (1994) shall preclude 'the use by a contracting party of exchange controls or exchange restrictions in accordance with the Articles of Agreement of the International Monetary Fund'.

With respect to the WTO's GATS, Article XI(2) states that nothing in GATS shall affect 'the rights and obligations of the members of the International

48. Author's interview with Switzerland's Ambassador to the WTO Pierre-Louis Girard, 19 May 2005, Geneva.
49. Part I, Art. 9 (1–3), draft protocol for China's accession to the WTO, February 1996 version; on file with the author.
50. Statement of the IMF Representative to the Working Party on China's Accession to the WTO, 22 Mar. 1996; document on file with the author.

Monetary Fund under the Articles of Agreement of the Fund, including the use of exchange actions which are in conformity with the Articles of Agreement'. The IMF expressed 'serious concerns' over the draft foreign exchange provisions and questioned 'their consistency with the rights and obligations of Fund members under the Fund's Articles, and with established practice for dealing with the exchange systems of common members'.[51]

The IMF came close to criticizing WTO members for applying double standards and violating the WTO's principle of non-discrimination. Specifically, the IMF argued that the draft protocol as such would create 'an unfortunate precedent, which would conflict with the principle of uniformity of treatment under the Fund's Articles by establishing two classes of Fund members in respect of their exchange regimes'. The WTO members' desire to restrict China's foreign exchange system also conflicted with the IMF's jurisdiction and articles and its ability to approve Fund members' temporary exchange restrictions in the event of balance-of-payments need: 'The incorporation of the exchange clause (as currently drafted) in the protocol on China's membership in the WTO' would mean that 'a member enjoying its rights under the Fund's Articles could be subject to punitive action under the rules of another international body. It could also mean that this Board's judgment on a member's exchange system could be disregarded by the judgment of WTO bodies. This is not consistent with the established pattern of jurisdiction between the Fund and the GATT', the IMF emphasized. It further suggested that the draft protocol should 'drop all references to exchange measures under Fund jurisdiction'.[52]

China supported the IMF's position and reiterated that it had expressed similar views to WTO members on various occasions: 'As there is a clear division of responsibility between the IMF and the WTO, China does not wish to be trapped in a legal conflict of obligations arising from a WTO protocol clause on foreign exchange policy',[53] *Long Yongtu* argued in 1992 in response to the IMF statement. In the end, foreign exchange provisions included in the commitment paragraphs of the Working Party Report for China's accession were by and large in line with the IMF Articles:

> The representative of China stated that China would implement its obligations with respect to forex matters in accordance with the provisions of the WTO Agreement and related declarations and decisions of the WTO that concerned the IMF. The representative further recalled China's acceptance of Article VIII of the IMF's Articles of Agreement, which provided that 'no member shall, without the approval of the Fund, impose restrictions on the making of payments and transfers for current international transactions'. He stated that, in accordance with these obligations, and unless otherwise provided for in the

51. *Ibid.*
52. *Ibid.*
53. Statement by the Representative of China, Long Yongtu, at the WTO Working Party on China, 22 Mar. 1996; document on file with the author.

> IMF's Articles of Agreement, China would not resort to any laws, regulations or other measures, including any requirements with respect to contractual terms, that would restrict the availability to any individual or enterprise of forex for current international transactions within its customs territory to an amount related to the forex inflows attributable to that individual or enterprise. The Working Party took note of these commitments.... In addition, the representative of China stated that China would provide information on exchange measures as required under Article VIII, Section 5 of the IMF's Articles of Agreement, and such other information on its exchange measures as was deemed necessary in the context of the transitional review mechanism. The Working Party took note of this commitment.[54]

2 Systemic Guarantees

Many concerns of WTO members over whether China would implement its accession commitments were addressed through the multilateral track of the accession negotiations. One factor that further delayed China's WTO accession process was that some WTO members were unconvinced that China would implement its WTO commitments. *Long Yongtu* said that the 'suspicions' of members over China's determination and capacity to implement its WTO commitments, and to make efforts to prevent legal loopholes in the implementation stage, prolonged the final multilateral stage of the accession negotiations.[55] Systemic concerns translated into additional sub-sections in China's Accession Protocol, such as 'uniform administration of trade regime', 'transparency', 'non-discrimination', 'judicial review' and 'trading rights'. In addition, a ten-year long TRM, designed for China and applicable to China alone, was and agreed upon in the final stages of the negotiations to ensure additional and continuous monitor of China's implementation efforts. The concerns of WTO members over these systemic legal issues and China's commitments and actions in response will be discussed later.

A trade official who followed the Chinese and other acceding members' accession processes pointed out an interesting 'unusual' feature in China's case, with regard to systemic guarantees and an acceding country's legal system.[56] Contrary to outsiders' perception that the Chinese legal system was under stricter scrutiny and faced more demands during the accession process, he said that compared to other acceding members, unusually little attention was paid to the Chinese legal system and that there was only 'superficial' examination of whether China already had laws and systemic features in place to fulfil its WTO commitments.

The official further noted that for those who only followed China's accession, they looked at the numerous additional provisions and requirements written into

54. China Working Party Report, II (3) paras 35–36.
55. Hu Suli, 44.
56. Author's interview with a Geneva-based trade official who spoke on the condition of anonymity, 13 Jun. 2005.

China's protocol and Working Party Report and concluded that WTO members had set higher standards for and placed more demands on the Chinese legal system than on that of other acceding members. On the contrary, these additional requirements and systemic guarantees in China's accession package were in fact the result of the WTO members' lacklustre scrutiny of the Chinese legal system and their reluctance to insist that China should have met all the systemic legal standards before joining the WTO. The underlying reason was that WTO members were keen to see China, a growing economic power with a big market, in the WTO soon in order to protect their economic interests. Fully aware that the Chinese legal system did not yet meet the standards required under WTO rules, WTO members choose to ensure China's future compliance through additional provisions on systemic guarantees in the accession package, rather than delaying China's WTO membership by insisting further reform of the Chinese legal system.

Taking Croatia (which joined the WTO in November 2000) as an example, the same official suggested that many questions were asked and Croatia had to provide written answers and detailed evidence demonstrating that its legal system and judiciary could implement WTO rules and requirements. The same was not done in China's case: 'China was allowed into the WTO many years before other countries would have been allowed in by applying the same standards. Take Croatia, if China would have been required to meet the legal standards [applied to] Croatia, it would have taken China at least 5 more years [to join]',[57] the official affirmed.

A search of the WTO's document database corroborates the above observations. While there are numerous WTO documents recording written questions and replies during Croatia's seven-year long accession process, a similar search on China's fifteen-year long accession negotiations yields no document which records written questions from WTO members and written answers by China. A similar search of documents during the GATT period also does not produce similar written records.

A discussion between Chinese law officials and the WTO Secretariat over the treatment of laws and regulations inconsistent with WTO rules further illustrates the members' approach: 'Join first and implement through transitional periods.' In a meeting held on 16 February 2000, officials from the Treaty and Law Department of Ministry of Foreign Trade and Economic Cooperation (MOFTEC) 'expressed concern that it might be awkward to notify laws and regulations that they know to be inconsistent with WTO rules'. It was suggested to them that 'they nonetheless submit these notifications and propose reasonable transition periods for bringing their laws into conformity where immediate adaptation is not considered feasible'.[58] The WTO is a members-driven organization and its Secretariat does not routinely take decisions and make recommendations of such nature on its own. The Secretariat's response to this particular concern of Chinese law officials was

57. *Ibid.*
58. WTO Memo, 22 Feb. 2000, para. 2; document on file with the author.

a reflection on the WTO members' approach in dealing with China's WTO-incompatible laws and regulations prior to its accession.

3 The Transitional Review Mechanism

It is crucial to understand the WTO members' approach to accepting China as a WTO member before the Chinese legal system was fully compatible with WTO rules, to be able to put into context the numerous transitional periods and additional post-accession monitoring measures detailed in the Chinese Accession Protocol and the Working Party Report. A special TRM to monitor China's post-accession legal and trade measures was agreed to in the final stages of the multilateral negotiations. No other WTO member is subject to a similar mechanism; it is unlikely that newly acceding countries will be subject to it in the future. Thus, Chinese Taipei, which joined the WTO immediately after China, was not subject to such a transitional review. And Russia, itself a former Communist country and now almost equal to China in terms of the length of its accession process, has not been requested to accept a similar TRM in the accession negotiations. The TRM therefore does not only exemplify the unique nature of China's WTO accession negotiations, it is also indicative of the WTO members' particular fears over China's post-accession implementation.

Under the TRM, the WTO's subsidiary bodies must review China's implementation of WTO rules annually and submit their reports to the General Council for adoption and recommendations. During the review, WTO members can raise WTO-related issues[59] and China must provide information and answers in response. The review will take place annually for eight years after accession. There will be a final review in year ten or at an earlier date to be decided by the General Council. On systemic issues and related measures concerning laws, regulations and the Chinese legal system, the TRM requires China to provide, inter alia, the following information:[60]

- On non-discrimination, the repeal and cessation of all WTO inconsistent laws, regulations and other measures on national treatment, and the repeal or modification to provide full GATT national treatment in respect of laws, regulations and other measures applying to internal sale, offering for sale, purchase, transportation, distribution or use of a number of products.
- On foreign exchange, exchange measures as required under Article VIII, section 5 of the IMF's Articles of Agreement and such other information on China's exchange measures as was deemed necessary in the context of the TRM.
- On investment regime and trade-related investment measures, to notify to the WTO's Committee on Trade-Related Investment Measures on completed revisions to investment guidelines in conformity with the WTO

59. See China Accession Protocol, Art. 18, Annexes 1A and 1B for details.
60. Extracts from China's Accession Protocol, Art. 18 and Annex 1A.

Agreement; and elimination and cessation of enforcement of trade and foreign exchange balancing requirements, local content and export performance offsets and technology transfer requirements made effective through laws, regulations or other measures.

- On the Chinese government's framework for enforcing policies, structure and powers of the government/authority of sub-central governments/uniform administration; revision or enactment of domestic laws, regulations and other measures related to China's commitments under the WTO Agreement and protocol, including those of local governments at the sub-national level, that have been promulgated since accession or the previous meeting of the relevant body under the TRM; and the establishment and operation (upon accession) of a mechanism under which individuals and enterprises can bring cases of non-uniform application of the trade regime to the attention of national authorities.
- On licensing, implementation of the provisions of the Agreement on Import Licensing Procedures and the WTO Agreement applying the measures set out in China's Accession Protocol including provision of the time taken to grant an import license.
- On trade in services, regularly updated lists of all laws, regulations, administrative guidelines and other measures affecting trade in each service sector or sub-sector indicating, in each case, the service sectors or sub-sectors they apply to, the date of publication and the date of entry into force; licensing procedures and conditions, if any, between domestic and foreign service suppliers, measures implementing the free choice of partner; regularly updated lists of the authorities, at all levels of government (including organizations with delegated authority) which are responsible for the adoption and implementation of, and the reception of appeals against, laws, regulations, administrative guidelines and other measures affecting trade in services; independence of the regulatory authorities from the service suppliers; as well as foreign and domestic suppliers in sectors where specific commitments have been undertaken indicating the state of play of licensing applications at sector and sub-sector levels.
- On TRIPS, amendments to the Copyright, Trademark and Patent laws, as well as relevant implementing rules covering different areas of the TRIPS Agreement bringing all such measures into full compliance with and full application of the TRIPS Agreement and the protection of undisclosed information, and enhanced intellectual property rights enforcement efforts through application of more effective administrative sanctions.

4 Holding Out until the Last Moment

Once the issue of systemic guarantees was settled, China faced some final attempts from WTO members to negotiate further substantive concessions before wrapping up the accession package. *Long Yongtu* urged members 'not to raise unrealistic requests in this final stage',[61] after China had concluded its bilateral negotiations with the United States and the European Union, respectively.

China's bilateral agreements with the United States and the European Union did not prevent China's WTO bid from running into further hurdles during the final stages of the accession negotiations. Washington took issue with China's entitlement to agricultural subsidies, and after several months of deadlock China reached a fresh deal with the United States in June 2001. Another EU deal also reached in June 2001 involved market access for service industries, in particular the insurance sector, and a concession from China on the definition of chain stores.

The final sticking point involved an EU-US dispute over the access of foreign insurers to the Chinese market.[62] In the 1999 bilateral Sino-US agreement, the American International Group, a major US insurance company, had secured the rights to fully own its mainland China operations. The EU – under pressure from insurance companies such as Allianz Group of Germany and AXA of France – demanded that European insurers be treated no worse than their US counterparts. The EU companies would be restricted to 50%–50% joint ventures under the EU-China bilateral deal. Finally, a compromise[63] was reached shortly after the attacks of 11 September 2001 on the United States.

On the bilateral front, Mexico held out longest to secure further concessions from China. The two countries concluded their bilateral agreement, necessary for completing China's accession negotiations, only a few days before the entire package deal was ready in mid-September 2001. WTO members must establish time frames to phase out restrictions on Chinese imports including footwear, textiles, and clothing, and this was a key issue particularly for Mexico, which had sought to keep restrictions on Chinese imports for up to thirteen years and which eventually secured a compromise on a six-year phasing out period. On the night of 16 September 2001, more than fifteen years of arduous negotiations came to an end. The remaining steps were for the WTO's Ministerial Conference formally to approve China's accession package in November 2001 and for the Chinese legislature to ratify the accord. But the ratification arrangement was yet another surprise.

E An Unorthodox Ratification Arrangement

Before the Doha WTO Ministerial Conference, speculations abounded as to when the Chinese parliament, the NPC, would ratify the Accession Protocol, thirty days

61. John Zaracosta, 'China Toughens Stance in WTO Talks', *United Press International*, 23 Jun. 2000.
62. Esther Lam, 'China Near Success in Trade Grail', *South China Morning Post*, 17 Sep. 2001.
63. The compromise involved adding a footnote to the China Working Party Report restating MFN treatment to all foreign insurers. For details, see Daniel Pruzin, 'Insurance Agreement Ends Stalemate on China's Accession to the WTO', *WTO Reporter*, BNA, 18 Sep. 2001.

after which China would become a WTO member. The Chinese government, however, did not indicate how it intended to complete the necessary ratification process before the Ministerial Conference. Therefore it came as a big surprise when the Chinese delegation, on 11 November 2001, declared that no further ratification by the NPC would be required for the Accession Protocol, and China would officially become a WTO member thirty days after the signing ceremony in Doha, that is, on 10 December 2001.

According to Chinese officials present in Doha, the signature by President *Jiang Zemin*, which indicated that the domestic ratification process had been completed, was to be deposited with the WTO immediately after the signing ceremony of the Accession Protocol. They noted that already on 25 August 2000, the NPCSC had passed a resolution which delegated authority to the State Council to complete the procedures required for China to join the WTO. *Shi Guangseng*, then MOFTEC and Head of the Chinese delegation to the Ministerial Conference, brought *Jiang Zemin*'s signature to Doha to expedite the required domestic legal procedures for China to become effectively a WTO member.[64]

Under Chinese law, an international treaty requires ratification by the NPCSC to become a legally binding instrument. The Chinese government's unusually secretive way of handling the WTO protocol ratification drew concerns about transparency and due process, that is, the very principles the WTO accession package requires China to adhere to. However, Beijing's decision to follow this unorthodox ratification arrangement – the NPCSC's delegation of authority to the State Council and a pre-approval signature by the President – was partly in response to a suggestion made by the then WTO Director-General, Mike Moore. As indicated in an internal WTO memo[65] of 22 February 2000, during a meeting in Beijing on 17 February 2000 with Premier *Zhu Rongji*, Moore had suggested to *Zhu* that 'it could be helpful to the process if China were able to accept the terms of accession definitely upon signing' the protocol, 'without having to resort to domestic ratification procedures'.[66] *Zhu* took note of the suggestion, and Minister *Shi* indicated to Moore a day later that the government was indeed looking into the viability of such an approach.

According to two informed sources,[67] Moore's suggestion was made not on his own initiative but in response to two major concerns of Beijing over the necessary domestic ratification of the WTO Accession Protocol. Firstly, the Chinese leadership was concerned that widespread media reports about China's 'WTO-plus' concessions might prompt a public backlash against the WTO accession during the domestic ratification process. The leadership also wanted to avoid public manifestation of grievances among those parts of the population that were

64. Author's separate interviews with two Chinese officials who requested not to be quoted by name, 10 Nov. 2001, Doha, Qatar.
65. Memo on file with the author.
66. *Ibid.*, para. 2.
67. A trade official and a Chinese delegate both spoke to the author over the phone on the condition of anonymity when asked about the background of the memo; 18 Sep. 2005 and 22 Oct. 2005.

likely to loose from WTO membership, such as farmers and the laid off workers of SOEs.

Secondly, the leadership was worried that Taiwan might outwit Beijing by some imaginative pre-ratification measures which would enable it to become a WTO member before the PRC. Beijing had consistently maintained that it would not object to Taiwan's WTO accession, provided that in accordance with the One-China policy, Taiwan (as a province of China) could only join the WTO as a separate customs territory under the title of Chinese Taipei, and only *after* China had become a WTO member. Such arrangements had been agreed to between China and other major players, such as the United States and the European Union. Therefore, even though Chinese Taipei had completed its accession negotiations in 1998, its Accession Protocol was approved at the Doha Conference only after China had signed its own. Beijing did not want to leave it to chance that delays in the domestic ratification process or an acceleration in the domestic process of Taiwan might lead to the latter's accession before that of Beijing, which would have been considered an embarrassment. It was suggested that Chinese officials had expressed concerns over this possibility to the WTO Secretariat, and that this prompted Moore's suggestion to *Zhu Rongji*.

The end of the fifteen-year long negotiations marked the beginning of a new journey, a journey China would begin as a full member of the WTO. This means that China can use WTO rules and mechanisms to protect its rights. Meanwhile, China also must start implementing its accession commitments and comply with the WTO rules-based system.

Chapter 5

Accession Commitments and Systemic Requests

This chapter examines four major areas of requests which WTO members have placed on the Chinese legal system for it to improve and which China is bound to fulfil as obligations incurred under the accession package. These systemic requests include the uniform administration of China's WTO-related legal regime, the transparency and predictability of the Chinese legal system, the implementation of the principle of non-discrimination, and the availability of judicial review by impartial and independent tribunals. Before analyzing these requests, China's commitments in response and the resulting challenges for the Chinese legal system, we will first look at some legal issues and how the accession package and WTO rules are implemented in China.

I THE IMPLEMENTATION OF WTO RULES IN THE CHINESE LEGAL SYSTEM

There are key constitutional issues in analyzing the implications of China's WTO membership for its legal order. One key concern raised by WTO members was how WTO rules would be implemented in China. The Untied States, for example, at one point had requested that WTO rules be directly applicable in domestic Chinese courts.[1] This request was rejected by the Chinese government, but from a theoretical point of view, it raises the question of whether a monist or dualist approach should guide China in the implementation of the WTO Agreement.

---

1. Author's discussions with US and EU delegates who took part in the accession negotiations; they spoke on the condition of anonymity; 28 Jun. 2001, Geneva.

The WTO Agreement itself remains silent on the point, and in practice WTO members do not follow a purely monist or dualist approach.

In the European Union, Member States follow different practices with regard to the domestic implementation of international law, though Member States speak with one voice and follow a unified policy vis-à-vis traders outside the EU bloc. European jurisprudence remains inconsistent on the extent to which WTO rules and the governments' WTO obligations can be invoked directly in both national and European courts.[2] In the United States, which follows the dualist model, a debate continues over whether WTO rules and rulings can be enforced by non-state actors through the domestic court system.[3]

A DEBATES OVER DIRECT APPLICABILITY

The legal status of international treaties is not clearly defined in the PRC Constitution. In the case of the WTO agreements, Chinese officials have repeatedly stated that if there is a conflict between Chinese law and WTO rules, the latter would prevail. This approach is consistent with the doctrine of consistent interpretation, which means that whereas 'a national rule allows for different interpretations, national or regional law has to be construed in accordance with international obligations'.[4] During China's WTO accession negotiations, requests were made by other WTO members that it should be stated clearly in the Working Party Report that WTO rules would be directly and automatically applicable in domestic Chinese courts. *Long Yongtu* rejected these requests but agreed to include the following paragraph in the report:

> The representative of China stated that China has been consistently performing its international treaty obligations in good faith. According to the Constitution and the Law on the Procedure of Conclusion of Treaties, the WTO Agreement fell within the category of 'important international agreements' subject to the ratification by the Standing Committee of the National People's Congress (NPCSC). China would ensure that its laws and regulations pertaining to or affecting trade were in conformity with the WTO Agreement and with its commitments so as to fully perform its international obligations. For this purpose, China had commenced a plan to systematically revise its relevant domestic laws. Therefore, the WTO Agreement would be implemented by China in an effective and uniform manner through revising

2. See, for example, the *Kupferberg* case (Case 104/81, ECR 1982, 3659), the *Anheuserbusch Inc. v. B.Budvar* case (Case C-245/02), and the *Leon Van Parys NV v. Belgisch Interventie – en* Restitutiebureau (BIRB) case (Case C-377/02).
3. For comparison between practices in the United States, the European Union and Switzerland, see T. Cottier & K.N. Schefer, 'The Relationship of WTO Law, National and Regional Law', *Journal of International Economic Law* (1993): 83–17, 99–107.
4. *Ibid.*, 87.

its existing domestic laws and enacting new ones fully in compliance with the WTO Agreement.[5]

The exact implication of this paragraph is subject to interpretation. Performing international treaty obligations in 'good faith' is a concept laid down in the *Vienna Convention on the Law of Treaties*.[6] The Convention stipulates that 'a party may not invoke the provisions of its internal law as justification for its failure to perform a treaty' (Article 27). In the PRC Constitution, the exact terminology is 'treaties and important agreements', for which decisions about ratification and abrogation rest with the NPCSC (Article 67(14)) and with the PRC President pursuant to decisions of the NPCSC (Article 81). The *Law on the Procedure of Conclusion of Treaties*[7] sets out the procedures for concluding international and multilateral treaties, without specifying their legal effect or the modalities of implementation.

The Chinese *Civil Procedure Law*[8] (Article 238) and the *General Principles of the Civil Law*[9] (Article 142), though not specifically governing domestic Chinese trade laws, clearly state China's approach in dealing with conflicts between provisions of domestic law and international law. Both stipulate that if an international treaty concluded by or acceded to by the PRC contains provisions which differ from those in the civil laws of the PRC, the provisions of the international treaty shall apply, unless the provisions in question are subject to reservations made by the PRC. In addition to these statutory provisions, judicial interpretations, legally binding guidelines for the lower courts issued by the SPC, are widely used in China to fill in legislative gaps. Evidence shows that the SPC has frequently used judicial interpretations both to clarify and to implement WTO rules and obligations in the Chinese legal system.

B DUALIST OR MONIST APPROACH

The WTO Agreement requires each WTO member to 'ensure the conformity of its laws, regulations and administrative procedures with its obligations as provided in the annexed Agreements' (Article XVI(4)). The WTO system therefore obliges its members to specific performance in accordance with WTO rules.[10] It nonetheless remains the prerogative of each member government whether to make the WTO rules directly applicable in its domestic legal system (monist approach) or to

---

5. Working Party Report, para. 67.
6. For meaning and implications of 'good faith', see R. Bernhardt (ed.), *Encyclopaedia of Public International Law*, vol. 1 (North-Holland: Elsevier, 1992) on 'Vienna Convention on the Law of Treaties', 1308–1317.
7. Adopted by the 17th session of the Standing Committee of the 7th NPC on 28 Dec. 1990, promulgated and made effective on the same date.
8. Adopted and made effective 9 Apr. 1991.
9. Adopted by the NPC on 12 Apr. 1986, effective as of 1 Jan. 1987.
10. J.H. Jackson, 'The WTO Dispute Settlement Understanding: Misunderstandings on the Nature of Legal Obligation', *The American Journal of International Law* 91, no. 1 (1997): 60–64, 63.

implement them indirectly through domestic legislation (dualist approach). The WTO's TRIPS Agreement specifically requires WTO members to adopt or to adapt domestic law to enforce TRIPS provisions and to provide for a judicial review opportunity of final administrative decisions concerning intellectual property rights (Articles 41–50). Even so, TRIPS does not impose substantial rules on the WTO members' domestic legal systems.

In China's case, in addition to requirements applicable to all WTO members, further obligations are placed on the government to bring its legal, administrative, and judicial system into conformity with WTO rules. These additional requests are detailed in the China Accession Protocol and the Working Party Report. But apart from unsuccessful attempts by members during the accession negotiations to urge Beijing to make WTO rules directly applicable in the Chinese legal system, nothing in the accession package obliges China to implement WTO law through a monist or dualist approach.

The PRC Constitution and the *Law on Legislation* are silent on the issue of direct application or the self-executing nature of international agreements. Past Chinese government practices have been inconsistent. When China ratified the *United Nations Convention on Contracts for the International Sale of Goods* in 1980, the SPC ordered the courts at different levels to apply the Convention directly in relevant cases. In 1987, China allowed for the direct application of the provisions of the *Convention on the Recognition and Enforcement of Foreign Arbitral Awards (New York Convention)*, through a SPC notice on implementation, without adopting implementing legislation.[11] For the implementation of the WTO Agreement and to bring its laws into conformity with WTO rules, Beijing has opted for domestic legislation.

C JUDICIAL INTERPRETATIONS

On 27 August 2002, the SPC issued a document about the implementation of the WTO Agreement, entitled *The SPC's Provisions on Certain Questions Concerning the Hearing and Handling of International Trade Administrative Cases*,[12] effective 1 October 2002. In explaining China's approach to implementation of the WTO Agreement, *Li Guoguang* (李国光), Vice President of the SPC, said the aforementioned regulations show that WTO rules are not directly applicable in Chinese courts. He recalled that individuals or companies cannot invoke WTO rules directly in the Chinese courts, nor can domestic judges directly apply WTO rules in their judgments. Instead, the Chinese authorities have adopted laws and regulations to implement China's obligations under the WTO Agreement.

---

11. Q. Kong, *China and the World Trade Organization: A Legal Perspective* (River Edge, NJ: World Scientific Publishing, 2002), 39–40.
12. In Chinese: '關於審理國際貿易行政案件若干問題的規定', issued on 27 Aug. 2002 and made effective as of 1 Oct. 2002.

As stipulated in the Provisions (Article 9), should more than one reasonable interpretation of domestic law be allowed, judges who adjudicate trade-related cases should interpret domestic law in a way consistent with WTO rules, *Li Guoguang* explained.[13] This was the first time a senior judge clearly took position on the issue of direct applicability of WTO rules since China joined the world trade body.

Individuals or corporations have no legal standing before a WTO dispute settlement panel or before the Appellate Body. If, for example, a company considers that a foreign government has breached WTO rules, it cannot initiate a case before the WTO dispute settlement mechanism but must instead ask its government to defend its interests in the appropriate WTO forum. It is up to the government to decide whether to follow this course of action.

Among WTO members, practice varies widely in as much as the preference for a monist or dualist approach is concerned.[14] In theory, the dualist approach usually emphasizes the supremacy of state sovereignty. The rationale is that matters concerning foreign relations are the responsibility of the executive branch, and barring a formal act of parliament, no international or foreign undertaking shall become legally binding domestically. In some dualist systems, this is clearly stated in the Constitution. For example, the Irish Constitution stimulates that no other legislative authority other than the Irish Parliament has the power to adopt laws for the state and that no international agreement shall be part of domestic law, except as may be determined by Parliament (Article 29(6)). The United Kingdom also follows a doctrine of parliamentary sovereignty in which domestic legislation is required for provisions of international agreements to become legally binding.[15]

In other jurisdictions such as Belgium, France, and Luxembourg, and in many Latin American countries, where a monist approach prevails, international agreements become legally binding domestically upon ratification. Under the monist vision of law, as spelled out in Kelsen's theory of law and his concept of the 'Grundnorm', the rationale for direct applicability lies in the hierarchy of law, and some fundamental international rules are superior to national ones.

In practice, however, few countries follow a purely monist or dualist approach. Jurisprudence in the United States and the European Union remains inconsistent on whether WTO rules or rulings can be enforced by non-state actors via the domestic courts. The EU Treaty creates its own system of direct applicability in EU Member States, but WTO rules do not have the same status in the domestic legal systems of different EU members. Articles 2 and 3 of the GATT, for example, were applied directly in several judgments of the Italian Supreme Court and

---

13. 中國法院將受理外國人提出的行政訴訟案件, 新華社 2002年08月29日 ('Chinese Courts to Accept Administrative Litigations from Foreigners', *Xinhua*, 29 Aug. 2002).
14. F. Roessler, 'Competition and Trade Policies: The Constitutional Function of International Economic Law', *Aussenwirtschaft*, 41 Jahrgang (1986), Heft II/III, Grusch: Ruegger, 467–474, 473.
15. Henry G. Schermers & Niels M. Blokker, *International Institutional Law – Unity within Diversity*, 3rd edn (The Hague: Kluwer Law International and Martinus Nijhoff Publishers, 1995), 1522–1525.

of several American courts, whereas direct application was refused by some German courts.[16] The European Court of Justice's jurisprudence on the direct applicability of WTO rules is also inconsistent.[17] Effectively, in the United States and the European Union, if a citizen or a company feels that their own government breaches its international legal obligations under WTO rules, there is no general right for them to invoke and enforce WTO rules or WTO rulings directly through their domestic courts.[18] In sum, the United States and the European Union do not give direct effect to WTO rules.

In the case of China, to the present day, there has been no test case to probe whether WTO rules can be directly invoked before and applied by domestic courts. While the Chinese government opted for a dualist approach in implementing its WTO obligations and commitments, nothing in Chinese law explicitly prohibits the direct application of WTO rules by domestic courts, nor can one rule out the possibility that Chinese courts will apply WTO principles and jurisprudence in interpreting domestic laws designed to implement China's WTO obligations. Even the 2002 Regulations of the SPC,[19] which lay down principles for the adjudication of cases involving international trade, do not *explicitly*[20] prohibit the direct application of WTO rules.

D LIMITED RELEVANT CASE LAW

On strictly WTO-related areas, so far foreign private enterprises remain reluctant to resort to Chinese courts to resolve their commercial disputes. This is partly explained by the fact that many foreign companies have become accustomed to

16. *Ibid.*
17. See, for example, the *Kupferberg* case (Case 104/81, ECR 1982, 3659), the *Anheuserbusch Inc. v. B.Budvar* case (Case C-245/02), and the *Leon Van Parys NV v. Belgisch Interventie-en Restitutiebureau* (BIRB) case (Case C-377/02). Judgment of the BIRB case, 1 Mar. 2005, para. 39–40 states that '[i]t is settled case-law in that regard that, given their nature and structure, the WTO agreements are not in principle among the rules in the light of which the Court is to review the legality of measures adopted by the Community Institutions. It is only where the Community has intended to implement a particular obligation assumed in the context of the WTO, or where the Community measure refers expressly to the precise provisions of the WTO agreements, that it is for the Court to review the legality of the Community measure in question in the light of the WTO rules.'
18. See, for example, a series of publications by Ernst-Ulrich Petersmann, 'Implementation of WTO Rulings: The Role of Courts and Legislatures in the US and Other Jurisdictions (EC, China)', Draft Discussion Paper, presented at the Columbia University Conference on the WTO, April 2006; *Constitutional Functions and Constitutional Problems of International Economic Law* (Higher Education Press, 2004), E.U. Petersmann & M.A. Pollack (eds), *Transatlantic Economic Disputes: The EU, the US and the WTO* (Oxford: Oxford University Press, 2003).
19. The SPC's Provisions on Certain Questions Concerning the Hearing and Handling of International Trade Administrative Cases.
20. Emphasis added; see also Part III, Ch. 6 Section II.C.2 on the issue of direct applicability of WTO international property rights rules in Chinese courts.

the traditional Chinese perception that going to court means a break-off of friendly relations and a refusal to resolve disputes through informal channels in an amicable manner[21]or through arbitration. In arbitration, parties in dispute can appoint arbitrators of their choice. But if they go to court, as plaintiffs and respondents they cannot pick and choose judges of the court to settle their disputes. In addition, China and many countries are parties to the New York Convention on the recognition and enforcement of foreign arbitral awards. Comparatively, there are fewer mutual judicial assistant agreements between China and other countries. The development of arbitration in China in itself is an important topic. This book, however, does not further discuss the subject for the following reasons: Since the entry into force the PRC Arbitration Law in 1995, arbitration practices have been developing quickly in China. Both the New York Convention and the Washington Convention became effective in China, in 1987 and 1992 respectively, way before China joined the WTO. Secondly, While Chinese courts play a role in the enforcement of arbitration awards, arbitration hearings and practices are usually held behind closed door and independent of judicial practices. The ways of which an arbitration case is handled, such as the applicable law and jurisdiction, are often dependent on a specific arbitration clause or agreement between contractual parties. All these make arbitration less relevant to the present study as it examines the impact of WTO membership on the Chinese legal system, focusing on the changing role of law and systemic impact. Another reason that accounts for the limited number of court cases invoking WTO-related Chinese laws in domestic courts is that firms prefer to lobby their respective governments to take up their issues at the WTO level, rather than confronting the Chinese authorities on their own.

However, the limited WTO case-law in Chinese courts does not mean that the impact of the WTO rules-based system on the Chinese legal system is in turn limited. On the contrary, the WTO's impact on the Chinese legal order and its reform preceded Beijing's WTO accession. Ambassador Girard has pointed out that a much earlier version of the draft China Accession Protocol,[22] from the days of the GATT, had a significant influence in guiding China's legal reform in the 1990s:

> If you follow what happened from 1992 to 2001, you realize that basically what the Chinese did was to accept most of the structure and the basic elements in the [GATT] protocol. But why did they not accept that sooner? What happened during that period in China [was that] they put into place, as least partially, the mechanism which would permit them to respond to the provisions of the GATT and the WTO.... They knew very well where they were going.[23]

The WTO rules-based system continues to exert a very multi-faceted influence on the Chinese legal system and its way of functioning, in its legislative, judicial,

21. Author's interview with Tao Jingzhou, China Practice Managing Partner, Coudert Brothers LLP, 7 Sep. 2004, Beijing.
22. A 1994 draft of China's WTO accession protocol, document on file with the author.
23. Author's interview with Ambassador Pierre-Louis Girard, 19 May 2005, Geneva.

administrative, and enforcement aspects. The following section focuses on the WTO's specific systemic requirements on the Chinese legal system, as stipulated in the WTO Agreement, China's Accession Protocol, and Working Party Report. These requirements can be broadly categorized into four areas, namely uniform administration of law, transparency, non-discrimination, and impartial judicial review. China's commitments and concrete actions in response are also addressed.

This book has so far discussed the salient features of the Chinese legal system, constraints of the on-going legal reform, the diverse Chinese WTO accession motivations, and the significant moments and issues of the accession negotiations. The commitments and challenges to be addressed here are the end products of this continuous cumulative process, during which a significant stage came to an end with the end of the accession process. The following section provides the basic but necessary information and foundation for Part III, which examines the WTO impact from wider and systemic perspectives, such as the growing importance of law in policy-making and daily functioning of Chinese society, the redistribution of influence between law and politics, and the prevalence of some underlining rule of law principles in China.

II WTO CHALLENGES TO THE CHINESE LEGAL SYSTEM

No matter how WTO rules and China's WTO commitments are implemented domestically, specific demands for the systemic improvement of the Chinese legal system test both the capacity of the system itself and the Chinese government's determination to proceed with tough and long-term legal reform. Given the systemic nature of these requests, entrenched in the WTO accession agreement, the implementation of these commitments inevitably raises significant challenges for the Chinese legal system and the existing constraints which domestic reform efforts could not overcome. If successfully implemented, WTO-driven legal principles can steer Chinese legal reform into a direction more compatible with the international standards.

A DECIPHERING THE ACCESSION PACKAGE

The WTO agreements and rules form a unique set in international law with its own enforcement mechanism. The Marrakech Agreement Establishing the WTO Agreement stipulates that 'each member shall ensure the conformity of its laws, regulations and administrative procedures with its obligations as provided in the annexed Agreements' (Article XVI).[24] The WTO has a quasi-judicial dispute

24. 'Annexed Agreements' refers to the Multilateral Trade Agreements and, where applicable, the Plurilateral Trade Agreements.

settlement mechanism, as set out in the Understanding on Rules and Procedures Governing the Settlement of Disputes (DSU), pursuant to which final decisions are of compulsory nature by authorizing trade retaliation measures, or 'suspension of concessions' in WTO terms. The WTO also administers a regular review mechanism, the TPRM, designed to improve the members' transparency in trade policy matters and their adherence to WTO rules and commitments.

As discussed earlier, China went through an unusual WTO accession process. According to Ambassador Girard who chaired the Chinese WTO accession negotiations, the China Working Party Report must be read together with the Accession Protocol. Specifically, the seventy-three-page long Working Party Report, consisting of 343 paragraphs, is not all about commitments of a binding nature, as is the text of the Accession Protocol itself.[25] Some simply identify concerns expressed by WTO members and explanations given by China.[26] Commitment paragraphs are those which end with the sentence '[t]he Working Party took note of this/these commitments', and paragraph 342 of the Working Party Report, which is incorporated into paragraph 1(2) of the Accession Protocol, lists all commitment paragraphs in the China Working Party Report.[27] These commitments specific to China, of course,

---

25. For an overview of China's WTO commitments by subjects, including trade in goods, trade in services and intellectual property rights, see C. Cheong & C.H. Yee, *Handbook on China's WTO Accession and Its Impact* (River Edge, NJ: World Scientific Publishing, 2003); for an assessment of China's WTO commitments on its socio-economic development by sectors, see D. Bhattasali, S. Li & W.J. Martin (eds), *China and the WTO: Accession, Policy Reform, and Poverty Reduction Strategies* (Washington, DC: World Bank, 2004), and K.T. Lee, Justin Yifu Lin & S.J. Kim (eds), *China's Integration with the World Economy: Repercussions of China's Accession to the WTO* (Seoul: KIEP, 2001).
26. Author's interview with Ambassador Pierre-Louis Girard, 19 May 2005, Geneva.
27. The main text of the China WTO Accession Protocol, not its annexes, is annexed to the present book. WTO document symbols of the China Accession Protocol and the China Working Party Report are WT/L/432 and WT/ACC/CHN/49 respectively; Goods Schedule: WT/ACC/CHN/49/Add.1 and WT/MIN(01)/3/Add.1; Services Schedule: WT/ACC/CHN/49/Add.2 WT/MIN(01)/3/Add.2.

    Paragraph 342 of the China Working Party Report reads: 'The Working Party took note of the explanations and statements of China concerning its foreign trade regime, as reflected in this Report. The Working Party took note of the commitments given by China in relation to certain specific matters which are reproduced in paras 18–19, 22–23, 35–36, 40, 42, 46–47, 49, 60, 62, 64, 68, 70, 73, 75, 78–79, 83–84, 86, 91–93, 96, 100–103, 107, 111, 115–117, 119–120, 122–123, 126–132, 136, 138, 140, 143, 145, 146, 148, 152, 154, 157, 162, 165, 167–168, 170–174, 177–178, 180, 182, 184–185, 187, 190–197, 199–200, 203–207, 210, 212–213, 215, 217, 222–223, 225, 227–228, 231–235, 238, 240–242, 252, 256, 259, 263, 265, 270, 275, 284, 286, 288, 291, 292, 296, 299, 302, 304–305, 307–310, 312–318, 320, 322, 331–334, 336, 339 and 341 of this Report and noted that these commitments are incorporated in paragraph 1.2 of the Draft Protocol.'

    Paragraph 1(2) of China's Accession Protocol reads:

    'The WTO Agreement to which China accedes shall be the WTO Agreement as rectified, amended or otherwise modified by such legal instruments as may have entered into force before the date of accession. This Protocol, which shall include the commitments referred to in paragraph 342 of the Working Party Report, shall be an integral part of the WTO Agreement.'

must be read together with the WTO Agreement and its annexes, which binds all WTO members.[28]

In examining the commitments that China undertook when joining the WTO, it is worth noting that for commitments to open its market of different sectors, China benefits from a two to five-year transitional period, with the specific time-frames depending on specific industries. But for China's commitments to comply with the specific legal standards set out in the WTO Agreement and the accession package, there is no transitional period as such. The United States, for example, took an unusual step to initiate WTO dispute settlement procedures over what it charged as systemic failure in the enforcement of TRIPS.[29] In this sense, challenges to the Chinese legal system can be broader and deeper than compared to those related to economic issues.

In its first ruling on a dispute settlement case (auto parts) against China, the WTO Appellate Body recalled that all parties to the dispute agreed that 'China's commitments under its Working Party Report are enforceable in WTO dispute settlement proceedings'.[30] The Appellate Body further affirmed that China's commitments under its Working Party Report, as they have been incorporated into the Accession Protocol, form an 'integral part of the WTO Agreement'.[31] The panel of the auto parts case proceeded on the basis that the commitment in dispute in the Working Party Report was 'enforceable in WTO dispute settlement proceedings and should be interpreted in accordance with the customary rules of interpretation',[32] as codified in Articles 31 and 32 of the *Vienna Convention on the Law of Treaties*. 'Neither of these propositions has been disputed at any point in these proceedings, including in this appeal',[33] the Appellate Body added.

It is clear that China's WTO Accession Protocol and Working Party Report (the accession package) are part and parcel of China's WTO legal obligations. For the purpose of the present research, it is necessary to identify the commitment paragraphs concerning specific WTO's requirements on the Chinese legal system. The following provides a detailed textual analysis of China's legal systemic WTO commitments in four main areas, concrete actions in response by the Chinese government, and subsequent changes in Chinese law.

---

28. Should different interpretations arise between provisions in the Chinese WTO accession package and that of the WTO Agreement, the *lex specialis* rule probably means that the former would prevail in determining China's exact legal obligations in the WTO.
29. See, for example, Kathleen E. McLaughlin, 'China Says U.S. Decision to Start Complaints over IPR at WTO to "Severely Harm" Relations', *WTO Reporter*, BNA, 11 Apr. 2007; issues related to TRIPS and its implementation in China will be discussed in Part III, Ch.6 Section II.C of the book.
30. The decision of the WTO Appellate Body in *China – Measures Affecting Imports of Automobile Parts*, WT/DS339/AB/R, WT/DS340/AB/R and WT/DS342/AB/R, 15 Dec. 2008, para. 213.
31. *Ibid.*
32. *Ibid.*, para. 214.
33. *Ibid.*

B UNIFORMITY IN ADMINISTRATION OF CHINA'S TRADE AND LEGAL REGIME

China has to repeal, amend and enact legislation to comply with WTO rules and the country's specific commitments. Chinese state media reported that at the central level, some thirty departments under the authority of the State Council have processed or amended up to 2300 distinct rules and regulations to this effect. The SPC has issued over 1,200 judicial explanations so that future adjudication of trade-related matters will be in line with WTO principles. At the local level, municipal authorities have simultaneously reviewed local rules, guidelines and instructions to bring them in line with the WTO requirements.[34] A close reading of the accession package documents reveals at least four systemic aspects of law in relation to which China will have to improve implementation throughout its legal system as a result of WTO membership. These include are:

– uniformity in the administration of the trade-related legal regime throughout the country;
– transparency and predictability;
– non-discrimination; and
– judicial review by impartial and independent tribunals.

This section examines the legal challenges the WTO poses to the Chinese legal system in line with the above principles and the immediate steps taken by China in response. For further analysis of the WTO's systemic long-term impact on the Chinese legal order and other theoretical issues, refer to Part III.

1 WTO Requirements and China's Commitments

The first challenge consists in the uniform administration of laws and regulations in relation to the trade regime throughout China. The Accession Protocol makes it clear that the WTO package agreements 'shall apply to the entire customs territory of China'.[35] This includes border trade regions and minority autonomous areas, such as Tibet and Xinjiang, Special Economic Zones, open coastal cities, economic and technical development zones, and other areas enjoying special regimes for tariffs, taxes, and regulations (collectively referred to as 'special economic areas' hereafter). The requirement of uniformity in the administration of all laws covers rules and measures pertaining to or affecting trade in goods, services and TRIPS. China shall 'apply and administer in a uniform, impartial and reasonable manner all its laws, regulations and other measures of the central government as

34. Liu Ren Min, 'How to Improve the Contemporary Chinese Legal System?', *People's Court Journal*, 2 Apr. 2002; for a report on specific cases and details of judicial explanations, see Wang Yin Bin & Wang Ye Peng, 'Judicial Preparations for the WTO – The Forth Round of Judicial Explanations and Related', *People's Court Journal*, 10 Jan. 2002.
35. Protocol of the Accession of the People's Republic of China,('Accession Protocol', hereafter), WT/L/432, 2 (A) 1.

well as local regulations, rules and other measures issued or applied at the sub-national level'.[36]

Furthermore, 'China's local regulations, rules and other measures of local governments at the sub-national level shall conform to the obligations undertaken in the WTO Agreement' and China's Accession Protocol.[37] China commits itself to notify the WTO of all the relevant laws, regulations, and other measures relating to special economic areas. Any modifications or additions to these areas and their related laws and measures shall be notified to the WTO within sixty days.[38] Except as provided for in the Accession Protocol, WTO provisions on non-discrimination and national treatment shall be fully observed in providing preferential arrangements for enterprises within special economic areas[39] – that is, such preferential treatment should be extended to foreign and local enterprises alike on a non-discriminatory basis.

Beijing also committed itself to establishing 'a mechanism under which individuals and enterprises can bring to the attention of the national authorities cases of non-uniform application of the trade regime'.[40] According to China's commitments in the Working Party Report, this mechanism would be operative upon accession. Under its terms, all individuals and entities could bring to the attention of central government authorities cases of non-uniform application of China's trade regime, including its commitments under the WTO Agreement and the Accession Protocol: 'Such cases would be referred promptly to the responsible government agency, and when non-uniform application was established, the authorities would act promptly to address the situation utilizing the remedies available under China's laws, taking into consideration China's international obligations and the need to provide a meaningful remedy. The individual or entity notifying China's authorities would be informed promptly in writing of any decision and action taken.'[41]

During China's accession negotiations, some WTO members questioned the central government's ability to ensure effectively a uniform trade regime throughout the country, fearing that multiple trade instruments used by different levels of government and sub-national governments' authority over fiscal, financial, and budgetary areas, such as subsidies and taxation, might diminish the predictability of China's trade regime. In response, China committed itself to annul local regulations, government rules, and other local measures inconsistent with China's WTO obligations. Beijing confirmed that the central government would ensure that China's laws, regulations, and other measures, including those of local governments, would conform to China's obligations under the WTO Agreement and the

36. Accession Protocol, 2 (A) 2.
37. Accession Protocol, 2 (A) 3; see also Working Party Report, paras 71–72.
38. Accession Protocol, 2 (B) 1.
39. Accession Protocol, 2 (B) 3.
40. Accession Protocol, 2 (A) 4.
41. Working Party Report, para. 75.

Accession Protocol,[42] and that the provisions of both would be applied uniformly throughout its special economic areas.[43]

2 Concrete Chinese Actions and Their Significance

In November 1999, after the Chinese government had concluded bilateral accession negotiations with the United States, it started to review trade-related laws, administrative rules, departmental regulations, decrees, and guidelines issued by the State Council. *Wu Hao*, Deputy Director-General of the Chinese Department of Foreign Affairs, the Legislative Affairs Office of the State Council, said that according to the results of the review, 1,150 laws, administrative rules, departmental regulations, and other policy measures at the national level were brought into line with WTO requirements before the end of December 2001. Among them, thirty-four administrative rules were amended or introduced, and twelve were repealed. At the departmental level, over 1,000 regulations were annulled, amended, or introduced, and thirty-four related documents issued by the State Council had been declared null and void by the time China became a WTO member.[44]

At the local level, the Central Office of the CPC and the State Council issued a guidance document entitled Opinion on the Clearance of Local Laws, Local Government Regulations and Other Policy Measures in Preparation for Our Accession to the WTO[45] in September 2001. This prompted an unprecedented campaign to bring order into a maze of Chinese local laws, regulations, and policy measures. Further to this Opinion, MOFTEC, the predecessor of the MOFCOM, issued a circular[46] to all local trade departments in November 2001, ordering that concrete steps be taken to review and clear trade-related laws and regulations to ensure compatibility with the WTO Agreement. The Opinion requires local authorities to complete this thorough review within a one year timeframe, in line with the above-mentioned guiding principles spelled out in China's WTO Accession Protocol.

A reliable source in the NPC's Legislative Office suggests that some years before 2001, the Office had sought the cooperation of local people's congresses in the review of local laws to iron out inconsistencies among regional laws and to eliminate irregularities between central and local laws, but the effort had met with limited success. The State Council's November 2001 Opinion just prior to China's WTO accession, however, was more effective in six months than the several years of effort by the NPC, both in terms of the volume of local laws reviewed and the

42. Working Party Report, paras 69–70.
43. Working Party Report, para. 73.
44. Author's interview with Wu Hao, Deputy Director-General, Chinese Department of Foreign Affairs, the Legislative Affairs Office of the State Council, 9 Sep. 2004, Beijing.
45. Available in Chinese, '关于适应我国加入世界贸易组织进程清理地方性法规, 地方政府规章和其他政策措施的意见', 中办发[2001]22号, issued by the Central Office of the Communist Party of China and the PRC State Council, 19 Sep. 2001.
46. Available in Chinese, '关于适应我国加入世界贸易组织进程, 清理地方性外经贸法规, 规章的通知', issued by the MOFTEC, 5 Nov. 2001.

degree of uniformity achieved between local and central laws. This situation, it was suggested, shows that in the Chinese system, measures introduced and backed by the executive branch and the ruling party are far more effective than the legal authority granted to the NPC and its offices under the Constitution and the laws.[47]

More importantly, according to *Wu Hao*,[48] the WTO accession prompted further momentum for Chinese legal reform. On the issue of the uniformity of the legal regime, the Chinese government designed new mechanisms, which continue to evolve, to ensure that future legislation and policy measures at both central and local levels are compatible with WTO commitments. Such mechanisms help ensure the consistency of laws throughout China in areas outside the WTO realm. This is an area where WTO membership affects the dynamics of the Chinese legal system and the domestic legal process as a whole. Regarding the uniform administration of trade-related legal regimes throughout China, the existing system of filing and reviewing of legislation, regulations, and judicial interpretations has been amended to allow companies, citizens, and investors to participate in the filing and review process.

The reasons for the number of conflicting laws and lack of uniformity in the Chinese legal regime are twofold: multiple and confusing legislative authorities both vertically, from central to local levels, and horizontally, across different government agencies and administrative organs at all level; as well as local protectionism.[49] The central government primarily seeks to address these problems and to ensure legal uniformity through a system of 'central archiving and review'[50] (备案审查, *Bi An Shen Cha*), under which local authorities and government departments must notify the central government of any new laws and administrative regulations within thirty days of their introduction by filing the new laws with the State Council. The system, first introduced by circulars of the State Council Office during the late 1980s,[51] was vague and implemented arbitrarily. *The Rules on the Archives Filing of Legislations and Government Rules*,[52] issued in 1990, consolidated the system by setting out further details for the implementation of the filing and review requirements throughout the country.

However, it was not until 1 July 2000, when the *Law on Legislation* took effect, that the subjects and procedures for issuing legally binding rules were

---

47. Author's interview with a Chinese official who spoke on condition of anonymity, 21 Aug. 2005, Geneva.
48. Author's interview with Wu Hao, Deputy Director-General, Chinese Department of Foreign Affairs, the Legislative Affairs Office of the State Council, 9 Sep. 2004, Beijing.
49. See Part I, Ch.2, Section II.D for details.
50. See 赵振华: 法规规章备案制度的建立和发展, 中国法制信息网, 8 Mar. 2006 (Zhao Zheng Hua, 'The Development of Archives Filing System', *China Legal News*, 8 Mar. 2006, <www.chinalaw.gov.cn/article/fzjd/bagz/200603/20060300056598.shtml>, 8 Apr. 2009).
51. In Chinese, '关于地方政府规章和国务院各部门规章备案工作的通知', issued on 7 Mar. 1987.
52. Rules on the Archives Filing of Legislations and Government Rules, promulgated by the State Council, 18 Feb. 1990.

properly defined. Partly because of China's commitments set out in the WTO Accession Protocol,[53] the State Council, on 14 December 2001,[54] promulgated the *Ordinance on the Archives Filing of Regulations and Government Rules*, which gave private companies, citizens, public institutions, social organizations, in addition to government organs, the right to inform and request the State Council to review any local regulations they deem to be in contradiction or inconsistent with national laws and regulations (Article 9).[55]

The Ordinance became effective 1 January 2002. It was designed to implement China's WTO commitments by establishing 'a mechanism under which individuals and enterprises bring to the attention of the national authorities cases of non-uniform application of the trade regime'.[56] The Ordinance is of general application and does not restrict the right of private entities and citizens to notify the central authorities of inconsistent or non-uniform application of law in the area of trade-related laws only.

Put differently, the WTO requirement of uniform administration of trade-related laws throughout China produces a spill-over effect, which allows both governmental and non-governmental entities, citizens, and public institutions to petition the central authorities and to challenge the legitimacy of numerous local laws and regulations, if they are deemed inconsistent with national laws and the Constitution. From 2002 to March 2004, the central authorities received twenty-three suggestions and notifications for review of rules and regulations regarding their consistency; among these, over ten were from private citizens and companies.[57] The Ordinance, together with the NPCSC *Working Procedures for Filing and Reviewing Administrative Rules and Regulations, Local Regulations, Autonomous Regulations and Specific Regulations, and Special Economic Zone Regulations* ('Working Procedures for Filing and Reviewing Legislation') and the introduction of *Working Procedures for Filing and Reviewing Judicial*

53. Author's interview with Wu Hao, Deputy Director-General, Chinese Department of Foreign Affairs, the Legislative Affairs Office of the State Council, 9 Sep. 2004, Beijing.

54. Three days after China became a WTO member.

55. Article 9 of the *Ordinance on the Archives Filing of Regulations and Government Rules* reads: 'In case any state organ, social organization, enterprise, public institution or citizen believes that a local regulation is inconsistent with any administrative regulation or believes that the government rule or any other universally binding administrative decision or order issued by the departments of the State Council or the people's governments of the provinces, autonomous regions, municipalities directly under the Central Government or the comparatively large cities is in contradiction with any law or administrative regulation, it or he may suggest in written form to the State Council for reviewing, and the legislative affairs organ of the State Council shall study the suggestion and put forward opinions about how to deal with the regulation or government rule and shall deal with them according to prescribed procedures.'

56. Accession Protocol, 2 (A) 4 and Working Party Report, para. 75.

57. 宋锐, 关于全国人大常委会法规备案审查工作的几个问题, '中国人大' 2004年第3期 (Sun Ren, 'Several Issues Concerning Filing and Review of Legislation', *NPC*, 3rd Issue, 15 Jul. 2004).

Interpretations, have furthered the filing and review system.[58] This, in turn, has had implications for the development of a Chinese constitutional review system, as is discussed in Part III.[59]

C TRANSPARENCY AND PREDICTABILITY

Another major challenge the WTO poses to China's legal system concerns the extent of its transparency. Chinese laws include a wide range of regulations and measures issued at different times pursuant to different laws and at different levels of authority. In some cases, their existence is unknown to the local population, not to mention foreign investors, unless and until these laws are invoked. During the accession negotiations, as indicated, WTO members expressed concerns over the lack of transparency of China's legal system, noting 'the difficulty in finding and obtaining copies of regulations and other measures undertaken by various ministries as well as those taken by provincial and other local authorities'.[60] They noted that '[t]ransparency of regulations and other measures, particularly of sub-national authorities, was essential, since these authorities often provided the details on how the more general laws, regulations, and other measures of the central government would be implemented and often differed among various jurisdictions.' In response, China pledged, in the Accession Protocol, to change the situation and enhance the transparency of trade-related laws and of legal process. The measures adopted so far suggest that the WTO-induced overhaul of legal transparency has far-reaching impacts which go far beyond the realm of trade.

1 WTO Requirements and China's Commitments

Most significantly, China undertakes that 'only those laws, regulations and other measures pertaining to or affecting trade in goods, services, TRIPS or the control of foreign exchange that are published and readily available to other WTO members, individuals and enterprises shall be enforced'.[61] For the first time in PRC history, the term 'published and readily available' was indeed made a criterion for the enforceability of laws. In addition, the protocol requires China to 'make available to WTO Members, upon request, all laws, regulations and other measures pertaining to or affecting trade in goods, services, TRIPS or the control of foreign exchange before such measures are implemented or enforced'.[62] To this effect, China pledges to create 'an official journal dedicated to the publication of all laws,

58. Shi Guosheng, 'System For Filing and Reviewing Legislation and Judicial Interpretations Goes a Step Further', *People's Web* <www.people.com.cn>, 20 Dec. 2005.
59. Chapter 7, Section II.D.
60. Working Party Report, para. 324; see in addition paras 325–330.
61. Accession Protocol, 2 (C) 1. It also allows for emergency situations that laws should be made available at the latest when implemented.
62. *Ibid.*, 2 (C) 1.

regulations and other measures pertaining to or affecting' WTO-related areas; and after the publication of these laws and measures, China shall 'provide a reasonable period for comment to the appropriate authorities before such measures are implemented'.[63] This journal shall be published on a regular basis, and copies of its issues shall be made readily available to individuals and companies.

To facilitate the flow of information and the implementation of such transparency measures, China pledges to establish 'an enquiry point' through which, at the request of any individual, enterprise, or WTO member, all information relating to the aforementioned measures required to be published can be provided. 'Replies to WTO Members shall be complete and shall represent the authoritative view of the Chinese government. Accurate and reliable information shall be provided to individuals and enterprises.'[64] Replies to such requests shall generally be provided within thirty days after receipt and no later than forty-five days in exceptional cases, in which case a notice of delay and the reasons therefore must be provided in writing.

The Working Party Report gives further details on China's commitment to transparency in specific areas, such as state pricing and licensing procedures. China confirmed that it would 'publish in the official journal the list of goods and services subject to state pricing and changes thereto, together with price-setting mechanisms and policies'.[65] About licensing procedures related to trade in services, WTO members expressed concerns during the accession negotiations over 'the lack of transparency in China's current services regime, in particular with respect to obtaining, extending, renewing, denying and terminating licenses and other approvals required to provide services in China's market and appeals of such actions'.[66] In response, China accepted a list of measures to enhance the transparency of the licensing procedures for those services sectors for which it had made liberalization commitments in its services schedule. For example, China's licensing procedures and conditions must be published prior to their becoming effective, within reasonable timeframes for review, and with the decision specified. All applicants should be informed in writing of any decision taken.[67]

Very often, laws and regulations are adopted and published in Mandarin Chinese only and are not available in any other language, thereby making it difficult for foreign traders and researchers to obtain accurate and up-to-date information about the Chinese legal system. In the WTO context, China committed itself to making available to WTO members translations into one or more official WTO languages – English, French, and/or Spanish – of all laws, regulations, and other measures pertaining to or affecting trade in goods, services, TRIPS, or the

63. Accession Protocol, 2 (C) 2; it allows for exceptions for those laws, regulations, and other measures involving national security, specific measures setting foreign exchange rates, or monetary policy and other measures the publication of which would impede law enforcement.
64. Accession Protocol, s. 2 (C) 3, see also Working Party Report paras 331–333, and 336 for further details.
65. Working Party Report, para. 60.
66. Working Party Report, para. 306.
67. Working Party Report, para. 308, see in particular para. 308 (a), (b), (g) and (h).

control of foreign exchange, preferably before their enforcement and in any case no later than ninety days thereafter.[68]

In the accession Working Party Report, it transpires from the commitment paragraphs and the header 'transparency' that WTO members also requested China to make available information on judicial decisions and administrative rulings of both general application, as well as those related to the WTO Agreement. Apparently China refused to accept. This request remains on the record of the Working Party.[69] This, however, remains a non-commitment paragraph in the Working Party Report, and China was not legally bound to provide the information requested.

At the WTO level, a special TRM was designed to ensure a continuous supply of information from China, to be reviewed annually during the first eight years after accession.[70] Such information must be provided to various WTO bodies, where other WTO members can raise questions and request further information and clarifications from China. This review mechanism is unprecedented in WTO history; and it was specifically designed to enhance the transparency and predictability of China's trade and related legal regimes and applies only to China.

In addition, China is subject to the TPRM, which applies to all WTO members. Under the TRM, China is requested to provide information on economic data and policies, the framework for adopting and enforcing policies, which includes the revision or the enactment of WTO-related domestic laws, trade in goods, services, TRIPS, and so forth. The six-page list of information items to be provided is annexed to China's Accession Protocol.[71]

2 Concrete Chinese Actions and Their Significance

Two new ordinances[72] issued by the State Council in late 2001 set out new transparency requirements and procedures for public consultations and for inputs into the process of adoption of Chinese rules and regulations.[73] These ordinances, in

68. Working Party Report, para. 334.
69. Working Party Report, para. 335, '[m]embers of the Working Party also requested that China set up an enquiry point where information relating to all laws, regulations, judicial decisions and administrative rulings of general application and other measures pertaining to or affecting trade in goods, services, TRIPS or the control of forex could be obtained.'
70. Accession Protocol, 18 (1–4), and Working Party Report.
71. Accession Protocol, Annex 1A.
72. *The Ordinance on Procedural Rules for Formulating Administrative Regulations* and *the Ordinance on Procedural Rules for Formulating of Departmental Rules*, both issued by the State Council on 16 Nov. 2001, and made effective after China's WTO accession, on 1 Jan. 2002.
73. There are different categories of laws or rules with legal effect in China. To simplify, laws (Fa Lu, 法律) are those laws of national application enacted by the NPC or its Standing Committee; administrative regulations (*Xing Zheng Fa Gui*, 行政法规) are those issued by the State Council, which can be called regulations (*Tiao Li*, 条例), rules (*Gui Ding*, 规定) or measures (*Ban Fa* 办法), usually of national application as well; another source of nationally applicable law are judicial interpretations (*Shi Fa Jie Si*, 司法解释) issued by the SPC. There are other

addition to the above-mentioned *Ordinance on the Archives Filing of Regulations and Government Rules*, supplement the *Law on Legislation*, in that they reform the legislative and rule-making aspect of the Chinese legal system. Neither the ordinances themselves nor the Law specifically mention the WTO, nor is their application restricted to trade-related areas only. While these new norms and legislative requirements can be seen as part of on-going Chinese legal reform, the timing of their introduction and the terminology used in relation to transparency and public consultation requirements clearly suggest that the WTO accession process gave the Chinese government a decisive external push to achieve a more holistic approach towards legislative reform.

The *Law on Legislation* provides opportunities for public comments on important draft bills pending before the NPCSC, though this is not made a compulsory procedure before any bill can be enacted into law. Comments from various agencies, organizations, and citizens should then be submitted to the office of the NPCSC (Article 35). An illustrative example of the potential impact of public consultations is the draft *Property Law.*[74] This draft law has aroused such comprehensive and heated debates that the NPC decided to postpone its adoption and directed that it be subject to further studies and consultations. The official media favourably commented on the process as 'a remarkable example of public participation in legislation', noting that the national legislature had received over 10,000 suggestions concerning the draft bill.[75]

The two ordinances of 16 November 2001 provide for a compulsory public consultation procedure (Articles 12, 20, 22 and 28) whenever a new administrative regulation is initially introduced and later reviewed at the State Council level. Both ordinances clearly state that new regulations and rules only are effective thirty days after their publication (Article 29 of the ordinance on administrative regulations and Article 32 of the ordinance on departmental rules). Exceptions are allowed for those laws, regulations, and other measures which involve national security, specific measures setting foreign exchange rates, or monetary policy, which can be made effective immediately upon issuing them to the public – a direct import of wording used in the WTO Accession Protocol, Articles 2(C)2.

On WTO-specific measures, the MOFTEC promulgated and made effective the *Measures on China WTO Enquiry Offices* on 1 January 2002. Implementation on a trial basis was to begin on 14 January 2002. The Measures clearly state that the new enquiry system seeks to establish an open and transparent trade administration system and to meet China's obligations under the WTO Accession

departmental rules (*Gui Zhang*, 规章) in the form of rule, notice or guidance, issued by ministries, commissions, or regulatory agencies directly under the State Council on specific areas of administration. See Xiaohu Ma, 'China's Commitment to Transparency Under WTO – Concepts of China's Law and Administrative Regulations', Legal Updates and News, December 2001, Morrison & Foerster, for a succinct explanation at <mofo.com/news/news/files/article622.html>, 12 Jul. 2006.

74. A more thorough analysis of the Property Law can be found in Part III, Ch. 8 Section IA.
75. 'Patience Is a Virtue for Key Property Law', *China Daily*, Hong Kong edition, 3 Mar. 2006.

Protocol.[76] WTO members, Chinese and foreign enterprises, and individuals can request '[a]ll of China's information about laws, regulations, judicial orders or judgments, administrative decisions and other measures pertaining to or affecting trade in goods, services, TRIPS or the control of foreign exchange.'[77] The time-frame for official written responses is the same as per China's commitments set out in the Accession Protocol.[78] The new enquiry system and the WTO Enquiry and Notification Centre, now operated by the WTO department in the MOFCOM, the successor of MOFTEC, remains operational. Other ministries also have created enquiry points for specific matters and so far received positive feedback from foreign investors. Most 'U.S. companies have generally found the enquiry points to be responsive and helpful, and they have generally received timely replies. In addition, some ministries and agencies have created websites to provide answers to frequently asked questions as well as further guidance and information.'[79]

D NON-DISCRIMINATION

This issue concerns the WTO principle of non-discrimination, most commonly characterized by the notions of MFN and national treatment. China accepted that 'except as otherwise provided for in this Protocol, foreign individuals and enterprises and foreign-funded enterprises shall be accorded treatment no less favourable than that accorded to other individuals and enterprises....'[80] In particular, the Accession Protocol guarantees that this treatment is accorded in relation to the procurement of goods and inputs and price and availability of goods and services.

Consistent adherence to the principle of non-discrimination helps bring equality closer to becoming a reality in China. Existing Chinese laws incompatible with this principle have to be repealed or amended. That in itself is a formidable task, given the number and variety of rules, regulations, and measures considered to be laws in China. An even bigger difficulty is to ensure a change of working methods and culture throughout the country, so that the non-discrimination principle is respected in daily law enforcement. The real challenge will be to change the working culture and practices of government departments and officials.

1 WTO Requirements and China's Commitments

The WTO China Working Party Report registers members' concern over 'the application of the principle of non-discrimination in relation to foreign individuals

76. Measures on China WTO Enquiry Offices, promulgated by the Ministry of Foreign Trade and Economic Cooperation (MOFTEC), 1 Jan. 2002, Art. 1.
77. *Ibid.*, Arts 2 & 3.
78. That is, within thirty to forty-five days upon receipt of an enquiry, see Accession Protocol, 2 (C) 3.
79. US Trade Representative's report to Congress on China's WTO Compliance, 11 Dec. 2004, 86; available on USTR website <www.ustr.gov>.
80. Accession Protocol, 3(a)(b).

and enterprises', in particular 'China's practice of conditioning or imposing restrictions upon participation in the Chinese economy based upon the nationality of the entity concerned'.[81] Specific to the Chinese legal system, some WTO members expressed concern about 'certain provisions of Chinese laws, regulations, administrative notices and other requirements which could, directly or indirectly, result in less favourable treatment of imported products, in contravention of Article III of the General Agreement on Tariffs and Trade (GATT 1994)'.[82] Most of these requirements relate to product registration and certification, internal taxation, price and profit controls and hugely diverse licensing procedures for imports, and distribution or sale of imported goods. Even though some of these requirements apply nominally to Chinese goods as well, WTO members 'reiterated that any de facto or de jure less favourable treatment of imported goods had to be eliminated in order to ensure full conformity with the principle of national treatment'.[83]

In response, China pledged that it would provide 'non-discriminatory treatment to all WTO members' and 'the same treatment to Chinese enterprises, including foreign-funded enterprises, and foreign enterprises and individuals in China. China would eliminate dual pricing practices as well as differences in treatment accorded to goods produced for sale in China, in comparison to those produced for export'.[84] With respect to WTO members' concern over Chinese laws, the government confirmed that 'full respect of all laws, regulations and administrative requirements with the principle of non-discrimination between domestically produced and imported products would be ensured and enforced by the date of China's accession', unless otherwise provided in the Working Party Report. Furthermore, China undertook, by the time of accession, to 'repeal and cease to apply all such existing laws, regulations and other measures whose effect was inconsistent with WTO rules on national treatment'.[85] This commitment also applies to provisional laws, administrative measures, rules and notices, or any other form of guidelines.

China confirmed that measures would be taken at both national and regional levels, including the repeal or the modification of legislation, to provide full GATT national treatment in respect of laws, regulations, and other measures applying to the internal sale, offering for sale, purchase, transportation, distribution or use of a wide range of products.

The principle of non-discrimination, when applied to the right to trade, requires that 'within three years after accession, all enterprises in China shall have the right to trade in all goods throughout the customs territory of China', with some exceptions as agreed in the Accession Protocol, and 'all such goods shall be accorded national treatment under Article III of the GATT 1994, especially

81. Working Party Report, II (1), paras 15–16.
82. Working Party Report, II (1), para. 20.
83. Working Party Report, II (1), para. 21.
84. Working Party Report, II (1), paras 18–19.
85. Working Party Report, II (1), para. 22.

paragraph 4 thereof, in respect of their internal sale, offering for sale, purchase, transportation, distribution or use, including their direct access to end-users'.[86] In addition, all foreign individuals and enterprises, including those not investing or registered in China, shall be accorded treatment no less favourable than that accorded to enterprises in China with respect to the right to trade.[87]

2 Concrete Chinese Actions and Their Significance

In order to comply with the WTO requirements of transparency and uniform administration of laws, existing laws were also scrutinized for their compatibility with the non-discrimination principle, by virtue of a massive program of nation-wide legislative review by the time of China's WTO accession. 'The State Council initiated a thorough screening of all the 756 existing administrative regulations promulgated before the end of 2000, and issued the result in Decree No. 319 in 2001. All local governments also conducted a review of all local regulations, rules and administrative measures for their compliance with the principles of uniform application, non-discrimination and transparency.'[88] This was what the Chinese government told the WTO's TPRB during the first review in 2006. While the review of all existing laws and regulations for their compliance with the non-discrimination principle was an immense project, this was a one-off effort by the time China joined the WTO. The more significant aspects of incorporating the principle involve continuous efforts to ensure that the principle is adhered to in new legislation, judicial decisions and law enforcement. An equally big challenge concerns the changing role of the government as an impartial referee of the interaction amongst various players and market forces when it comes to ensuring non-discriminatory treatment.

Key to the implementation of the non-discrimination principle is the redistribution of competing existing interests in China, through WTO-consistent laws and rules that are equally applicable to all – the same treatment given to domestic and foreign entities and individuals (national treatment) as well as to different foreign players (MFN). The concept of equality, impartial application and enforcement of laws, introduced in China via the WTO, will have far-reaching implications for the Chinese legal system and the citizens' perception of their entitlement to equal treatment before the law.

It is interesting to note that the US Congressional-Executive Commission on China, in its 2005 annual report, documented a non-trade related case in which Chinese scholars used the WTO terminology of non-discrimination to urge the government to change its regulations and to give migrant workers the same rights to equal treatment and benefits than urban residents. The report noted that '[t]he principles of non-discrimination and transparency, introduced to government

86. Accession Protocol, Art. 5(1).
87. Accession Protocol, Art. 5(2).
88. Minutes of the TPRB, April 2006, WTO Document: WT/TPR/S/161, s. III(4) vii (d)(e).

officials at all levels by new commercial laws, have positive repercussions for some aspects of non-commercial public policy as well.'[89] WTO transparency requirements have put pressure on officials to curb the use of internal and non-public rules. Chinese citizens, private companies, and government agencies have used WTO terminology regarding national treatment when criticizing discrimination in regulations. The report further stated that both the central government and local governments, in the discussion of discrimination of rural residents as compared to urban residents, also used WTO-inspired terms such as promising expanded 'urban resident treatment' to all citizens.[90]

The first case against China in the WTO's Dispute Settlement Body (DSB) further publicized the principle of non-discrimination. Central to the complaint was the alleged violation of the principle of national treatment by the Chinese government in its administration of tariffs on automobiles and car parts. On 15 September 2006, the United States, the European Union, and Canada submitted separate requests for the establishment of a dispute panel, which would determine whether China violates global trade rules by imposing a tariff surcharge on imported automobile parts.[91] The plaintiffs argued that China violated WTO rules by imposing discriminatory tariffs on imported car parts, which favoured China-based car parts manufacturers. China, in response, maintained that the measures were necessary to stop importers from circumventing higher tariffs by importing automobiles under the guise of car parts.

The panel, established in late October 2006, was the first WTO dispute panel adjudication against China since it joined the WTO.[92] At issue was China's May 2004 *Policy on Development of Automotive Industry* (Order No. 8 of the National Development and Reform Commission (NDRC)) and two subsequent implementing regulations adopted on 1 April 2005. Under these regulations, tariffs on imported car parts were equivalent to the tariff imposed on complete vehicles if the imported parts exceeded a certain percentage of the completed vehicle's content or its price, or if specific combinations of imported car parts were used in the final vehicle. The tariff surcharge sought to encourage car part manufacturers to establish production facilities in China and to protect the producers already based in China. The complainants contended that the surcharge exceeded the maximum tariff in China's WTO schedule of commitments and amounted to a discriminatory

89. Annual Report, Section V.F, Commercial Rule of Law and the Impact of the WTO, US Congressional-Executive Commission on China, 2005.

90. *Ibid.*, citing Ge Yanfeng, Wang Xu & Tian Kai, 'The Impact of WTO Accession on China's Society and Government Policy Choices-Completely Strengthens the Protection of Disadvantaged Communities', State Council Development Research Center, 16 May 2002; 'Xiamen's People's Congress Twelfth Session First Government Work Report', Xiamen People's Government, 3 Dec. 2002. See Part III, Ch. 7, Section II.C.2 for concrete examples.

91. Measures affecting imports of automobile parts (WTO case: DS339, 340, 342).

92. A previous WTO case brought against China over value-added taxes applied to semiconductors, brought by the United States in 2003, was settled before a dispute settlement panel was established.

tax that favoured domestic over imported goods, and that, in effect, it provided a subsidy to those using domestic rather than imported car parts.

In late 2008, the WTO Appellate Body ruled against China[93] and upheld the panel's finding that the measures at issue indeed subjected imported auto parts to an internal charge that was not applied to 'like domestic auto parts',[94] and that they were inconsistent with China's obligations under GATT Article III(2).[95] It also upheld the panel's finding that the measures accorded imported auto parts 'less favourable treatment than like domestic auto parts'[96] and hence in violation of the national treatment obligation under GATT Article III(4). The Appellate Body's report was later adopted by the WTO DSB, which requested China to implement the report's findings and to bring its measures into conformity with its WTO obligations.

On the domestic front, China has taken measures to minimize the likelihood of discrimination against foreign litigants. The SPC has assigned commercial cases involving foreigners or foreign enterprises to specific middle-level courts, effective as of 1 March 2002. According to the *China Daily*, this measure 'will help China conform to the WTO principle of non-discrimination'.[97] In the past, any 'grassroots'[98] or intermediate courts – that is, the lower level courts which are frequently plagued by procedural irregularities and discrimination against non-locals – could hear commercial cases involving foreign litigants. The new measure seeks to act against local protectionism and reduces the risk of undue interference with judicial orders when foreigners are involved in court cases. In Zhejiang Province, there were at one point eleven intermediate courts and eighty-eight lower courts competent to hear foreign cases. With the new measure in place, only two intermediate courts may do so.[99]

E JUDICIAL REVIEW BY IMPARTIAL AND INDEPENDENT TRIBUNALS

Finally, both the Accession Protocol and the Working Party Report set out clear standards for judicial review of WTO-related matters. This introduces elements of accountability as well as checks and balances into the Chinese legal system, which were long alien to the PRC's notion of 'socialist legality'. By subscribing to the legal standards of the WTO regime, the Chinese government has shown its willingness to incorporate into its legal system elements that underpin the ideas fundamental to the notion of separation of powers – such as an impartial and

93. The decision of the WTO Appellate Body in *China – Measures Affecting Imports of Automobile Parts*, WT/DS339/AB/R, WT/DS340/AB/R and WT/DS342/AB/R, 15 Dec. 2008.
94. *Ibid.*, para. 253(b).
95. *Ibid.*, para. 253(a) & (b).
96. *Ibid.*, paras 197 and 253(c).
97. 'Judicial Reform Meets WTO Rules', *China Daily*, 19 Mar. 2002.
98. A term used in the *China Daily* article, meaning the lowest level courts.
99. *Ibid.*

independent process in the review of executive and administrative actions. This is remarkable as the political rhetoric of former President *Jiang Zemin* had ruled out Western-style democracy for China.[100]

The above observation does not mean to suggest that China has committed itself to any specific formula of political or democratic reform in the WTO accession package. As pointed out by a Chinese official involved in the negotiations,[101] judicial independence – a principle which implies the separation of powers incompatible with the unitary PRC structure and not accepted by the Chinese government – requires more than simply putting into place independent and impartial tribunals. China's commitments to the WTO require that the impartiality and independence of administrative and judicial organs in making their decisions is safeguarded. Whichever label it is given, the impartiality of judicial process is an important and necessary, although insufficient, condition for achieving judicial independence. With this, China moves closer to the ideal of a rule of law system, even though its state hierarchy, with the dual role of the NPC, remains incompatible with the systemic and institutional aspects of judicial independence guaranteed and practised in most Western democracies by in-built structural checks and balances.

China's commitments in relation to impartial and independent judicial and administrative reviews in the WTO context, however, indicate that the WTO, a trade body, acts as a catalyst in introducing elements of separation of powers and judicial process compatible with international standards in China.

1 WTO Requirements and China's Commitments

The Accession Protocol and the Working Party Report devote a section to 'Judicial Review'. During the accession negotiations, some WTO members stated that 'China should designate independent tribunals, contact points, and procedures for the prompt review of all administrative actions relating to the implementation of laws, regulations, judicial decisions and administrative rulings of general application',[102] as referred to in Article X(1) of the GATT 1994. They also insisted that 'the administrative actions subject to review should also include any actions required to be reviewed under the relevant provisions of the TRIPS Agreement and the GATS', whereas 'such tribunals should be independent of the agencies entrusted with administrative enforcement of the matter and should not have any substantial interest in the outcome of the matter'.[103]

The WTO members' requests go beyond administrative review bodies and extend to appeals to judicial bodies, as well as transparency in their deliberations and decision-making. According to the Working Party Report, such review

100. 'Jiang Rules Out Western-style Democracy', *South China Morning Post*, 18 Dec. 1998.
101. Author's interview with a Chinese official who spoke on the condition of anonymity, 19 Jul. 2005, Geneva.
102. Working Party Report, para. 76.
103. *Ibid.*

procedures should include the opportunity for appeal, without penalty, by individuals or enterprises affected by any administrative action subject to review. If an initial appeal is heard by an administrative body, there should be an opportunity for further appeal to a judicial body. Any decision by any appellate body, and its reasons, must be communicated in writing to the appellant, together with the notification of any right to further appeal.[104]

In response, China confirmed that it would revise relevant laws and regulations to ensure that they are consistent with the requirements of the WTO Agreement and its Accession Protocol on procedures for judicial review of administrative actions. China further pledged that 'the tribunals responsible for such reviews would be impartial and independent of the agency entrusted with administrative enforcement, and would not have any substantial interest in the outcome of the matter'.[105] The Accession Protocol contains similar guarantees with regard to the impartiality and independence of these tribunals.[106]

China also pledged that:

> administrative actions related to the implementation of laws, regulations, judicial decisions and administrative rulings of general application referred to in Article X(1) of the GATT 1994, Article VI of the GATS and the relevant provisions of the TRIPS Agreement included those relating to the implementation of national treatment, conformity assessment, the regulation, control, supply or promotion of a service, including the grant or denial of a license to provide a service and other matters, and that such administrative actions would be subject to the procedures established for prompt review.[107]

Under section 2(D)(2) of the Accession Protocol, the relevant provision stipulates that these:

> [r]eview procedures shall include the opportunity for appeal, without penalty, by individuals or enterprises affected by any administrative action subject to review. If the initial right of appeal is to an administrative body, there shall in all cases be the opportunity to choose to appeal the decision to a judicial body. Notice of the decision on appeal shall be given to the appellant and the reasons for such decision shall be provided in writing. The appellant shall also be informed of any right to further appeal.[108]

Given the breadth of the aforementioned commitments, we may justifiably suggest that under the WTO, the Chinese government has committed itself to achieving and maintaining minimum international standards designed to guarantee basic independence of judicial bodies. For the first time, the attributes of 'impartiality' and 'independence' are legally required of Chinese courts and tribunals. Indeed,

104. Working Party Report, para. 77.
105. *Ibid.*, para. 78.
106. Accession Protocol, 2(D)(1).
107. Working Party Report, para. 79; see also Accession Protocol, Art. 2(D)(1).
108. Accession Protocol Art. 2(D)(2).

the central government could be held accountable in the WTO, should there be a systemic failure in ensuring the impartiality and independence of Chinese courts.

China normally practices a so-called 'two-tier judicial supervision system', which means that if a litigant wishes to challenge a court decision, an appeal can at most reach a court two levels higher. But in the accession package, China committed itself to allowing appeals of both administrative and judicial decisions. The accession package required the Chinese government to introduce the right to appeal by individuals or enterprises without penalty. Contrary to a customary practice in many Chinese courts, litigants who choose to appeal a court decision should not be punished for doing so. In addition, if the right of appeal is dealt with by an administrative body, there shall always be the opportunity for appeal to a judicial body.

Another element required of Chinese judicial practices relates to openness and accountability. Justice has to be seen to be done, and the reasoning of court decisions must be given to the parties concerned. Both the reasons and decisions on appeal shall be provided in writing to the appellant. Even though the Chinese government rejected requests that the WTO rules should be automatically and directly applicable in domestic courts, it nevertheless pledged to revise all relevant laws and regulations in order to comply with the requirements of the WTO Agreement and relevant provisions in the Accession Protocol. In pre-WTO accession times, only administrative review and very limited judicial review were permissible, and the possibility of establishing a constitutional review mechanism remained remote. China's commitment to introduce procedures in line with standards of judicial review, including impartiality and independence of courts and tribunals, comes close to complying with the principles enshrined in Article 14, paragraph 1, of the *International Covenant on Civil and Political Rights* (ICCPR) – to which China is not a party. This development is indeed unprecedented.

2 Concrete Chinese Actions and Their Significance

The Chinese government has sought to help implement its judicial review-related WTO commitments through a massive overhaul of the Chinese court system. The government was well aware of the challenges the WTO commitments posed to its judicial system. Chinese media have published articles urging prompt reform, to help curb judicial corruption and enhance both the professionalism and the qualifications of judges. The five-year plan of judicial reform initiated in 1999 was partly prompted by the PRC's preparations to join the WTO. It sought to improve the efficiency, transparency, and impartiality of the judiciary.

The reform package seeks to correct past practices of hearing cases and handing down judgments in closed proceedings. More significantly, the reform package tries to tackle deep-rooted problems of the PRC's judicial recruitment and personnel policies, which are partly responsible for the irregular practices and low professional qualifications of most Chinese judges. This is especially true for lower courts, where officers discharged from the PLA or persons with good personal relations (*guanxi*) can be arbitrarily and conveniently appointed as judges.[109] Any reform of judicial personnel policy would necessarily affect the vested interests of those in power and prompt resistance, especially at local levels. Only in early 2002, largely due to the pressing need for better qualified judges after China's WTO accession, did the central government succeed in introducing a number of amendments to the *Law of Judges*. One of the key changes of the law was to introduce a national judicial examination for recruitment of judges, assessed by a set of uniform criteria.[110]

Notwithstanding these recent improvements, judicial irregularities remain rampant at the regional and local levels. To reduce the pressure of numerous foreign complaints about this situation, the Chinese government has sought to prevent the lower-level courts from hearing cases involving foreigners. The *Provisions of the Supreme People's Court on Some Issues Concerning the Jurisdiction of Civil and Commercial Cases Involving Foreign Elements* were introduced in early 2002. This judicial interpretation, issued by the Judicial Committee of the SPC, clearly stated that the changes were introduced '[i]n order to try civil and commercial cases involving foreign elements correctly, and protect the legitimate rights and interests of both Chinese and foreign parties in accordance with the law.'[111]

As a result, cases concerning disputes over contracts or torts involving foreign elements; disputes over letters of credit; application for revocation, recognition and compulsory enforcement of international arbitration award; examination of the effectiveness of the relevant provisions of civil and commercial arbitration involving foreign elements; and application for recognition and compulsory enforcement of the civil and commercial judgments and orders rendered by foreign courts, can henceforth only be heard by high courts, by intermediate courts in municipalities, the capitals of provinces, autonomous regions, and special economic zones, as well as by some courts in economic and technological development areas in large cities.[112] The Provisions, however, do not apply to cases concerning border trade, real estate, and violation of intellectual property rights involving foreign parties, and the lower-level local courts may still hear such cases.[113]

---

109. Liu Mei Hseung; see also Part I, Ch. 2 Section II.D.
110. *The Lawyer's Law of the People's Republic of China* was also revised at the end of 2001 and made effective on 1 Jan. 2002; for more on the legal profession in China, and its post-WTO legal education system, see Y. Gu, 'Entering the Chinese Legal Market: A Guide for American Lawyers Interested in Practicing Law in China', *Drake Law Review* 48 (1999): 173–211 and L. Guo, 'What Makes a Lawyer in China? The Chinese Legal Education System after China's Entry into the WTO', *Willamette Journal of International Law and Dispute Resolution* 10 (2002): 197–229.
111. Provisions of the Supreme People's Court on Some Issues Concerning the Jurisdiction of Civil and Commercial Cases Involving Foreign Elements, No. 5, 2002, of the Interpretations of the Supreme People's Court, adopted by the Judicial Committee of the Supreme People's Court, 25 Dec. 2001, in force 1 Mar. 2002.
112. Articles 2 and 3 of the Provisions.
113. Article 4 of the Provisions.

China has four levels of judicial instances: the grassroots courts, the intermediate courts, the high courts, and the SPC. Under its two-tier judicial supervision system, if a case is first heard by a low-level grassroots court, a party to the case can never appeal to the SPC. New measures which allocate foreign-related cases to courts no lower than middle-level courts are part of efforts to ensure that final decisions on such cases should not be left to the local courts.

In connection with China's judicial review-related commitments under the WTO, the SPC issued another judicial interpretation in August 2002, entitled *The SPC's Provisions on Certain Questions Concerning the Hearing and Handling of International Trade Administrative Cases*.[114] It became effective on 1 October 2002 and stipulates that the *Administrative Litigation Law*, inforce since 1990, as well as other relevant laws and regulations, are the legal basis for any judicial review of administrative acts on WTO-related issues (Article 3). Such administrative cases, including those related to international trade in goods, services, intellectual property rights, and others (Article 1), must be heard by courts not lower than intermediate courts (Article 5). Pursuant to this judicial interpretation, those with *locus standi* to sue are 'natural persons', 'legal persons', and 'other organizations' who consider that their legal rights have been breached by 'concrete acts' of PRC state organs entrusted with administrative authority or of administrative officials (Article 3). In line with the WTO's principles of non-discrimination and national treatment, Article 10 provides that foreign plaintiffs and organizations have the same rights and obligations in the judicial review of administrative acts related to international trade. If there is more than one reasonable interpretation of domestic legal rules, judges who adjudicate cases related to international trade should interpret Chinese law in a way consistent with international agreements to which China is a party (Article 9), that is, the WTO Agreement.

The SPC has issued two other judicial interpretations specific to the judicial review of anti-dumping and countervailing cases: the *Provisions of the Supreme People's Court on Certain Issues Concerning the Applicability of Laws in the Hearing and Handling of Antidumping Administrative Cases*; and the *Provisions of the Supreme People's Court on Certain Issues Concerning the Applicability of Laws in the Hearing and Handling of Countervailing Administrative Cases*. Both Provisions stipulate that such cases must be heard by high courts or by designated intermediate courts.[115]

Several restrictions in the conduct of administrative reviews, as stipulated in the *Administrative Litigation Law*, on whose basis any WTO-related judicial review must be conducted, may either render the *Administrative Litigation Law* inadequate or even inconsistent with China's judicial review-related commitments

---

114. '關於審理國際貿易行政案件若干問題的規定'; [No. 1239] meeting of the Judicial Committee of Supreme People's Court , 27 August, made effective on 1 Oct. 2002: available at <www.law-lib.com>.
115. In Chinese, '關于審理反傾銷行政案件應用法律若干問題的規定', and '關于審理反補貼行政案件應用法律若干問題的規定', both issued on 21 Nov. 2002 and made effective 1 Jan. 2003: available at <www.law-lib.com>.

in the WTO. This law only allows the courts to review administrative decisions themselves, but not the rules or the laws on which such decisions are based. WTO members, however, may challenge both the decisions and whichever domestic Chinese rules or laws they consider to be incompatible with WTO rules. The *Administrative Litigation Law* specifically states that the courts shall not accept cases against 'administrative rules and regulations, regulations, or decisions and orders with general binding force formulated and announced by administrative organs' (Article 12(2)). China's WTO accession commitments do not allow for any such exceptions. Nor do China's judicial review-related WTO commitments protect 'specific administrative acts that shall, as provided for by law, be finally decided by an administrative organ' from a potential challenge in impartial and independent courts, as set out in Article 12(4) of the *Administrative Litigation Law*. A 2004 study[116] indicated that it was 'still too early to see any pattern of judicial practices emerging from WTO-related' *Administrative Litigation Law* cases in China. It suggested that the *Administrative Litigation Law* system was not independent by giving examples of 'how interference, inter-court and intra-court influence, and bribery weaken the independence of the judiciary in administrative litigation'.[117] The study concluded that despite the 'quite impressive' efforts undertaken by the Chinese government, including 'steps taken to combat judicial bribery, bolster judicial competence, and make existing legislation and judicial interpretations more consistent with WTO rules', to fulfil its WTO commitments relating to judicial review, these efforts cannot 'eliminate the fundamental obstacles to an independent judicial review system in China'.[118]

III CONCLUDING REMARKS

The four aspects of systemic requirements on the Chinese legal system and the Chinese government's corresponding commitments and concrete actions discussed in this section have multi-faceted significance. First and foremost, these domestic laws, judicial interpretations, and rules represent the largest scale project so far in modern Chinese history which aims to incorporate China's international commitments into Chinese laws. China's ratification of other international treaties administered by international organizations, for example those under the auspices of the United Nations, had never before led to such cross-cutting and extensive domestic legislative changes. Secondly, the unique post-accession WTO monitoring mechanism on China's compliance means that these legislative changes are

116. V.M.Y. Hung, 'China's WTO Commitment on Independent Judicial Review: Impact on Legal and Political Reform', *The American Journal of Comparative Law* 52 (2004): 77–132; see also two articles on the subject: C. Li, 'The Impact of the WTO Rules on the Judicial Review System in China', and L. Zeng, 'China's Accession to the WTO and the Improvement of its Judicial Review System', in *China and the WTO: Going West*, eds D. Smith & G. Zhu (Hong Kong: Sweet and Maxwell Asia, 2002), 19–33 and 60–74, respectively.
117. V.M.Y. Hung, 82.
118. *Ibid.*, 84.

under close scrutiny of WTO members, both in relation to their content and implementation. They also provide an important foundation and model for further changes in non-WTO related areas of Chinese laws in line with international standards as far as systemic legal principles are concerned, such as uniformity of laws and legal administration, non-discrimination, transparency, and impartial mechanisms for challenging government decisions and actions.

The lengthy WTO negotiations process, the subsequent amendments of Chinese laws, and regular scrutiny by the WTO are familiarizing the Chinese public with these important legal principles. This continuous process brings home to Chinese society international principles to an extent that no government-sponsored legal education campaign had managed to achieve in the past. This has long-term implications for the development of a much stronger role for law to play in Chinese society, and for the incorporation of international principles into the Chinese legal system.

Part III

The Impact of China's WTO Membership on the Chinese Legal System

WTO accession is a strategic decision made by the Chinese Government under economic globalization and is in line with China's reform and opening-up policy and the goal of establishing a socialist market economic system..., the efforts made by China for its WTO accession have greatly accelerated the reform and opening-up process in China.[1]

Long Yongtu

The last part of this book examines the long-term impact of China's WTO membership on the development of the Chinese legal system. While the latter sections of Part II already discussed some of the concrete implementation actions taken by the Chinese government, Part III here concentrates on the 'spill-over' effects of the Chinese WTO membership. This part, therefore, focuses on the bigger picture and is forward-looking in the analysis.

This conceptual framework assesses the WTO's impact on the Chinese legal system through two major perspectives: Firstly, to what extent and in what ways does China's WTO membership affect the role of law in the Chinese society. This analytic dimension essentially addresses the relationship between legal authority and political power. It is important to recall that, as illustrated in Part I, law always played a secondary role in traditional Chinese society and was made subordinate to political power. By examining concrete examples, Part III seeks to demonstrate

1. Statement by Long Yongtu, Head of the Chinese Delegation to the WTO's Working Party on China, on the completion of China's accession negotiations, Geneva, 17 Sep. 2001; on file with the author.

that the relationship between politics and law is undergoing significant changes in China, with the latter playing a much stronger role in policy-making and guiding the daily functioning of Chinese society. The role played by law, the Chinese government and the market, with its rules of the game prescribed by law, also experiences a paradigm shift unprecedented in Chinese history.

The second analytic dimension focuses on the impact of the WTO on the systemic aspects of the Chinese legal system. Chapter 7 of this book examines the scope and extent to which four of the major principles underpinning the rule of law, namely due process and procedural fairness, transparency, equality, and justiciability of government action, are present in the post-WTO Chinese legal system. These four principles are chosen as benchmarks for assessment for two principal reasons. Firstly, they are considered fundamental principles underpinning the rule of law. Secondly, all of them are related to, directly or indirectly, the WTO's systemic accession requirements on the Chinese legal system.

It is beyond the scope of this study to demonstrate whether or not the post-WTO Chinese legal system fully complies with standards underlying the rule of law. This study seeks to establish that the WTO has served as an external impetus that guides the ongoing Chinese legal reform and orients it in ways that domestic forces alone could not have achieved and sustained. It further argues that Chinese WTO accession has also enabled its domestic legal reform to incorporate the above four principles fundamental to the rule of law. The last chapter of this book examines challenges and opportunities for the future of Chinese legal reform.

Chapter 6

Changing Relationship between Legal Authority and Political Power

This chapter examines the transformation of the role of law in China. By giving concrete examples in the areas of China's foreign trade law, administrative law, foreign investment legal regime, legal tools for trade-related remedies such as anti-dumping and safeguard laws, and the new intellectual property rights regime adopted after the WTO accession, it argues that as a result of the implementation of China's WTO commitments, the role of law is undergoing significant changes in Chinese society.

The transformation of the role of law is also present in decision and policy-making processes in China. More importantly, in the area of TRIPS, the constant monitoring by WTO members and the potential Damocles sword of a WTO dispute settlement case[1] in the event of non-compliance forced China to confront a persistent problem of its legal reform – weak enforcement. In other words, the Chinese government has realized that law is a continuum,[2] and that the existence

1. Since China became a WTO member in December 2001, as of April 2009 there have been seven WTO dispute settlement proceedings against China, concerning value-added tax on integrated circuits (WTO case: DS 309), measures affecting imports of automobile parts (WTO case: DS339, DS340, DS342), certain measures granting refunds, reductions, or exemptions from taxes and other payments (WTO case: DS358–DS359), measures affecting the protection and enforcement of intellectual property rights (WTO case: DS362), measures affecting trading rights and distribution services for certain publications and audiovisual entertainment products (WTO case: DS363), measures affecting financial information services and foreign financial information services suppliers (WTO case: DS372–DS373, 378), and export tax breaks (WTO case: DS387DS388, 390). In the case of integrated circuits, the complainant, the United States, did not proceed to requesting the establishment of a dispute settlement panel after holding consultations with China to resolve their dispute. China also settled the foreign information services disputes with the United States, the European Union and Canada before a panel was established.
2. For the concept on law as a continuum or process, see n. 3 in the introduction of this book.

of new laws without appropriate enforcement mechanisms will not produce tangible changes on the ground.

The aforementioned areas of laws are chosen as examples to illustrate these significant changes for several reasons. In some cases, such as the new *Foreign Trade Law* (FTL) and *Administrative Licensing Law* (ALL), it is because they embody unprecedented concepts concerning the role of the Chinese government, citizens' legally guaranteed rights to trade and to conduct their businesses. In other cases, such as the newly introduced laws governing trade remedies, the laws illustrate a direct transplant of WTO disciplines into the Chinese legal system. For the area of intellectual property laws, it is modelled after provisions of the WTO's TRIPS Agreement, and its implementation in China is controversial. The difficulties China faces in the implementation of TRIPS are illustrative of the much more prevalent enforcement problems in the Chinese legal system.

These significant changes and legal awareness are evident in the role of law vis-à-vis the role of the Chinese government in its relation to the market. The growing importance of legal authority as a means to regulate and check political power, under the notion of 'ruling the country in accordance with law',[3] is remarkable. The new laws used as examples in this chapter are clearly the result of China's WTO accession. It is because the immediate reasons for their introduction, key amendments, or implementation represent of the Chinese government's efforts to fulfil its WTO commitments. It is equally important to remember that these legal reform measures, accelerated by the WTO specific requirements, are in line with China's reform and opening-up policy. Indeed, China urgently needs these changes to help overcome its reform bottlenecks but had been unable to address them primarily because of domestic resistance and a lack of orientation.

I REDEFINING THE ROLE BETWEEN THE MARKET AND THE GOVERNMENT

Both the FTL and the ALL, in force since 2004, are important examples to illustrate how the WTO system and its rules impact and help transform the roles of the law, the market, and the government in Chinese society. The FTL does not only concern the role of the Chinese government in dealing with foreign trade issues but also in the daily life of its citizens. It is through the FTL that for the first time in Chinese history, the individual's right to trade became legally stipulated and protected. It also illustrates the growing Chinese awareness that rights and freedoms, especially in the economic realm, require the guarantee of law to be viable. In the past, while Chinese citizens engaged in business activities, Chinese law did not recognize their right to trade as such and hence made their activities vulnerable to arbitrary administrative or government interference.

3. See, for example, R. Peerenboom, 'Ruling the Country in accordance with Law: Reflections on the Rule and Role of Law in Contemporary China', *Cultural Dynamics* 11 (1999): 315–316.

Significant changes also take place in the area of administrative law, where most of the Chinese government's regulatory role in the daily life of citizens has been taken over by law and by market forces. Central to this transformation has been a change in philosophy that is reflected in the new ALL: from the previous motto that everything was prohibited unless explicitly permitted to an administrative system in which everything is permitted unless explicitly prohibited. The new law, applicable to Chinese and to foreigners alike, represents a paradigm shift – from controller/designer to facilitator/regulator – in the role of the Chinese government, and has far-reaching implications for Chinese society.

A THE *FOREIGN TRADE LAW*:[4] A LEGALLY GUARANTEED RIGHT TO TRADE

The FTL, first adopted in 1994, was thoroughly revised after China's accession to the WTO. The law as amended became effective in July 2004. It provides the principal legal basis for China's foreign trade policies. The old FTL was ill adapted to the fast-changing economic situation of China and its interaction with foreign trading partners, and thus required fundamental amendments. It took an external push by the WTO's requirements to provide the necessary political momentum to revise the FTL in 2004 and orient it towards WTO-compatible standards.[5] Official media reports[6] covering the new law noted its significance as a basic legal and policy instrument for introducing WTO rules and to make all Chinese rules and regulations WTO-compatible. Without mentioning the term 'WTO', the revised FTL defines foreign trade in line with the major areas governed by the WTO's multilateral agreements, including the import and export of goods, technology, international trade in services, as well as foreign TRIPS (Article 2, FTL). The revised FTL states that the PRC will grant MFN treatment and national treatment to other parties or members 'according to the international treaties and agreements' that it has concluded or acceded to (Article 6). It thus incorporates the WTO's principle of non-discrimination as a basis to govern China's foreign trade legal regime. When explaining the revised law to the NPC, Vice-Minister of Commerce *Yu Guangzhou* stated that 'the main aim of the revision is to implement our WTO commitments and to promote the healthy development of foreign trade according to the WTO rules'.[7]

---

4. Foreign Trade Law of the People's Republic of China, first promulgated in 1994, amended and promulgated by the NPC on 6 Apr. 2004, made effective 1 Jul. 2004; English version available at <www.law-bridge.net/english/LAW/20065/1322245098315.html>, 13 Jul. 2007.
5. For example, the Chinese WTO accession package requires China to grant all enterprises the right to trade in all goods, except those permitted under state trading, within three years of the accession, that is, 2004. Accession Protocol, Art. 5(1) and Working Party Report, paras 80–86.
6. See, for example, Xu Bingian, 'New Trade Law to Fit WTO Rules', *China Daily*, 9 Mar. 2004, China's new Foreign Trade Law receives Warm Welcome', *Xinhua*, 9 Apr. 2004, and 'China Introduces Overall WTO Rules by Foreign Trade Law amendment', *People's Daily*, 25 Jun. 2004.
7. *Xu Bingian.*

Specific to the changing role of government, the revised FTL recognizes the right of 'any legal person, other organizations, or individuals' (Article 8), that is, both foreign and Chinese, to engage in foreign trade. Under the old FTL, foreign legal persons or organizations (Article 8) required prior permission by the government to engage in trading activities in or with China (Article 9). 'Foreign trade operators' as defined (Article 8) and regulated by the old FTL did not include individuals, whether foreign or Chinese, which meant that individuals had no legal standing and hence were not permitted to conduct foreign trade under the old definitions of the old law. Under the revised FTL, 'foreign trade business operators' include 'any legal person, other organization or *individual*'[8] (Article 8), therefore granting both foreign and Chinese individuals the right to engage in foreign trade. Another major philosophy shift concerns the role of the Chinese government in foreign trade – it moves from a controller to a registrar. Individuals and organizations no longer require advance government approval to engage in foreign trade in goods and technology. They only need to register with relevant government authorities for 'archival purposes' (Articles 9 and 15).

Commenting on the new FTL, the *China Daily* stated that:

> [w]hat is more important is that the revision has a different spirit … . The old law, promulgated 10 years ago, was intended to address the administrative needs of the booming foreign trade business. So the law is mainly about giving the government the legal tools required to *supervise* and *manage* the foreign trade sector. You can say that it [the old law] does not put sufficient emphasis on *protecting* normal foreign trade and protecting domestic industry.[9]

As reflected in the General Provisions chapter of the revised FTL, additional elements including 'broadening the opening to the outside world' and 'protecting the lawful rights and interests of the foreign trade business operators' (Article 1) are added as overarching objectives of the FTL.

Other notable additions include a separate chapter on the protection of foreign trade-related intellectual property (Chapter V), two new chapters on foreign trade investigation and foreign trade relief (Chapters VII and VIII), which are designed to bring the FTL up to date with the Chinese obligations under the WTO's TRIPS Agreement, as well as with WTO rules on anti-dumping, countervailing, and safeguards measures. Efforts to enhance transparency in foreign trade are legally prescribed in the revised FTL, which stipulates that '[t]he state establishes a foreign public information service system so as to provide information services to the foreign trade business operators and the general public' (Article 54). So far there are no domestic judicial decisions on the application of the revised FTL, and it is too soon to assess how the revised FTL is applied in practice. At the WTO, the United States raised questions about the relationship between certain provisions of the revised FTL and Chinese state trading enterprises during China's first WTO

8. Emphasis added.
9. *Xu Bingian*, emphasis added.

trade policy review in 2006.[10] The implementation of the revised FTL did not become an issue of concern during China's first trade policy review.

B THE *ADMINISTRATIVE LICENSING LAW*: A PARADIGM SHIFT[11]

The promulgation of this important law illustrates the significance of the legal challenges that the WTO poses, and how they prompt Chinese authorities to deal with some deep-rooted problems affecting the Chinese legal system. According to a legal scholar familiar with the legislative process of the ALL, the new law[12] was meant to tackle the problems posed by 'excessive regulation with little regularity' in China.[13] There were 'intolerably excessive licensing requirements by the government and extreme irregularity and massive corruption in the exercise of licensing power', which was 'an outright challenge to the rule of law'. 'If people are regulated by the government from the cradle to the grave in the West, the Chinese people are controlled from pregnancy to death',[14] wrote *Chen Duanhong*, a law professor at the University of Beijing. His research revealed that more than three thousand types of licenses existed under various names before the ALL came into effect. Licenses were required in many areas of Chinese daily life, ranging from parking space for bicycles, driving a taxi, to constructing a building.[15] To address these problems, a group of legal scholars closely linked to the Legal Working Commission working under the NPCSC initiated the drafting process in 1997 for a general law which would regulate all licensing types, with the objectives of 'dramatically cutting' the total number of licensing types and setting out clear and transparent procedures for the issuance of licenses.[16]

However, the State Council took over the drafting project in 1998 and '[f]or some time there was no progress. Thanks to the challenge brought by China's

---

10. China's answer to intellectual property rights questions raised by the United States during the first WTO Trade Policy Review of China, Trade Policy Review Body, Minutes of Meeting 19–21 Apr. 2006, WTO Document: WT/TPR/M/161/Add.1, 15 Jun. 2006, 7, 172, 194–195 and 202.
11. Promulgated by NPCSC 23 Aug. 2003, made effective 1 Jul. 2004, available at <www.lehmanlaw.com/resource-centre/laws-and-regulations/administration/administrative-license-law-of-the-peoples-republic-of-china-2003.html>, 13 Jul. 2007.
12. In the past, government departments, especially those at local level, could establish licensing requirements arbitrarily without following any due process or procedures. The ALL in 2004 became the first national law in China to regulate licensing activities.
13. D. Chen, 'Reasonable Government or Limited Government in Licensing?, A Critical Survey of the Draft Administrative Licensing Law of P.R.C.', paper given at Asian Law Centre, The University of Melbourne (Australia, 6 Aug. 2002), 2, available at <www.law.unimelb.edu.au/alc/assets/chen%20duanhong.pdf>; 9 Jul. 2007.
14. *Ibid.*, 2–3.
15. For example, a taxi driver in Shenyang City was required to carry with him over twenty permits and licenses ready for inspection any time on road. Normally more than a hundred stamps were needed for the construction of a building in cities. See D. Chen, 2.
16. See also Part I, Ch. 2 Section II.D 'Arbitrary Administrative Power'.

re-entry to the WTO, the State Council was forced to reactivate the reform of the licensing system.'[17] As licensing brings additional fees and revenues to government departments and agencies both at the central and local levels, any overhaul of the licensing system and any attempt to oblige officials to follow a set of legal rules and procedures in issuing licenses was met with strong resistance from all those with vested interests in the persistence of the 'licensing jungle'. The WTO's requirements for uniform administration of laws with transparency, due process, and impartial judicial review of administrative acts meant that the Chinese authorities were forced to address the problems in a radical way. The draft law eventually was adopted by the NPCSC in 2003 and became effective on 1 July 2004.

The ALL represents a remarkable philosophy shift for the Chinese government's regulatory role in society. It is also a vital legal tool to facilitate the redefinition of roles between the government and the market because it sets out key principles and detailed rules which administrative authorities must follow. This means the government can no longer arbitrarily interfere with market activities and people's daily life through licensing. The previous assumption had been for Chinese citizens to ask for permission and licenses for everything unless otherwise stated. Under the new Law, the government's role in administrative licensing is quite simply reversed. From the citizens' perspective, everything is permitted and no prior approval or license is required unless it is prescribed by law. According to a knowledgeable observer of the Chinese legal system, the ALL Law represents an important advance in the promotion of the Chinese leadership's goal of 'small or limited government':

> Chinese leaders and scholars now view administrative law as an important instrument for transforming government functions and increasing the predictability, openness and fairness of China's immense regulatory bureaucracy in its dealings with citizens, businesses and other organizations. China's commitments to market-based regulatory reforms upon its entry into the WTO in 2001 further bolstered these efforts....
>
> This unique law, with no counterpart anywhere in the world, establishes the foundational principle that government should intervene only where individual initiative, private associations or the market cannot adequately address a situation. It seeks to restrain government interference with market activity by restricting the number of government agencies that have authority to issue approvals in the form of licensing and limiting the types of activity that can be so regulated.[18]

Horsley pointed out that the number of subjects requiring licensing approval has almost been halved since the introduction of the ALL. Indeed, the Chinese 'licensing jungle' existing prior to the adoption of the ALL was all but meant to restrict

---

17. D. Chen, 3–4.
18. J. P. Horsley, 'Rule of Law in China: Incremental Progress', 4 Mar. 2006; the article was written as a background paper for incorporation in *China*: *The Balance Sheet,* eds C.F. Bergsten, B. Gill, N.R. Lardy & D. Mitchell (New York: Public Affairs Press, 2006).

the citizens in their daily activities; whereas the ALL is designed to restrict the government from arbitrarily intervening in the daily life of Chinese citizens through licensing requirements.

Significantly, the changes introduced by the ALL are not limited to WTO-related areas alone. The law is of general application and regulates 'the behaviour of administrative authorities to permit citizens, corporations or other organizations to conduct specific activities after the review and approval of their applications in accordance with law' (ALL, Article 2). It sets out several broad areas which may be subject to administrative licensing, such as specific activities related to public security, personal health and environmental protection, the development and utilization of limited natural resources, professions and sectors providing services for the general public which require the recognition of specific qualifications, as well as equipment and facilities related to public security and safety that require inspection for technical standards (Article 12). The ALL adds, however, that if the above areas can be regulated through 'the mechanism of market competition',[19] decisions by citizens, corporations, or other organizations, or industrial organizations exercising management through their own rules, administrative licensing is no longer required (Article 13).

The ALL also sets out new transparency, due process, accountability and review requirements and legal standards in government licensing. To that end, it provides that '[a]ny regulations on administrative license shall be made pubic. Any regulations that have not been made public may not be used as the basis for granting administrative licenses' (Article 5). In addition, it designates the government departments and agencies with authority to grant administrative licenses (Chapter III of the ALL). These agencies shall do so in accordance with procedures provided by law (Chapter IV) and follow due process requirements (Article 18) within legally prescribed time frames (Section III) and fees (Chapter V); they must provide opportunities for pubic hearings (Chapter IV, Section IV) and for review of the legality of administrative decisions (Chapter VII). All government departments are required to review their existing practices of administrative licensing to ensure their compatibility with the ALL, and cease to implement previous incompatible practices (Article 83).

The ALL clearly represents a major effort by the Chinese leadership to recast the distribution of legal authority and political power. Commenting on the ALL, the official *People's Daily* suggested that the law embodies an 'important concept' involving 'the transformation from *power orientation* to *rules orientation*'[20] through 'the restraint on power', which promotes the gradual establishment of a concept of administration according to legal rules in China.[21]

In March 2004, the State Council issued a guiding document entitled *Program for Comprehensively Implementing Government Administration in*

---

19. Emphasis added.
20. Emphasis added.
21. 'Law on Administrative Licenses and Change of Concept: Commentary', *People's Daily,* 5 Jul. 2004, an English version is available on the newspaper's website <www.peopledaily.com.cn>.

Accordance with the Law.[22] The document spelled out the implementation measures for a State Council 1999 decision[23] according to which China was to achieve the goal of building a government subject to the rule of law within a decade. While the ALL, together with other new administrative laws, is an important legislative step that will help tilt the power dynamics towards the emphasis on legal authority vis-à-vis political power, other recent research[24] suggests that institutional weaknesses, especially the judiciary, cushion the impact of new legal instruments in checking and balancing political power through legal authority. This is especially true at local levels. Long-standing protectionism continues to compromise China's top-down approach when it comes to introducing rule of law reforms. Despite the handicaps faced by the Chinese judiciary[25] in conducting judicial and constitutional reviews, some legislative review mechanisms, introduced or strengthened as a result of China's WTO commitments, have created new possibilities for balancing political power through law and legitimacy acquired through legal authority.[26]

The above analyses of the FTL and the ALL demonstrate that law is increasingly used in China to define and limit political power and administrative authority. It is doing so through legally prescribed rights of individuals, such as the right to trade and the right to be heard in the process of administrative decision-making, and legally set procedures for individuals to claim their rights through administrative and judicial review. Both laws clearly stipulate the domains in which government departments can play a role and must do so pursuant to legal rules and within the limits defined by law. The two laws illustrate this current trend in the changing balance of power between law and politics in China.

II A STRONGER ROLE OF LAW IN POLICY-MAKING

In order to fully appreciate the WTO's impact on strengthen the role of law in Chinese policy-making, it is necessary to understand how China used to make and implement government policies. For the period between the establishment of the PRC in 1949 and the end of *Mao*'s rule in the late 1970s, political slogans and announcements by the ruling Communist party were the basis of government policies. Law was put aside and hardly played a role in running the country.[27] Since the onset of *Deng*'s economic reform, pronouncements by the central leadership

22. In Chinese, '全面推进依法行政实施纲要', issued by the State Council 22 Mar. 2004, Chinese version available at the PRC government website: <www.gov.cn>.
23. In Chinese, '国务院关于全面推进依法行政的决定', adopted by the State Council in November 1999, Chinese version available at the PRC government website: <www.gov.cn>.
24. See for instance, B.K.P. Chou, *Downsizing Administrative Licensing System and Private Sector Development in the PRC, A Preliminary Assessment*, Discussion Paper 52 (Asia Development Bank Institute, 2006), 1–30, especially the examples cited in 21–24.
25. See Part I, Ch. 2 Section II.
26. See more in Part III, Ch. 7 Section II.
27. See Part I, Ch. 2 Section II.

remained the primary basis of government policies, although an increasing number of laws was introduced to regulate economic activities and to regulate interaction with foreign investors. It is fair to argue that before the WTO accession, Chinese legal development was constantly and unsuccessfully trying to catch up with fast developing economic activities but structures. Under this piece-meal approach to handling the relationship between the law and the economy, regulations were introduced on an ad hoc basis to deal with regulatory necessities.

Law was not used pro-actively as a policy-making instrument to provide a guiding framework for economic activities. Nor was it used to introduce, in an anticipatory manner, measures coherent with China's development needs. Such an improvised approach triggered undesirable side effects, such as local protectionism and inconsistencies among different regulatory regimes that obstructed China's further development.[28] However, a paradigm shift in the role of law in policy-making and implementation began to surface once China prepared for imminent WTO accession.

Three areas of law – foreign investment laws, trade remedy laws, and intellectual property rights laws – are examined below to illustrate these important changes. The examples are chosen because they are all directly linked to China's WTO commitments and closely monitored by WTO members. In addition, each of them illustrates different dimensions of the paradigm shift of the role of law in policy-making. In the case of foreign investment, the pro-active use of laws represents a clear departure from China's previous ad hoc approach, when law played a passive role in trying to catch up with the changing regulatory needs of the Chinese economy.[29] Each area of law also witnessed an unprecedented participation of both local and foreign stakeholders in the law-making process. In the area of trade remedy laws, noticeably anti-dumping and safeguards regulations, the Chinese government almost directly transplanted the corresponding WTO agreements into its legal regime because such legal tools previously were either non-existent or in an embryonic stage before China joined the WTO. Intellectual property laws in China underwent a similar transplantation process, yet this area of law offers an additional analytical perspective in tracking the changing role of law in China. This is because of the specific design of the WTO's TRIPS Agreement, which sets out detailed minimum standards for the protection of intellectual property rights. All WTO members are required to provide in their domestic legal systems legislation and enforcement procedures for the protection of intellectual property rights pursuant to the TRIPS standards. While China's legislative regime in this regard is by and large compatible with TRIPS, the WTO members' mounting concern over enforcement procedures highlight the weakest link in China's current legal reform – the domain of enforcement, which also exists in other areas of Chinese law.

---

28. See Part I, Ch. 2 Section II.D.1 on regionalism.
29. For an overview of China's foreign investment legal regime before its WTO accession, see *Compilation of Laws and Regulations Concerning Foreign Investment in China*, 2nd edn (China International Press, 2001).

The Chinese government has used the WTO accession as a momentum to introduce new laws to achieve policy purposes, even though they are not part of China's WTO commitments. The new *Law of the People's Republic of China on Government Procurement*[30] is an illustrative example. This law represents a comprehensive attempt by the central authorities to regulate and standardize government procurement practices at all levels of the administration, to increase the efficiency of government spending, to eliminate malpractices, and to prevent corruption in government procurement.[31] China is an observer but not a party to the WTO Agreement on Government Procurement (GPA).[32] An observer, China is not legally obliged to implement the GPA; the new law does not provide foreign suppliers with equal access to its government procurement market. However, the Chinese government undertook voluntarily to notify the WTO of relevant rules and regulations on government procurement. By doing so, the central government clearly sought to benefit from the momentum generated by its WTO membership to introduce the new law for standardizing government procurement practices.

A THE FOREIGN INVESTMENT REGIME

During the transitional period, when the Chinese government is gradually implementing its WTO schedules and commitments, law has clearly taken on a more important role in policy-making in China. The transformation of China's foreign investment regime best captures the changing role of law in steering foreign investment in China in ways compatible with the WTO's rules-based system while simultaneously suiting the country's development needs.

Despite numerous restrictions, different Chinese regions have actively granted preferential treatment to foreign investors, in comparison to their Chinese counterparts, for attracting foreign capital and transfer of technology and business know-how. While these needs remain crucial to the development of certain Chinese regions, notably the North-Western parts of the country, local industries have called for an overhaul of the foreign investment regime to achieve equal conditions of operation for Chinese and foreign investors alike.

No decisive policy change took place on this front until 1999, when the Chinese government began to amend and introduce laws consistent with the WTO's Agreement on TRIMs, especially its Article 2, which governs national treatment and quantitative restrictions. In 2000 and 2001, the NPCSC adopted

30. 中華人民共和國政府採購法 (Procurement Law), promulgated on 29 Jun. 2002, effective since 1 Jan. 2003, English version available at <english.gov.cn/laws/2005-10/08/content_75023.htm>, 13 Jul. 2007.
31. F. Cheung, *New Regime for Government Procurement in the PRC*, Deacons Beijing Office; available at <www.deacons.com.hk/eng/knowledge/knowledge_147.htm>,16 Jun. 2007.
32. The Government Procurement Agreement (GPA) is one of the WTO's plurilateral agreements, which bind and apply only to its signatories. See B. Hoekman & M. Kostecki, *The Political Economy of the World Trading System: From GATT to WTO* (Oxford: Oxford University Press, 1997), 122–126, for more details on the GPA.

crucial amendments to three laws which constituted the general regulatory framework for foreign investment, namely the *Law on Chinese-Foreign Equity Joint Ventures*, the *Law on Chinese-Foreign Cooperative Joint Ventures* and the *Law on Foreign-Capital Enterprises*,[33] as well as their implementing regulations. The amendments to these laws, first promulgated in the late 1980s and in 1990 respectively, reduced market access limitations and export balancing requirements and relaxed restrictions on foreign-invested enterprises and technology transfer requirements.[34]

1 Provisions on Guiding Foreign Investment Direction

In the later stage of China's accession negotiations, the WTO already had an impact on the trade policy-making process in China. A Chinese trade official who participated in the process made the following observations:

> To summarize briefly those changes or features recorded in China's trade policy making during the process of WTO accession negotiations, we can say that they represented unprecedented participation of foreign stakeholders in the formulation of trade policies of China covering a wide range of sectors and areas. Hundreds of domestic and foreign organizations were involved in the consultative process, and thousands of individuals from various countries and circles contributed to it. Tons of data, statistics and other written materials were collected and compiled by the interested parties, among whom China and the WTO secretariat were the principal sources of information. Within China, there were extensive inputs by dozens of government agencies and hundreds of industrial associations and academic institutions. Major transnational corporations lobbied hard for their interests in China and many of them were successful in securing improved market access for their areas of particular concern.[35]

The revised *Provisions on Guiding Foreign Investment Direction*,[36] which entered into force in April 2002, represents one of the early post-accession efforts by the Chinese government to legally prescribe measures tailored to its development

33. In Chinese, '中外合资经营企业法', promulgated by the NPC on 8 Jul. 1979, amended on 4 Apr. 1990 and 15 Mar. 2001; '中外合作经营企业法', promulgated by the NPC on 13 Apr. 1988, amended on 31 Oct. 2000; and '外资企业法', promulgated by the NPC on 12 Apr. 1986, amended on 31 Oct. 2000; their English version available at <www.lehmanlaw.com/resource-centre/laws-and-regulations/foreign-investment.html>, 13 Jul. 2007.
34. 季文华，中国涉外法律体系的变革回顾：WTO压力下的突破 (W. Ji, A Review of China's Changing Foreign-Related Laws: Breakthrough under WTO Pressure, in Chinese), unpublished paper, 12–13, on file with the author.
35. R. Huang, Minister Counsellor, Permanent Mission of the PRC to the WTO, Geneva, 'How has accession to the WTO changed trade policy making in China?', paper given at Workshop on Trade Policy Making in Developing Countries, London School of Economics and Political Science (London, 25 May 2005), 9, document on file with the author.
36. Adopted 11 Feb. 2002, available at the website of *China Daily*, at <www.chinadaily.com.cn/bizchina/2006-04/18/content_570818.htm>, 13 Jul. 2007.

needs. The Provisions divide foreign investment projects into four categories: 'encouraged'; 'permitted'; 'restricted'; and 'prohibited'. Following this framework, the *Decision of the State Council concerning the Reform of the Investment Regime* was adopted to give provincial governments more power to approve projects in accordance with the above four categories.[37] It also simplified the approval process by requiring only filing 'for the record' for most projects, except for those relating to economic security, environmental protection, and use of natural resources.

After the WTO accession, the Chinese government further restructured its trade policy ministries, which resulted in the establishment of the MOFCOM in 2003. This was done 'to formulate development strategies, guidelines and policies of domestic and foreign trade and international economic cooperation, draft laws and regulations governing domestic and foreign trade, economic cooperation and foreign investment, [and] devise implementation rules and regulations'.[38] MOFCOM is also tasked with studying and putting forward 'proposals [for] harmonizing domestic legislations on trade and economic affairs as well as bringing Chinese economic and trade laws into conformity with multilateral and bilateral treaties and agreements'.[39] Meanwhile, the State Development and Planning Commission (SDPC) were restructured into the NDRC; whereas the former State Economic and Trade Commission (SETC) and the MOFTEC were abolished.

With a simpler structure and clearer mandate for trade policy formulation, the Chinese authorities have started to actively use legal instruments to guide investment activities in a way that meets both the WTO's legal parameters and is conducive to China's specific development needs.

2 Catalogue for the Guidance of Foreign Investment Industries

According to the WTO Secretariat, 'China has used its trade and foreign investment policy actively to meet its industrial and development goals, most notably the development of the private sector.'[40] In early 2005, the State Council issued the *Guidelines on Encouraging and Supporting the Development of the Non-Public Sector including Individual and Private Enterprises*, which were designed to improve market access to previously restricted industries by private companies, both domestic and foreign.[41] The *Provisions on Guiding Foreign Investment*

---

37. V. Bath, 'Changes to China's Foreign Investment Regime following China's Accession to the World Trade Organisation and the Implications for Australian Investors', paper given at the 26th International Trade Law Conference (Sydney, 23 Sep. 2004), <www.ag.gov.au/www/agd/agd.nsf/Page/RWPC0753E825DA6E020CA257196000A5F45>, 13 Jul. 2007.
38. From MOFCOM's mission statement, available at its official website <english.mofcom.gov.cn/>, 13 Jul. 2007.
39. *Ibid.*
40. China's First Trade Policy Review under the WTO, Report by the Secretariat, 17 Mar. 2006 document symbol: WT/TPR/S/161, 29.
41. *Ibid.*, 52.

Direction and the *Catalogue for the Guidance of Foreign Investment Industries*[42] sets out China's foreign investment policy and seeks to guide foreign investment towards industries that are compatible with China's development needs. The amended Catalogue increased the number of 'encouraged industries' from 186 to 262 and reduced the 'restricted industries' from 112 to seventy-five. Some previous prohibitions on foreign investment in services sectors, such as telecommunications, gas, and water supplies, were lifted.[43]

The latest changes in the foreign investment regime, together with the new FTL, indicate that new laws are drafted following a much wider consultation process and that they enhance transparency in their enforcement. They are also used more pro-actively as an instrument in policy-making, in contrast to the previously prevalent piece-meal regulatory approach to addressing changing economic needs.

China's commitments to grant foreign investors market access to its domestic services sectors have long-lasting implications for China's changing foreign investment regime.[44] These commitments, entrenched in the Chinese WTO accession package, mean that China must abide by WTO rules when formulating its foreign investment policy. For example, while it is the Chinese government's prerogative to categorize foreign investment projects into four categories, those falling under the category 'prohibited' cannot include services sectors that China has committed to opening to foreign investors.[45] China made market opening accession commitments in a number of services sectors, including financial, legal, telecommunications, architectural and engineering, distribution, air transport, and express delivery services.

On financial services, China has committed to gradually opening its banking sector to foreign competition, with specific minimum working capital requirements for direct branches of foreign banks operating in China. The Chinese authorities require that the head office of the foreign bank guarantee all liabilities of its branches in China. In late 2004, China allowed for an expansion of geographical scope for foreign-funded financial institutions and lifted geographic and product restrictions in the insurance sector. Beijing also simplified the application process for foreign financial institutions planning to set up representative offices in China, granted preferential review and approval procedures for foreign banks' applications to establish new entities or offer new lines of business in China's Western and North-Eastern regions, and expedited foreign bank applications for setting up sub-branches within big cities.

---

42. Promulgated on 11 Mar. 2002, amended on 30 Nov. 2004, and entered into force 1 Jan. 2005, available at <english.mofcom.gov.cn/aarticle/topic/lawsdata/ForeignInvestment/200501/20050100015843.html>, 13 Jul. 2007. The Catalogue was further revised in October 2007.
43. WTO Secretariat Report on China's First Trade Policy Review, 53–54.
44. See, for example, B.F. Hsu, D. Arner, Q. Wan & Wei Wang, 'Banking Liberalization and Restructuring in Post-WTO China', *Banking & Finance Law Review* October (2005), 23–59.
45. R. Peerenboom, 'The New Foreign Investment Guidelines', *China Law & Practice* April (2002), 19–22; on the opening financial service, see J.D. Langlois Jr, 'The WTO and China's Financial System', *The China Quarterly* 167 (2001): 610–629.

On legal services, under China's accession commitments, foreign law firms are allowed to establish offices in China. But they cannot provide legal opinions on 'Chinese legal affairs', which have to be entrusted to local Chinese firms. On telecommunications, China allows foreign investors to establish joint ventures in basic telecommunication services, under the condition that they enter into partnership with a main Chinese partner already active in the sector. On distribution services, a Chinese directive entitled *Measures for the Administration of Foreign Investment in the Commercial Sector*, effective since June 2004, affects retail services of several products for service suppliers with more than thirty stores. The law established a limitation of 49% foreign ownership for distribution of books, pharmaceutical, and other products. China's accession commitments required this limitation to be phased out by January 2007.[46]

As this example illustrates, the increased importance of law in Chinese policy-making should be considered at two levels – both international law and domestic law. China's WTO membership has provided domestic law with a much stronger role in society, whether trade-related or not. Meanwhile, the formulation and implementation of domestic laws, as long as it is related to China's commitments at the WTO, must be compatible with international trade law and with WTO rules.

B A Direct Transplant of WTO Rules

The WTO's impact on Chinese legislation is strongest in areas where WTO agreements provide new policy tools for trade measures little known or used by the PRC before it joined the WTO. China's recent domestic laws on anti-dumping, countervailing, and safeguards, which together form the basic Chinese trade remedy system, are direct transplants of the contents of WTO agreements covering those same areas, namely the Agreement on Implementation of Article VI of the GATT 1994 (the 'Anti-Dumping Agreement', ADA), the Agreement on Subsidies and Countervailing Measures, and the Agreement on Safeguards. These are commonly known as the 'trilogy of trade remedy regimes' in the WTO system.[47] There are additional operational provisions mirroring those of the European Union and the United States, since both traders frequently resort to these trade remedy tools to protect their domestic industries. Trade remedy laws in post-WTO China illustrate the convergence between the content of Chinese laws and WTO rules in this area,

46. For details of China's market opening commitments in trade in services, see the Services Schedule in China's WTO accession package. For progress and concerns of their implementation, see, for example, Esther Lam, 'EU Questions China on Burdensome Rules On Banks, Law Firms, Phones, Other Services', *WTO Reporter*, BNA, 16 Aug. 2005; Daniel Pruzin, 'U.S. Reiterates Its Concerns at WTO over Chinese Market Access Restrictions', *WTO Reporter*, BNA, 9 Sep. 2005; and Jason Subler, 'China Opens More Cities to Foreign Banks Ahead of WTO Pledge, Cuts Capital Minimum', *WTO Reporter*, BNA, 9 Dec. 2005.
47. Michael J. Trebilcock & Robert Howse, *The Regulation of International Trade* (London: Routledge, 1998), 166; for a general introduction of the trade remedy regimes, see Chs 7–9.

as well as the Western model of using laws in guiding and implementing trade remedy policy.

The WTO Agreement itself does not oblige members to put in place domestic legislation for trade remedy tools, nor does the WTO require China to introduce laws governing anti-dumping and safeguards measures. The WTO system allows for such trade remedy measures, but the introduction of such measures must fulfil both substantive and procedural requirements, as set out in the WTO's ADA and the Safeguards Agreement, and be notified to the WTO. China's speedy introduction of domestic laws in these areas illustrates that the Chinese government and domestic industries were and remain keen to avail themselves of WTO-compatible measures to protect their commercial interests. In so doing, the Chinese government also brings its laws into convergence with WTO standards.

1 Anti-dumping Regulations

Chinese exports have always been among the main targets of anti-dumping investigations and duties by WTO members.[48] WTO statistics indicate that the annual number of anti-dumping measures initiated against Chinese exports increased after China joined the WTO.[49] From 2002 to 2004, WTO members initiated 756 anti-dumping cases in total, and among which about one fifth (152 cases) targeted Chinese exports.[50] This partly reflected the rapid expansion of Chinese exports after China's WTO accession. Chinese authorities have in turn started to use anti-dumping measures more actively to protect domestic industries. They have notified the WTO of a total of sixty-eight anti-dumping measures against foreign exports between 2002 to 2005, but the figures remain behind those of other active users, such as India, the United States, and the European Union, which initiated 316, 234, and 219 anti-dumping measures respectively between 1995 and 2005.[51]

The Chinese government has actively lobbied WTO members to recognize its market economy status sooner than it had accepted this in its accession commitments.[52] So far, it has done so, for example, with regard to Brazil and the Republic of Korea, but it remains unsuccessful with the three principal users of anti-dumping measures.

48. See for example, Daniel Pruzin, 'China Remains Target of Antidumping Investigations, Orders, WTO Report Says', *WTO Reporter*, BNA, 2 Nov. 2006.
49. WTO statistics, available at <www.wto.org/english/tratop_e/adp_e/adp_stattab6_e.xls>, 14 Nov. 2006. From 1995 to 2005, there were 338 anti-dumping measures against Chinese exports, by far the largest among all WTO members; the number of anti-dumping measures at South Korean exports came as a distant second, registering 127 during the same period, followed by Chinese Taipei (99), the United States (95) and Japan (89).
50. WTO Secretariat Report on China's First Trade Policy Review, 110.
51. WTO statistics, available at <www.wto.org/english/tratop_e/adp_e/adp_stattab7_e.xls>, 14 Nov. 2006.
52. WTO members can treat Chinese exports as those from a non-market economy, therefore a third-country price level can be used in determining whether dumping is occurring, for fifteen years after China's accession.

In March 1997, faced with a mounting number of anti-dumping cases against Chinese exports, the State Council rushed through the *Anti-Dumping and Anti-Subsidy Regulations*.[53] In response to a complaint filed by nine newsprint producers from the United States, Canada, and the Republic of Korea against Chinese exports, MOFTEC, then in charge of deciding on dumping margins, initiated an investigation in December 1997, even before the implementing rules of the regulations were announced. Some provisions of the regulations were considered to be 'imprecisely worded' or 'lacked the detail of the WTO ADA'[54] and fell short of the required procedural and transparency standards spelled out in the WTO Agreement.[55] Under these rather primitive regulations, the Chinese authorities initiated approximately a dozen anti-dumping investigations between 1997 and the end of 2001. Foreign lawyers noted that 'the complete lack of transparency and substantiation mean that few, if any, of China's pre-WTO anti-dumping determinations would have been able to withstand the scrutiny of a WTO panel'.[56]

On 26 November 2001, the State Council issued the Regulations of the PRC on Anti-Dumping and the separate Regulations of the PRC on Countervailing Measures; both became effective on 1 January 2002; the 1997 regulations were repealed.[57] The new anti-dumping regulations closely mirror provisions of the WTO's ADA, and in some cases they directly transplant the relevant provisions of the latter into Chinese law, such as the definitions of 'dumping', 'domestic industry', and 'like product' (Articles 2 to 6, 11 and 12 of the Chinese regulations and Articles 2 and 4 of the WTO's ADA), and the determination of what constitutes 'dumping' and 'injury' (Articles 7 to 10 of the Chinese regulations and Article 3 of the ADA).

In addition to directly transplanting substantive WTO elements such as definitions, the Chinese regulations follow the procedural requirements and standards of the WTO's ADA, such as about evidence gathering and access to information (Article 6), public notice and transparency (Article 12 of the ADA and Articles 19 and 20 of the Chinese regulations), timeframe (Article 9 of the ADA and Article 26 of the Chinese regulations), and possibilities of judicial review. Of particular interest was the addition of a judicial review option in the new Chinese regulations. It is because the lack of such a mechanism in the previous regulations had been severely criticized as being incompatible with WTO requirements.[58] The WTO's ADA stipulates that '[e]ach Member whose national legislation contains provisions on anti-dumping measures shall maintain judicial, arbitral, or administrative

53. W. Ji, 8.
54. Patrick M. Norton & Kermit W. Almstedt, 'China's New Anti-Dumping Rules: Battleground for New Protectionism', originally published in *China Law & Practice* 16 (2002): 79–83; available at the website of the law firm of O'Melveny & Myers LLP <www.omm.com/Webcode/webdata/content/publications/Topics_2002_0201.pdf>, 3.
55. *Ibid.*, 2 and W. Ji, 8.
56. *Ibid.*, 4.
57. State Council Decrees, Nos 328 and 329 respectively, both were amended subsequently on 31 Mar. 2004.
58. W. Ji, 8.

tribunals or procedures for the purpose, inter alia, of the prompt review of administrative actions relating to final determinations and reviews of determinations' (Article 13). The Chinese regulations now allow for any party 'not satisfied with antidumping decisions to apply, in accordance with the law … for administrative reconsideration or file a lawsuit in the people's courts' (Article 53).

While the Chinese regulations basically follow the ADA standards, their operational structure, a feature not set out in the ADA, more resembles the relevant US mechanism – with the Investigation Bureau for Industry Injury (IBII) and Bureau of Fair Trade (BOFT) under the MOFCOM responsible for injury determination and anti-dumping investigations. They perform a role similar to that of the US International Trade Commission (ITC) and the Department of Commerce (DOC) in US anti-dumping proceedings. As in other areas related to Chinese implementation of WTO rules, the Chinese anti-dumping legal regime, consisting of the main 2001 regulations, the related *Provisions of the Supreme People's Court on Certain Issues Concerning the Applicability of Laws in the Hearing and Handling of Anti-Dumping Administrative Cases*, the *Regulations on Information Access and Information Disclosure in Industry Injury Investigations,*[59] and the *Rules on Public Hearings with Regard to Investigations of Injury to Industry*[60] are considered strong in terms of 'legislative implementation'. This means that China has done well so far in introducing legislation compatible with WTO standards and requirements, but that it did less well in terms of their enforcement.

In October 2006, the United States challenged what it called 'a lack of transparency' in China's anti-dumping proceedings, and urged Beijing to take specific steps to ensure timely and transparent disclosures to interested parties in anti-dumping investigations. During the 2006 transitional review of China's implementation of its accession commitments, the US government stated that it continued to receive complaints from parties to Chinese anti-dumping proceedings about the lack of transparency concerning the facts used in the BOFT's consideration, and about the absence of any adequate explanation of BOFT's evaluation of those facts. The United States complained that the disclosure of anti-dumping margin calculations in preliminary and final determinations did not contain the information required to repeat certain calculations and identify specific adjustments that might have been made. In addition, the United States charged that MOFCOM's IBII 'does not regularly provide in a timely manner sufficiently detailed non-confidential summaries of information submitted to IBII during antidumping investigations',[61] as required by Article 6(5) of the WTO's ADA. There is, so far, no dispute settlement case on this particular issue.

59. China's notification to the WTO dated 14 Apr. 2003, document symbol: G/ADP/N/1/CHN/2/Suppl.2.
60. *Ibid.*
61. Questions from the United States to China, Transitional Review Mechanism in Connection with Art. 18 of the Accession Protocol of the PRC, WTO's Committee on Anti-dumping Practices, 5 Oct. 2006, Document Symbol: G/ADP/W/459; see also Esther Lam, 'U.S. Complains to WTO of China's Nontransparent Antidumping Proceedings', *WTO Reporter*, BNA, 10 Oct. 2006.

Meanwhile, China initiated WTO dispute proceedings against the United States to challenge US anti-dumping and countervailing duties imposed on imports of Chinese coated-free sheet paper. In a communication[62] dated 14 September 2007, China requested consultations with the United States to discuss its claims that the investigations leading to the imposition of these duties were not carried out in accordance with WTO rules. If the two sides are unable to settle their differences within sixty days, China has the right to request a WTO dispute panel to rule on its claims.

2 Safeguards Regulations

The *Regulations of the People's Republic of China on Safeguards*[63] present many elements similar to the case of anti-dumping, that is, the desire to use WTO-compatible trade remedies by adopting legally prescribed policies designed to protect domestic industries. China had no experience in using safeguards measures prior to the WTO accession. While anti-dumping duties are designed for protecting domestic industries from dumped imported products,[64] safeguards measures may be used if a specific product is imported in such increased quantities which 'cause or threaten to cause serious injury to the domestic industry that produces like or directly competitive products'.[65]

Under the WTO system, safeguards measures are normally used on a MFN basis (Agreement on Safeguards, Article 2), which means that such measures are applied to an imported product regardless of its source. The WTO rules generally do not allow the imposition of safeguards measures which target exports of some particular members. However, China had been subject to particular treatment during the accession negotiations and agreed to two transitional safeguards mechanisms. These allowed WTO members to impose safeguards measures, under less stringent criteria those set out in the WTO's Agreement on Safeguards, to Chinese apparel and textiles exports until the end of 2008,[66] and for other

62. Request for Consultations by China: United States – Preliminary Anti-dumping and Countervailing Duty Determinations on Coated Free Sheet Paper from China, WTO Document: WT/DS368/1, 14 Sep. 2007.
63. Decree No. 330, promulgated by the State Council on 26 Nov. 2001, effective 1 Jan. 2002, amended 31 Mar. 2004.
64. That is, below the price levels as in the exporter's markets.
65. The WTO's Agreement on Safeguards, Art. 2.
66. Working Party Report of China's Accession, para. 242; under this paragraph, a WTO member which finds that imports of Chinese textile and apparel products are, due to market disruption, 'threatening to impede the orderly development of trade in these products', may request consultations with China with a view to easing or avoiding such market disruption. Upon receipt of the consultations request, China must restrain its shipments for the products in question to a level no greater than 7.5% (6% for wool product categories) above the amount entered during the first twelve months of the most recent fourteen months proceeding the month in which the request for consultations was made. In addition, every effort must be made to reach a mutually satisfactory solution within ninety days; if no agreement is reached in that time, 'consultations

specific products[67] until twelve years after China's WTO accession. The European Union and the United States, for example, invoked the textiles provisions in China's accession Working Party Report to reintroduce quotas on Chinese exports after the end of the WTO textiles quota system in 2005. Under China's accession terms, these measures need not even be notified to the WTO.

In relation to transitional product-specific safeguards, measures which must be notified to the WTO, the list of WTO members invoking this Chinese concession is long and will grow further. By November 2006, Turkey had imposed provisional measures on porcelain tiles, polyvinyl chloride, and float glass; Colombia had imposed provisional measures on made-up parts started an investigation into men's underwear products while Ecuador begun an investigation into imports of taps, locks, and valves for domestic use and textiles. The United States has requested consultations on certain welded non-alloy steel pipes, certain iron water works fittings, steel wire garment hangers, and pedestal actuators; Peru has requested consultations to initiate such measures on textile products; and India on industrial sewing needles.

China has realized that its booming exports may heighten protectionist sentiments in overseas markets and trigger possible abuses of China-specific 'WTO-plus' safeguards mechanisms. The Chinese delegation therefore insisted, during the accession negotiations, to put on record in the China Working Party Report that WTO members should afford due process when resorting to these mechanisms:

> With respect to implementation of the product-specific safeguard, the representative of China expressed particular concern that WTO Members provide *due process* and *use objective criteria*[68] in determining the existence of market disruption or trade diversion, because WTO Members did not have wide experience in implementing the provisions of Section 16 of the Draft Protocol. He stated that with respect to trade diversion, WTO Members needed to apply objective criteria to determine whether an action by China or another WTO Member under the product-specific safeguard to prevent or remedy market disruption caused or threatened to cause significant diversion of trade. Such criteria should include the actual or imminent increase in market share or

---

would continue and the Member requesting consultations could continue the limits' imposed on Chinese apparel and textile products.

67. China's Accession Protocol, Art. 16, Working Party Report, para. 245; under these provisions, a WTO member has the right to apply a safeguard in the event of market disruption, but only after an investigation is carried out by the responsible authorities. The authorities must establish a causal link between imports which are increasing rapidly, either absolutely or relatively, and any material injury or threat of material injury to the domestic industry. Also, WTO members have the right to take action against Chinese imports if a product-specific safeguard imposed by a third country leads to, or threatens to led to, significant diversion of trade to its market. The WTO member threatened by trade diversion must consult with China on remedying the situation; only if the talks do not lead to an agreement within sixty days may that member impose measures to limit imports and remedy the trade diversion, with the restrictions to be terminated within thirty days of the product-specific safeguard ending in the third country.
68. Emphasis added.

> volume of imports from China, the nature or extent of the action taken by China or the other WTO Member and other similar criteria. In addition, WTO Members should provide an opportunity for importers, exporters and all interested parties to submit their views on the matter.[69]

In addition to following the definitions and procedural requirements of the WTO's Agreement on Safeguards, China's own Safeguards Regulations included a provision which provides a legal basis for retaliating against what China considers to be discriminatory safeguards measures against its exports. Article 31 stipulates that '[w]here any country (region) discriminatorily applies safeguard measures on the exports from the People's Republic of China, the People's Republic of China may… take corresponding measures against that country (region).'

More than seven years after its accession and the entry into force of the safeguards regulations, China has not invoked the above provision. But the Chinese government has, on several occasions, threatened to invoke Article 31, read together with Article 7 of the FTL on countermeasures against discriminatory measures, in particular when faced with safeguards measures imposed by WTO members on Chinese products under the 'WTO-plus' mechanisms set out in China's accession package. Here, the Chinese government seeks to assert its legal rights as a WTO member, by invoking domestic legislation compatible with WTO rules, to protect its industries from unfair treatment. This approach has caused unrest among other WTO members and prompted many pertinent questions under the TRM for China. On this issue, the Chinese government has stood firm and consistently argued that its Safeguards Regulations are compatible and consistent with the WTO's Safeguards Agreement.[70]

The direct transplant approach adopted by China to formulate and implement its trade remedy policy through WTO-compatible rules is an important lesson for the Chinese government. Clearly, Chinese exports are prime targets of anti-dumping and safeguards measures by some WTO members. China's 'WTO-plus' accession concessions further complicate the government's task when it seeks to defend Chinese industries against discriminatory treatment. So far China has done so by closely following the corresponding WTO agreements in devising its own trade remedy laws. The Chinese government realizes that the first line of defence on this front must be that its own trade remedy system fully adheres to WTO rules. This is the basis upon which China has appealed to WTO members to respect due process and follow objective criteria when they in turn consider trade remedy measures against Chinese products.

Such a direct transplant approach in developing Chinese laws is most obvious for, but not limited to, trade remedy laws. It occurs in a wider area of

---

69. Working Party Report, para. 245.
70. See, for example, the questions and answers between China and Japan (Document No: G/SG/Q1/CHN/27) and the European Union (Document No: G/SG/Q1/CHN/27) under the WTO's Committee on Safeguards, 27 Apr. 2006.

business laws such as contract law[71] and company law. A legal practitioner pointed out that:

> [w]ith the promulgation of a series of business laws in recent years, an unsuspecting student of Chinese business law may find more similarities than differences between Chinese codes and Western laws. In their endeavour to join the club of developed nations, the Chinese have displayed genuine eagerness to introduce Western business law concepts into their legal framework, oftentimes resorting to verbatim copying.[72]

'Implementation, however, can be quite another story',[73] the same lawyer cautioned. Using China's compliance with the WTO's TRIPS Agreement as an example, the following will examine law implementation issues in China.

C INTELLECTUAL PROPERTY RIGHTS LAW

The real test for the relevance and impact of law comes with its enforcement and the regulatory and deterrent effects in the implementation of the law. It is a continuum and should be examined through the prism of legislative, adjudicating, and eventual enforcement activities. At the WTO level, some have suggested that the WTO has three principal methods of implementing its norms: surveillance, supervision, and dispute settlement, with each performing the functions of pre-emptive measures, ensuring compliance and correcting non-compliance respectively.[74]

Despite the considerable efforts deployed by China to introduce, amend, and repeal laws, rules, and regulations to meet its WTO accession commitments, much weaker judicial procedures and enforcement processes in the Chinese legal system have been major obstacles to the implementation of WTO-compatible law throughout China. Generally speaking, a pattern of strong legislative action but weak enforcement is discernible in many areas of China's legal reform. This is unsurprising considering the size of the country, the persistence of regional protectionism, a weak judiciary, and the lack of effective checks and balances in the Chinese state structure.[75] However, the problem remains most acute in the area of protecting intellectual property rights in accordance with the WTO's TRIPS Agreement.

---

71. For an overview of the 1999 Uniform Contract Law of the PRC and its post-WTO implementation, see Patricia Pattison and Daniel Herron, 'The Mountains Are High and the Emperor Is Far Away: Sanctity of Contract in China', *American Business Law Journal* 40 (2003): 459–487.
72. J.J. Zhang, 'Arbitration, China Style: Negotiating a Changing Legal Landscape', *International Law News* (2003), 32 American Bar Association, No. 2, on file with the author.
73. *Ibid.*
74. A.H. Qureshi, *The World Trade Organization: Implementing International Trade Norms* (Manchester: Manchester University Press, 1996), 48 & 63.
75. See Part I, Ch. 2 Sections II.C and II.D.

1 Legislative Efforts

The Chinese government prepared for a WTO-compatible intellectual property rights regime well before it joined the WTO in 2001. By March 2000, as set out in a 'comprehensive list of China's relevant laws and regulations'[76] which China had submitted to the WTO, legislation was already in place for most areas covered by TRIPS, and much of it became effective before China's WTO accession. The laws include the *Trademark Law* and the rules for its implementation, the *Interim Provisions on Claims for Priority in Applying for Registration of Trademarks*, the *Patent Law* as well as its implementing rules, the *Regulations on the Patent Agency*, the *Copyright Law* and its implementing regulations, the *Provisions on the Implementation of International Copyright Treaties*, the *Regulations for the Protection of Computer Software*, the *Regulations on Protection of New Varieties of Plants*, and finally, the *Regulations on the Customs Protection of Intellectual Property*.[77]

Under WTO rules, China would be, as a developing country, entitled to a five-year transitional period after accession before fully implementing the TRIPS provisions.[78] In response to demands from some WTO members and, more significantly, in the firm belief that its legislative efforts in the area of intellectual property rights *were already* compatible with WTO standards, the Chinese government agreed to be bound by TRIPS immediately upon accession: 'Noting the advanced state of protection [of] intellectual property rights in China, the representative of China confirmed that upon accession China would fully apply the provisions of the TRIPS Agreement.'[79]

Legislative efforts continued after China joined the WTO. The China Working Party Report lists those Chinese intellectual property rights laws, administrative regulations, and departmental rules which should be revised or repealed upon or after accession, among them the amendments to the existing patent, copyright, and trademark laws, and their implementing rules, the introduction of *Regulations on the Protection of Layout Designs of Integrated Circuits*. It also recommends the repeal of several departmental rules incompatible with TRIPS, such as the *Interim Rules on the Administration of Patents in Agriculture, Animal Husbandry and Fisheries*, the *Rules of Interim Regulations on the Protection of Copyright of Books and Magazines*, *Publication Intention Contracts*, and *Publication Contracts*.[80] These were legislative measures already scheduled by the time China joined the WTO; post-accession legislative efforts to make the Chinese intellectual property rights regime compatible with TRIPS continue to the present day.

---

76. Communication from China to the WTO China Accession Working Party, 20 Mar. 2000, document on file with the author.
77. The Chinese government had listed these eleven laws under the header 'Protection of Intellectual Property Rights', in its communication of 20 Mar. 2000 to the WTO China Accession Working Party, *Ibid.*
78. WTO TRIPS Agreement, Art. 65 (1), (2), (5).
79. Working Party Report, para. 305.
80. Working Party Report, 59, Table B, under para. 52.

So as to meet the substantive requirements set out in TRIPS and China's accession package, the Chinese government introduced several additional amendments to its intellectual property law panoply. Before joining the WTO, China was already a party to the principal international intellectual property rights conventions.[81] In 1980, China became a signatory to the *Convention Establishing the World Intellectual Property Organization* (WIPO); it acceded to the *Paris Convention for the Protection of Industrial Property* five years later. China is also a party to, for example, the *Madrid Agreement for the International Registration of Trademarks* (accession in 1989), the *Berne Convention for the Protection of Literary and Artistic Works*, the *Geneva Phonograms Convention*, the *Universal Copyright Convention* (accession in 1992), and *the Patent Cooperation Treaty* (accession in 1994). A basic regulatory framework for the protection of intellectual property rights thus already was in place in China.[82]

Legislative amendments were introduced to 'fill in the gaps' between the requirements and obligations under the existing intellectual property rights conventions and those under TRIPS, notably to comply with the MFN and national treatment principles. Amendments were also required for some substantive provisions. Thus, the Chinese *Patent Law* was amended in 2001, inter alia to make the unauthorized 'offering for sale' a violation of the patent holder's rights, to address issues of compulsory licensing, and to shift the burden of proof of infringement to the defendant, as required under TRIPS.[83] So as to fulfil TRIPS requirements in the areas of trademarks and copyrights, the *Trademark Law* and its implementing rules were amended to include the protection of 'geographical indicators', prior rights, and 'well-known marks', as prescribed by TRIPS. The *Copyright Law* was amended to extend protection to models and mask work, as well as the copyright holder's right to limit online transmissions of protected materials.[84]

Some have argued that when China joined the WTO in 2001, it had already, from the legislative point of view, 'established a comprehensive and high-standards IPRs regime that is modelled on international standards. As a matter of fact, China's IPRs laws not only meet, but also, on some points, exceed, the standards of the principal international treaties'.[85]

---

81. 何茂春, 中國對入世承諾要點及政策法律的調整, 中國物資出版社, 2002年, 361–362 (M. He, *China's WTO Commitments and Its Adjustments in Policies and Law* (China *Wuzhi* Publishing, 2002), 361–362).
82. 何茂春編, 國對外經濟貿易白皮書*2002*, 中國對外貿易經濟合作部, 2002年, 171–186 (He Maochun (ed.), *China's White Paper on Foreign Trade and Economic Cooperation Year 2002* (Ministry of Foreign Trade and Economic Cooperation, 2002), 171–186).
83. TRIPS, Arts 28 and 34.1, 'Recent Development in China's IP Laws in Relation to TRIPS', *China Law and Practice*, June 2005, s. 2, 2, available in ProQuest database at <www.proquest.com>.
84. *Ibid.*
85. 'Judicial Protection of Intellectual Property Rights in China: On the Eve of WTO Accession', in Kong Qingjiang, *China and the World Trade Organization: A Legal Perspective* (River Edge, NJ: World Scientific Publishing, 2002), 270.

2 Judicial Process and Efforts to Improve Intellectual Property Rights Adjudication

The toughest challenges for China under TRIPS, however, lie in the judicial and enforcement processes that TRIPS requires WTO members to introduce in their domestic legal systems. TRIPS lays down detailed obligations for WTO members, under Part III of the Agreement ('Enforcement of Intellectual Property Rights'), to provide effective protection of intellectual property rights. TRIPS is often described as introducing only 'minimum' intellectual property rights protection standards at the multilateral level. As intellectual property laws rarely existed or only in a rudimentary form in the domestic legal systems of many less developed countries before protection of intellectual property rights became a WTO area in 1995, it is arguable that TRIPS standards were far from minimum for most developing member states of the WTO. For these countries, it was difficult and they required technical assistance to establish an intellectual property rights legal regime fully compatible with TRIPS.

On the other hand, TRIPS is considered by many developed countries a set of minimum standards for intellectual property rights protection, since TRIPS states that '[m]embers may, but shall not be obliged to, implement in their law more extensive protection than is required by this Agreement.'[86] The Agreement clearly states that '[m]embers shall be free to determine the appropriate method of implementing the provisions of this Agreement with their own legal system and practice.' In their effect, the TRIPS enforcement requirements and standards are so rigorous and detailed that, in most cases, they all but dictate the domestic intellectual property rights regimes of WTO members. This is particularly true for developing country and LDC members of the WTO, which have neither the experience and expertise nor the resources to establish an intellectual property rights regime that both meets domestic needs and complies with WTO requirements.

For each of the six major substantive areas[87] of intellectual property rights covered by TRIPS (patents, copyrights, trademarks, geographical indications, industrial designs, and layout/designs (topographies) of integrated circuits), WTO members 'shall ensure that enforcement procedures as specified in this Part [Part III on enforcement] are available under their law so as to permit effective action against any act of infringement of intellectual property rights'. This includes 'expeditious remedies to prevent infringements and remedies which constitute a deterrent to further infringements'.[88] TRIPS enforcement procedures address due process issues such as transparency, adjudication without undue delay, and possibilities of judicial review of final administrative decisions. They prescribe judicial and enforcement standards in relation to civil and administrative procedures and

86. TRIPS, Art. 1.
87. There are also two separate sections in TRIPS governing the 'protection of undisclosed information', and the 'control of anti-competitive practices in contractual licenses'; see ss 7 and 8, TRIPS.
88. TRIPS, Part III, Section 1, Art. 41(1).

remedies, special requirements for border measures, criminal procedures, and dispute prevention and settlement.

Among the measures that China undertook to comply with TRIPS adjudication procedures were several judicial interpretations by the SPC related to the handling of intellectual property rights cases.[89] These judicial interpretations were issued before but also designed to pave the ground for China's WTO accession. Starting in 1992, China introduced new and improved intellectual property rights standards. That same year, it concluded a bilateral agreement on intellectual property rights with the United States and another one in 1995, after Washington had threatened trade sanctions because of non-compliance with the first agreement.[90] Both bilateral agreements were part of the Sino-US negotiations for China's WTO accession.

The Chinese judiciary also prepared for the application of TRIPS to China long before 2001. The SPC undertook to improve and strengthen the judicial process in intellectual property rights protection. Its pre-WTO accession measures included: (a) the designation of specific Intermediate People's Courts, generally better staffed and with more qualified judges than the lower-level courts, as the first instance courts for patent disputes; (b) the establishment of an intellectual property rights division within the SPC in 1996 to improve the standard of intellectual property trials throughout China; and (c) the creation of specialized intellectual property tribunals at the levels of high or intermediate people's courts, so that intellectual property rights cases were dealt with by specialized judges as these courts were designated courts of first instance, as per measure (a). By mid-2001, there were fifty intellectual property rights tribunals in China.[91]

With regard to judicial interpretations, the SPC issued a directive on the *Further Strengthening Judicial Protection of Intellectual Property* in 1994. In June 2001, the SPC promulgated *Several Provisions on Law Application for Stopping Patent Infringement before Litigation*.[92] These measures were designed to protect patent holders from losses incurred by patent infringement pending litigation. In response to pressure from WTO members who complained that penalties for intellectual property rights infringements were too lenient, the SPC, together with the SPP, revised the 2001 *Interpretation of Several Issues Regarding Specific Law Application in Handling Criminal Cases of Intellectual Property Rights*

89. The WTO's first Trade Policy Review of China, Report by the Government, Doc: WT/TPR/G/161, 17 Mar. 2006, 15, para. 62. There are judicial interpretations on, for example: *Several Issues of Concrete Application of Laws in Handling Civil Cases Concerning Dissension on Internet Domain Name*, *Several Issues of Concrete Application of Laws in Handling Civil Cases Concerning Dissension on Trademark Rights*, and *Several Issues of Concrete Application of Laws in Handling Criminal Cases of Infringing Intellectual Property*, jointly issued by the SPC and SPP, December 2004.
90. Q. Kong, 269.
91. *Ibid.*, 273.
92. *New Progress in China's Protection of Intellectual Property Rights*, Information Office of the State Council of the People's Republic of China, April 2005, 33, document on file with the author.

Infringement in December 2004. The revision included a lowering of the threshold for intellectual property rights cases subject to criminal prosecution.

To improve transparency in decisions concerning intellectual property rights cases, an official website[93] entitled *China Intellectual Property Rights Judgement Documents* was made accessible to the general public in March 2006. According to information China provided to WTO members, the website publishes judicial information about intellectual property rights, such as judgments, determinations, and reasoning of courts, from 2005 onwards. The website complements other transparency efforts made by courts from more developed areas, such as Beijing, which already make public their judgments.[94]

The Chinese judiciary has emphasized the importance of efficiency in the handling of intellectual property rights cases. In 2005, a total of 3,567 criminal cases of rights infringement were registered in Chinese courts, a 27.9% increase from 2004. The number of first instance intellectual property civil cases reached 13,424 in 2005, an increase of 44.1% from the previous year.[95] According to *Jiang Zhipei*, Chief Justice of the SPC's intellectual property rights tribunal, the number of cases involving overseas parties dealt with by Chinese courts increased 50% annually between 2002 and 2006.[96]

To further ease foreign pressure on China to improve its intellectual property rights protection, and in response to threats of WTO dispute settlement cases against China over TRIPS non-compliance, a senior Chinese judge recently argued for the first time that international intellectual property rights laws could be applied directly in domestic courts:[97]

> As for regulations… that China signed on accession to the World Trade Organization, such as the Agreement on Trade-Related Aspects of Intellectual Property Rights (TRIPS), the endeavour is to transform them into domestic laws. And for those that have already been enshrined in domestic laws, their execution is bound by international treaties.… Chinese IPR laws are typically in tune with international IPR laws, so equal protection is accorded to both overseas and domestic owners. But when they are not, China will give priority to international conventions that are directly applicable in domestic intellectual property rights trials, *Cao Jianming*, Vice-President of the SPC, was quoted in January 2007.[98]

---

93. <ipr.chinacourt.org>; thousands of judgments related to intellectual property rights are posted on the website, divided by categories including trademarks, patents, copyrights, new variety of plants, technology contracts, unfair competition, and others; last visited on 27 Apr. 2009.
94. China's answer to intellectual property rights questions raised by the European Union during the first WTO Trade Policy Review of China, Trade Policy Review Body, Minutes of Meeting 19–21 Apr. 2006, WTO Document: WT/TPR/M/161/Add.1, 15 Jun. 2006, 243–263.
95. Report of the Chinese government to the WTO's Trade Policy Review Body, para. 63.
96. Chuanjiao Xie, 'International Laws Applied in Local IPR Cases', *China Daily*, Hong Kong edition, 19 Jan. 2007.
97. *Ibid.*
98. C. Xie.

In what ways and to what extent such a pronouncement may effect a change in the application of the law and of jurisprudence in intellectual property rights cases remains to be seen. While China is not a common law system in which the lower courts are bound to follow the case law and judicial precedents developed by higher-level courts, Chinese judges tend to look to the SPC for judicial guidance and interpretation principles for the adjudication of cases. During the 1990s, the SPC handed down landmark judgments in a series of intellectual property rights cases which served as judicial precedents for and inspired the case law of all Chinese courts.[99]

3 WTO Focus of Concern: Enforcement Deficiency

Much like the implementation of other important policy initiatives in China, efforts to improve the enforcement of intellectual property rights protection took the form of a campaign. In August 2004, the Chinese government launched a one-year campaign to protect intellectual property rights across the country. It focused on law enforcement of intellectual property rights, with special campaigns cracking down on trademark, copyright, and patent rights infringements across the country. Since 2004, the week of 20–26 April has been designated the annual week for publicizing the importance of intellectual property rights protection.[100]

Institutionally, the State Intellectual Property Office, the State Administration for Industry and Commerce, the Press and Publication General Administration, the State Copyright Bureau, the Ministry of Culture, the Ministry of Agriculture, the Ministry of Public Security, the General Administration of Customs, the SPC itself, and the SPP are designated as the principal state organs involved in the protection of intellectual property rights. In 2004, China established a specialized 'State IPR Protection Work Team' headed by a Vice-premier of the State Council; it is responsible for the planning and the coordination of intellectual property rights protection throughout the country.[101] Also in 2004, these government bodies jointly issued *Opinions Increasing Works Contacts between Administrative Law Enforcement Organs, Public Security Organs and People's Procuratorates*. The document established a mechanism designed to ensure better coordination between the administrative law enforcement officers and criminal law enforcement authorities in their attempts to curb intellectual property rights infringement.[102]

In November 2004, the Ministry of Public Security launched a year-long national campaign against trademark infringements, with confiscation of the production of counterfeit brand name razors, sports shoes and electronic products in different provinces. Another operation, carried out in cooperation with the US Immigration and Customs Enforcement, Homeland Security, resulted in the

99. Q. Kong, 272.
100. New Progress in China's Protection of Intellectual Property Rights, 4–5.
101. *Ibid.*, 3.
102. For details, see *Ibid.*, 4 and Sections II to VII.

confiscation of over 210,000 pirated DVDs.[103] According to figures provided to the WTO, procuratorial organs at different levels 'have earnestly exercised their duties' in making arrests and prosecuting intellectual property rights violations. In 2005, public authorities investigated a total of 3,534 intellectual property rights breaches and solved 3,149 of them, in the context of a campaign labelled ShanYing or Mountain Eagle. The figures represent an increase of roughly 200% in comparison to the 2004 figures.[104]

Despite the above commendable efforts to strengthen the institutions involved in enforcing intellectual property rights laws, enforcement on the ground remains perhaps the weakest link in China's legal regime. In March 2006, the WTO Secretariat identified key intellectual property rights problems in China as follows:

> [t]he main problems identified by China's major trading partners include: lack of coordination among the main enforcement agencies; local protectionism and corruption; inadequate deterrence provided by the system of administrative, civil, and criminal penalties; and a lack of sufficient training of personnel....
>
> [I]t appears that enforcement remains weak and infringement of intellectual property rights widespread. In addition to inadequate deterrents provided through the prosecution system, it is also claimed that 'local protectionism' is a major cause of IPR infringement. Local protectionism may be the result of discretionary actions that give preference to local traders and producers, and of local corruption, which may provide local manufacturers or traders of counterfeit goods advance notice of police raids; there is also concern that regional administrative agencies lack sufficient knowledge and training in IPR enforcement.[105]

These problems match the list of constraints on China's legal reform already discussed in Part I. With China's efforts to introduce and implement a WTO and TRIPS compatible legal regime, the importance of law as a continuum and the challenges that this entails reveal themselves in their most acute form.

Three principal factors explain why the effective legal protection of intellectual property rights as required by TRIPS continues to stand out among the implementation issues confronting the Chinese government:

- first, protection of private property, especially intellectual property, is a relatively new concept in Chinese society;
- second and related, the TRIPS compatible Chinese intellectual property rights regime, at least its legislative element, is primarily an imported model prescribed by TRIPS, and fashioned after the intellectual property rights standards of developed countries; and

103. *Ibid.*, 30.
104. Report of the Chinese government to the WTO's Trade Policy Review Body, para. 61.
105. WTO Secretariat Report on the first Trade Policy Review of China, paras 303 & 313.

- third, as SPC Vice President *Cao* has summed it up: 'IPR protection has become a constant strategic topic in China's external affairs. On the one hand, China has made remarkable progress; while on the other hand, some developed countries keep applying pressure, as global IPR competition intensifies. It is impossible to solve in a short time the contradictions between China's economic and technical shortcomings as a developing country and the high IPR protection standards proposed by developed countries', and '[t]hese disputes will last for a long time.'[106]

In late 2005, the United States, together with Japan and Switzerland,[107] invoked a rarely used WTO information gathering procedure (TRIPS, Article 63(3)) requesting China to provide details of intellectual property rights judicial decisions and enforcement cases.[108] The United States argued that, under TRIPS Article 41(1), China must make available domestic enforcement procedures that 'permit effective action against any act of infringement' and include 'remedies which constitute a deterrent to further infringement'.[109] It had repeatedly threatened to file a case with the WTO's DSB and to challenge what it claimed to be a systemic failure, by the Chinese government, to enforce domestic law protecting intellectual property rights, as required by TRIPS.[110]

In April 2007, the United States took the first step to initiate the WTO dispute settlement procedures by requesting consultations with China over problems in Chinese enforcement of intellectual property rights.[111] A number of WTO members,

106. C. Xie.

107. Request for Information pursuant to Art. 63.3 of the TRIPS Agreement, Communication from the United States, 14 Nov. 2005, WTO Document: IP/C/W/461; Request for Information pursuant to Art. 63(3) of the TRIPS Agreement, Communication from Japan, 14 Nov. 2005, WTO Document: IP/C/W/463; and Request for Information pursuant to Art. 63(3) of the TRIPS Agreement, Communication from the Switzerland, 14 Nov. 2005, WTO Document: IP/C/W/462.

108. TRIPS Art. 63(3) states: 'Each member shall be prepared to supply, in response to a written request from another member, information of the sort referred to in paragraph 1. A member, having reason to believe that a specific judicial decision or administrative ruling or bilateral agreement in the area of intellectual property rights affects its rights under this agreement, may also request in writing to be given access to or be informed in sufficient detail of such specific judicial decisions or administrative rulings or bilateral agreements.'

109. A follow-up letter on the TRIPS information request by US ambassador to the WTO, Peter Allgeier, to his Chinese counterpart, Ambassador Sun Zhenyu, 20 Jan. 2006, letter on file with the author.

110. *Ibid.,* repeated requests by the United States for enforcement information on TRIPS compatible law in China, including judicial decisions and their implementation, which US officials said could be used for building a dispute case on systemic enforcement failure. See, for example, transcript of press conference by Rob Portman, US Trade Representative, US Embassy Beijing, 14 Nov. 2005, where Portman emphasized the need for the Chinese government to provide concrete law enforcement examples in fighting piracy; transcript on file with the author.

111. See Kathleen E. McLaughlin, and 'China – Measures Affecting the Protection and Enforcement of Intellectual Property Rights', Request for Consultations by the United States, 16 Apr. 2007, WTO Document: WT/DS362/1.

such as the European Union, Japan, Switzerland, and Canada have since requested to join the consultations as third parties. In August 2007, the United States decided to request the WTO to establish a dispute panel.[112] The panel was established on 25 September 2007.[113] It would be the first panel ever in WTO history to rule on whether or not a member's domestic legal enforcement procedures are compatible with TRIPS.

The panel in January 2009 issued a mixed ruling,[114] which prompted both the United States and China to claim victory over the dispute. In essence, the Panel agreed with the United States that a provision in the Chinese *Copyright Law* which denied copyright based on content – that is, works that failed official censorship review is not entitled to copyright protection – was incompatible with the TRIPS Agreement. The panel also ruled against China on permitting the release of counterfeit goods into the market after removing the unlawful trademark. However, the United States failed to provide adequate evidence to support its key complaint that China's thresholds for initiating criminal prosecution against counterfeit goods producers and sellers were too high to be WTO-consistent. None of the parties to the dispute appealed against the ruling, so the panel report was adopted as final by the WTO DSB on 20 March 2009.

Against the above background, the regime of intellectual property rights laws is examined as an example which illustrates the dynamics of law in policy-making and implementation in post-WTO China. This area of law illustrates not only the impact that WTO membership has had on the transformation of a substantive area of domestic law, but also how important it is to examine the changing role of law in China from the perspective of law as a continuum and a process. This is so because, unlike other WTO agreements, TRIPS imposes detailed obligations on WTO members to make available domestic legal mechanisms for the application, appeal, enforcement, and avenues for seeking compensation and remedies in promoting and protecting intellectual property rights.

Due to constant foreign pressure, senior leaders, including Premier *Wen Jiabao*, have publicly stated that the improvement of intellectual property protection is a 'strategic policy' for the country.[115] The lesson the Chinese government has learned from its struggle to meet its TRIPS-related WTO commitments, however, goes far beyond the protection of intellectual property rights. Top officials have realized that laws on the books alone are insufficient to transform China into a society based on the rule of law. Without an impartial and efficient judicial process, coupled with strong institutions for effective enforcement, legislative efforts alone do little to affect people's daily lives.

---

112. 'China – Measures Affecting the Protection and Enforcement of Intellectual Property Rights', Request for the Establishment of a Panel by the United States, WTO Document: WT/DS362/7, 22 Aug. 2007.
113. Daniel Pruzin, 'WTO Sets Up Dispute Panel to Decide U.S. Challenge to Chinese IP Enforcement', *WTO Reporter*, BNA, 26 Sep. 2007.
114. WTO Document: WT/DS362/R, 26 Jan. 2009.
115. Andrew Batson, 'As China Reins in Piracy, Some Seek Faster Results; Firms in U.S., EU Want Officials to Press Beijing for Stiffer Enforcement', *Wall Street Journal*, 27 Nov. 2006.

III CONCLUDING REMARKS

Analyses of the changing relationship between legal authority and political power in China as a result of its WTO accession have illustrated two significant aspects concerning the role played by law in Chinese society. Although the enforcement of laws remains weak, legal rules are assuming an unprecedented level of prescriptive power in post-WTO accession China. The impact of this enhanced prescriptive role of law is multi-faceted. It results in a new and clearer division of labour between the government and market forces by stipulating the areas and the manner in which government intervention is allowed by law. As a result, it provides, among other things, legal guarantees to individual freedom of actions and the right to trade, and it restricts political power from arbitrarily encroaching onto spheres where law does not prescribe it to do so. The FTL and the ALL are paradigm examples of these significant changes.

The stronger prescriptive power of law also means that law is becoming a significant tool in policy-making. It is incrementally replacing crude political power as a main source of legitimacy in policy formulation and implementation. Unlike in the past, pronouncements by political leaders or decisions of administrative authorities alone are now no longer sufficient as a source of legitimacy. Both foreign investors and Chinese citizens nowadays routinely demand whether these actions and policies are based on and prescribed by law. Legal legitimacy is gaining importance in post-WTO accession China. The next chapter examines some key emerging principles that govern the functioning of the post-WTO accession Chinese legal system.

Chapter 7

Incorporating Major Rule of Law Principles into the Chinese Legal System

This Chapter assesses the prevalence of four of the major principles that are fundamental to the rule of law, namely due process and procedural fairness, transparency, equality, and justiciability of government action in the post-WTO accession Chinese legal system. The four principles are chosen as evaluation criteria for two main reasons. They are all relatively foreign to the traditional Chinese legal order,[1] and, hence, arguably not home-grown but imported to China directly or indirectly through the WTO's systemic requirements on the Chinese legal system. Second, the implementation of these four basic principles has been recognized as a necessary condition for any society purporting to practise the rule of law. It is important, however, to note that the prevalence of these four conditions alone does not necessarily represent the sufficient conditions for the operation of a rule of law system.

Leïla Choukrounen rightly raises the question that while:

> [t]he underlying idea of the [WTO] negotiations was in fact to get China to accept a number of key principles that could, in the long term, modify its legal environment by bringing it into greater conformity with international standards, and why should that not head in the direction of a reform of the institutions and of the regime?[2]

---

1. See discussion in Part I, Ch. 1 Section II, and Ch. 2 Section II.D.
2. Leïla Choukrounen, 'Rule of Law Through Internationalisation: The Objective of the Reforms?', *China Perspectives* 40 (2002), Special Edition, China and WTO, French Centre for Research on Contemporary China, available <www.cefc.com.hk/uk/pc/sommaire.php?idsom=40>, 12 Jul. 2007.

She expresses a reservation that legal reform in China on account of its WTO accession, despite its undeniable advances, may result in the rule of law as conceptualized in a Western context. The *Rechtsstaat*, or constitutional state, used by German theorists; the *Etat de droit*[3] in France, which sets a framework for and hence limits the power of the state by law; and the rule of law and due process of law conceptions in the Anglo-Saxon legal tradition, for example, are concepts commonly used by the West in addressing or conceptualizing the rule of law. Indeed, China's accession to the WTO no doubt has led to greater convergence between WTO prescribed international legal standards and Chinese law. It is, however, important to bear in mind that the rule of law, in the context of Western democracies, encompasses elements far beyond WTO systemic legal requirements on China.

Other sceptics question whether the WTO-inspired rule of law practices and regulatory model are applicable in China. Dowdle, for example, has argued that while 'the notion of "rule of law" is deeply embedded in the WTO framework', the WTO requested legal practices, such as administrative and legal transparency, a 'rationalized set of legal rules regulating governmental behaviour', and 'consistent enforcement of the rules and other laws by the courts', which 'could actually impede the long-term development of China's legal system'.[4] Instead, he advocates a more 'pragmatic development' strategy for the Chinese legal system, which should take into account of 'China's own, unique experiences.'[5]

Against the background of these conceptual and methodological considerations, the following analysis does not purport to explore whether the WTO has brought to China all the elements of the rule of law, instead, it focuses on some key WTO-related rule of law principles which are slowly being incorporated into the Chinese legal system.

The following section also seeks to show that China's WTO accession has guided Chinese legal reform endeavours in a way that would otherwise be difficult to achieve and to sustain by the exclusive operation of domestic forces. Indeed, it would be hard to imagine the growing recognition of the above four legal principles in China without the WTO's accession requirements and the constant interaction between Chinese authorities and other WTO members on compliance and implementation issues. The WTO continues to serve as an external impetus that enables China to keep reforming its legal system in a way that allows these rule of law principles to take root incrementally in Chinese society, extending to areas

3. See, for example, the *Bamako Declaration*, adopted at Bamako, Mali, on 3 Nov. 2000, by the intergovernmental organization *L' organisation de la Francophonie*, in which the rule of law is defined as 'the submission to the law of all institutions, the separation of powers, the free exercise of human rights and fundamental freedoms, as well as the equality of citizens, men and women, before the law, all these representing constitutive elements of the democratic state', s. II(2); see also s. 4(A) 1–6 of the Declaration for measures to consolidate the rule of law.
4. M.W. Dowdle, 'The WTO as an Obstacle to Legal Development: The Need for a More Pragmatic Conceptualization of Development Processes', in *China and the WTO: Going West*, eds D. Smith & G. Zhu (Hong Kong: Sweet and Maxwell Asia, 2002), 35.
5. *Ibid.*, 37.

beyond trade and economics. The analytical approach of Part II[6] focuses on the detailed systemic requests derived from the WTO and concrete actions by the Chinese government in response. This chapter builds on the findings of Part II and assesses China's legal system through the above four rule of law principles, which have either underlined or further developed from the WTO's systemic requests on China.

I KEY RELEVANT RULE OF LAW PRINCIPLES

There are numerous definitions of the rule of law, but not a single one can claim universal acceptance. Some argue that the rule of law should encompass a list of core values, such as democratic enactment of laws, fair notice of rules, equality and non-discrimination in the administration of justice, due progress in ensuring procedural fairness, and justice in the substantive contents of laws.[7] This type of definition focuses on the substantive virtues of the rule of law, as argued for instance in John Rawls' theory of justice.[8] Others define the rule of law by differentiating the concept from 'rule by man' and 'rule by law', using formal theories to identify the institutional features of the rule of law or procedural models, with particular emphasis on due process to distinguish it from arbitrary forms of governments.[9] This definition tends to offer a value-free explanatory scheme of the rule of law, which is arguably without normative content.

Hayek's idea of a spontaneous order[10] in relation to the market economy and the rule of law postulates that the rule of law should consist of universal rules of just conduct that are by definition purpose-independent. He argues that if individuals can use their own knowledge and resources to their best advantage, they must do so in a context of known and predictable rules governed by law. The test of any system of rules is whether it maximizes an anonymous individual's chance of achieving his unknown potential.[11] It is no coincidence that Hayek's rule of law theory has gained support among Chinese legal theorists. It is because legal reform in China is primarily explained and prompted by market economy-driven reforms, and political realities often make the substantive rule of law definitions that originated in Western democracies inoperative or inapplicable.

Using Hayek's concept of law as a critique of the Western model of the rule of law which is being transplanted into non-Western cultures and nation-states

---

6. Part II, Ch. 5 Section II.
7. J.J. Shestack, 'The Rule of Law and Human Rights', speech given at the Institute for Corean-American Studies (Spring Symposium 2000), document on file with the author.
8. See, for example, J. Rawls, *A Theory of Justice* (Oxford: Oxford University Press, 1977).
9. D. Clark, 'The Many Meanings of the Rule of Law', in *Law, Capitalism and Power in Asia: The Rule of Law and Legal Institution*, ed. K. Jayasuriya (London: Routledge, 1999).
10. F.A. Hayek, *Law, Legislation, and Liberty, Vol. I: Rules and Order* (Chicago, IL: University of Chicago Press, 1973); see also J. Gray, *Hayek on Liberty* (New York: Basil Blackwell, 1984), Ch. 1.
11. J. Gray, 61–63.

through intergovernmental organizations such as the WTO, Killion charges that 'given its Western origins, [the] rule of law must necessarily be defined within the ambit of West[ern] centric political and economic forces and taxonomies'.[12] He describes the dynamics of WTO accession, citing China as an example, and argues that the institution building process of non-Western developing countries 'is for the most part dictated on Western terms of development and by Western theories of development'.[13] It is for these considerations that the present study adopts a pragmatic approach in assessing the impact of the Chinese WTO membership on the Chinese legal system. Instead of imposing onto the Chinese legal system a rule of law model – whether it is defined substantively or procedurally – and examine whether China is practicing the rule of law according to such a definition, the following analysis focuses on four WTO relevant rule of law principles and assess their prevalence in post-WTO China.

The forces of globalization further accelerate the process and widen the extent to which international law is transforming itself into transnational law. Insights into the political economy of the WTO and other international organizations serve as a timely reminder that a 'one size fits all' approach to rule of law analysis is likely to be misguided and counterproductive. It is with this caution that we analyse the applicability of some rule of law principles to the Chinese context.

A GLOBALIZATION: CONVERGING INTERNATIONAL AND DOMESTIC LAWS

Good governance is a concept underlying most international organizations, regardless of their core mandates. 'The ideal is … submitting some control of governance to the international system in order to secure lawful conduct and to check and balance the impact of domestic law. This is equally reflected in the WTO.'[14] Thomas Cottier has suggested that the significant number of transparency and judicial review provisions in WTO agreements actually represent a set of 'common and significant minimal standards of good governance'.[15] There are, of course, those who are less positive about the WTO's role in globalizing international norms. For example, Shukla asserts that the WTO's 'democratic deficit' is 'bourgeoning' because '[n]ational norms and standards established through

12. M.U. Killion, 'Western Institution Building: The War, Hayek's Cosmos and the WTO', *The Berkley Electronic Press* (2005), 454–500, 476; available at <law.bepress.com/expresso/eps/454>, 29 Jul. 2007.
13. *Ibid.*, 460.
14. T. Cottier, 'Emerging Doctrines of Good Governance: The Impact of the WTO and China's Accession', in *China in the World Trading System: Defining the Principles of Engagement*, ed. F. Abbott (The Hague; London; Boston: Kluwer Law International, 1998), 119–126.
15. T. Cottier & M. Oesch, 'The Paradox of Judicial Review in International Trade Regulation: Towards a Comprehensive Framework', in *The Role of the Judge in International Trade Regulation: Experience and Lessons for the WTO*, eds T. Cottier & P.C. Mavroidis (World Trade Forum, 2002), 293–312.

democratic procedures by sovereign parliaments are being trumped by global standards set at the behest of powerful transnational corporations.'[16]

By subscribing to WTO norms and the standards by which the multilateral trading system operates, the Chinese legal system is adapting to the WTO standards and its legal principles. It is necessary to take into account the forces of globalization in this process of the internationalization of Chinese law to fully appreciate the impact of the WTO on the Chinese legal system. Despite the uniqueness of the Chinese case, the subject of this study exemplifies the influence of an international organization (the WTO) on its member state's domestic legal order. Taking into consideration the fluidity and multi-dimensional nature of globalization equally helps illuminate the continuous 'spill-over' effects of the above four rule of law principles on the Chinese legal system.

International law, among its other functions, lays down rules applicable to the international community. WTO rules are normative[17] and binding on its 153 members, which taken together account for over 94% of total world trade.[18] To assess the long-term consequences of WTO membership on the Chinese legal system is, in a way, to articulate the concerted influence of globalization and international law on a domestic legal order.

1 Globalization Defined

The definition of 'globalization' is the subject of much debate, partly because the concept is so multi-dimensional, vague, and amenable to different definitions that different actors tend to use the term to suit their own agendas. Originally, the term became popular towards the end of the Cold War era, when the market economy was becoming hegemonic as a model for economic growth and development worldwide. For economists who define globalization narrowly, it refers to 'the activities of multinational enterprises engaged in foreign direct investment and the development of business networks to create value across national borders'.[19] A sociological definition of globalization covers a much broader spectrum.[20] Robertson describes globalization as 'the compression of the world, and the

16. S.P. Shukla, 'From the GATT to the WTO and Beyond', in *Governing Globalization: Issues and Institution*, ed. D. Nayyar (Delhi: Oxford University Press, 2002), 254–286, 275; see also C.E. Barfield, Ch. 4, 'Constitutional Problems and Substantive Deficiencies', 37–69.
17. See S.A. Voitovich, *International Economic Organizations in the International Legal Process* (The Hague: Martinus Nijhoff Publishers, 1995), Ch. 1, for a discussion of normative features of international economic organizations, being perceived as an 'autonomous legal system' but at the same time having an 'external' impact in law-making beyond its immediate domain, 11.
18. The Russian Federation, one of the principal non-WTO members, accounts for about 2.3% of total world trade.
19. A. Rugman, *The End of Globalization, Why Global Strategy Is a Myth & How to Profit from the Realities of Regional Markets* (New York: Amacom, 2001), 4.
20. Rugman, 5, citing A. Giddens, *Runaway World: How Globalization is Reshaping Our Lives* (London: Profile Books, 1999), 10.

intensification of consciousness of the world as a whole'.[21] A commonly accepted legal definition of globalization, however, has yet to emerge. Some legal scholars discuss globalization in the light of the concept of state sovereignty in international law.[22] Their discussions have focused on the role of nation states in an era of globalization, where the traditional notion of state sovereignty is challenged in the international law discourse. This occurs in the areas of human rights, trade and development, environmental protection, and in recent years, the use of force against a sovereign state. This conception allows researchers to take into account the growing influence of non-state players, such as members of civil society and international organizations, in shaping both international and domestic law.

This study, however, takes a different perspective in looking at globalization. Partly borrowing from the sociological definition of globalization, it emphasizes the standard-setting nature of law and examines the normative elements of globalization. It seeks to articulate the ways through which the forces of globalization, through the internationalization and 'internalization' of dominant norms at the local and global levels, affect the Chinese legal system. Globalization is a continuous process whereby local, national, and regional political, economic, social, cultural and legal phenomena are internationalized. Globalization transforms local norms into international ones, and plays a major role in transforming the local reality into what might become normative internationally. In turn, such globalized norms can affect practices and guide what should become normative locally.

2 Globalizing WTO Rules

The GATT and WTO rules-based system was primarily designed by, and modelled after, legal norms governing the type of market economy widely practised in Western industrialized countries. The WTO agreements are treaty laws. Substantive WTO agreements lay down the 'rules of obligation'[23] which bind WTO members. The WTO dispute settlement mechanism, as contained in the DSU, represents the 'rules of adjudication'. The so-called 'trade rounds', where Member States negotiate new agreements or amend existing rules, can be approximated to the 'rules of change'.

---

21. R.J. Holton, *Globalization and the Nation-State* (Macmillan Press, 1998), 15, citing M. Albrow, in *Globalization, Knowledge and Society*, eds M. Albrow & E. King (London: Sage, 1990), 8.
22. S. Sur, 'The State between Fragmentation and Globalization', *European Journal of International Law* 8, no. 3 (1997): 421–434, P. Alston, 'The Myopia of the Handmaidens: International Lawyers and Globalization', *European Journal of International Law* 8, no. 3 (1997): 435–448.
23. This is to borrow H.L.A. Hart's concept of law originally conceived in the context of domestic legal systems. His theory considers law as 'a union of primary and secondary rules'. The general public must generally obey those valid 'rules of obligation' and officials must accept the society's 'rules of recognition' which specifies the criteria of legal validity; and they must also effectively accept its 'rules of change' and 'rules of adjudication'. Under this conception, law represents those norms internalized in a given society. See H.L.A. Hart, *The Concept of Law* (Oxford: Clarendon Press, 1961).

For the purposes of this study, one can articulate the influence of the WTO rules-based system on the Chinese legal order as follows: The forces of globalization, as embodied in WTO rules and the legal principles underlying the modus operandi of the multilateral trading system, work in tandem with domestic Chinese forces to help the Chinese legal system converge with internationally recognized standards. Naturally, significant legal changes in China cannot and will not be confined to the remit of trade and economics only. The 'spill-over' effects of these legal changes gradually surface and become embedded in Chinese society. Previous sections examined new laws and concepts introduced as a result of China's WTO accession, which are designed to apply generally across the board, rather than affecting trade alone.[24] The following assesses the prevalence of the four WTO-related legal principles in China beyond trade realm.

B APPLICABILITY IN THE CHINESE CONTEXT

Different definitions of the rule of law can roughly be divided into two categories: Ends-based definitions or institutional-based ones.[25] Ends-based definitions emphasize the ends or goals, such as maintaining law and order, or a predictable and fair legal system and efficiency that the rule of law seeks to achieve in a society. Institutional-based definitions highlight the institutional attributes, such as comprehensive laws, well-functioning tribunals, and properly trained and effective law-enforcement agencies that are necessary for a society to be endowed with the rule of law attributes.[26] It will be argued here that ends-based definitions are better suited to assess the impact of China's WTO membership on the Chinese legal system.

First, as discussed in Part I, the rule of law as a concept did not exist in more than two thousand years of Chinese dynastic history until the very end of the twentieth century. Law, whether in ancient China or the republican era, was considered a means to an end rather than an end in itself. Efforts of legal reforms in China always were driven by instrumental motivations: be it to maintain social order throughout the dynastic period; to regain legal sovereignty and jurisdiction during the period of foreign occupation of the late *Qing* dynasty; to meet the practical needs of economic development starting with *Deng Xiaoping*'s reform policy; and, in the current context, to pursue WTO membership and fulfil WTO commitments. Ends-based definitions of the rule of law, therefore, are not only compatible with China's cultural and legal traditions in the perception of law. More importantly, they also reflect the Chinese government's motivations for continuous reform of its legal system before, during, and after China's WTO accession.

---

24. See Part II, Ch. 5 Section II.
25. R.K. Belton, 'Competing Definitions of the Rule of Law, Implications for Practitioners', Rule of Law Series, Democracy and Rule of Law Project, Carnegie Endowment for International Peace, No. 55, January 2005.
26. *Ibid.*, 3.

Second, China does not necessarily agree with the institutional features defined mostly for models of the rule of law practised in Western democracies. Practically, political reform in modern China lags behind economic and legal reform. Even though some ends of the rule of law could be achieved as a result of China's WTO guided legal reform, the institutions generally subsumed under institutions-based definitions of the rule of law would require even bigger efforts to establish. Some of them, such as genuine democratic institutions, would not be established before Chinese political reform genuinely catches up with economic and legal transformation.

1 A Pragmatic Approach

Does one have to conclude from the above that without these rule of law institutions, China cannot move closer to the ideal of the rule of law, despite its recent impressive legal reform measures? Such a dogmatic application of definitions and legal theoretical framework would prevent researchers from understanding the significant legal transformation that China undergoes. Randall Peerenboom suggested what he called 'a middle ground' in assessing China's development towards a rule of law system: 'While the footprint of the system's instrumental rule by law heritage remains visible, there is considerable evidence of a shift from a legal regime best characterized as rule by law, towards a system that complies with the basic elements of a thin rule of law.'[27] He divided theories of rule of law into two general types: 'thin and thick'. The former stresses the formal or institutional aspects of the rule of law, regardless whether the legal system in question is part of a democratic state structure, or if it functions in a capitalist or socialist system. A 'thick' theory would incorporate elements of political morality such as democracy, free market, or conceptions of human rights in defining the rule of law. Some also suggested that 'Chinese development of the rule of law may be separated from the development of Western-style democracy' and recommended the promotion of the rule of law as a 'normative' system in China.[28]

Third, unlike most institution-based definitions of the rule of law, to define the rule of law from the perspective of the goals it seeks to achieve avoids the trap of an all-or-nothing approach. Ends-based definitions allow us to assess the achievements and shortcomings of legal reforms in a pragmatic manner. This approach allows the practitioner to tailor reform efforts to different practical needs and priorities or to different stages of development of a country.

27. Randall Peerenboom, 'Let One Hundred Flowers Bloom, One Hundred Schools Contend: Debating Rule of Law in China', *Michigan Journal of International Law* 23 (Spring 2002): 471–519, 496; with a more focused discussion on the administrative law regime of China by the same author, see Randall Peerenboom, 'Globalization, Path Dependency and the Limits of Law: Administrative Law Reform and Rule of Law in the People's Republic of China', *Berkeley Journal of International Law* 19 (2001): 161–255.
28. Eric W. Orts, 'The Rule of Law in China', *Vanderbilt Journal of International Law* 34 (2001): 43–107, 43.

Belton summarizes ends-based definitions of the rule of law as including five separate and socially desirable goods or ends: (1) a government bound by law, (2) equality before the law, (3) law and order, (4) predictable and efficient rulings, and (5) human rights. She adds that:

> [t]hese ends are distinct, likely to meet different types of support and resistance within countries undergoing reform, and often in tension with one another in practice....By considering the rule of law as a series of separate goods that must advance together, practitioners can improve their measurements of the rule of law within and between various countries, better anticipate likely supporters of and opponents to different reform efforts.[29]

Among the five aforementioned ends, the promotion and protection of human rights was never among the fundamental reform goals in the Chinese context. This does not mean that, however, improvements in the Chinese legal system as a result of WTO accession have no impact whatsoever on the situation of human rights in China. Thus, the term 'human rights' was first included in the PRC Constitution in 2004. Similarly, as the WTO non-discrimination principle is implemented in Chinese law and takes root in Chinese society, it empowers Chinese citizens to acknowledge and claim their right to be treated equally. However, if one seeks to measure China's progress in moving towards the rule of law by focusing on human rights alone, one will reach a different conclusion than if the situation were assessed through the ends of, for example, 'a government bound by law', or the justiciability of government action.

Several factors explain this situation. China's legal reform is economically motivated; the WTO requires the Chinese government to implement its trade policies through transparent and predictable laws, and to provide for the judicial review of the legality of administrative acts and decisions. This has had direct impacts on the Chinese administrative legal regime and prompted the introduction of new laws and enforcement mechanisms in this area. Thus, 'a government bound by law' or legal restraints on government power, as one of the ends of the rule of law, has made big strides in China.

For the case of 'human rights' as one of the ends of the rule of law, the term itself is not used in any of the WTO agreements. While WTO rules and their implementation may have direct or indirect human rights repercussions,[30] the promotion and protection of human rights is not a primary mission of the WTO. Chinese legal reform, being primarily economics-motivated and WTO rules guided, is likely to have less of a direct impact on the human rights situation in the country. And yet, the indirect impacts and spin-offs even for selected human rights issues can be identified and are by no means insignificant. The interconnection between different subjects of law, or the 'cross-fertilization of international law',

29. R.K. Belton, 3.

30. For the impact of WTO rules on human rights, see, for example, Esther Lam et al., *A Practical Guide to the WTO for Human Rights Advocates* (3D: Trade–Human Rights–Equitable Economy and Asian Forum for Human Rights and Development, 2004).

as described by some academics and judges,[31] is also increasingly common in domestic legal systems.

It is important to recognize the current interplay between external and internal factors and their dynamics in shaping the Chinese legal system. The rule of law, and indeed law as a concept, does not only refer to static rules but to a continuous and dynamic process in which laws are adopted, applied, and enforced in response to the ever changing challenges that society faces.

2 Four WTO-Induced Principles

The above analysis suggests that a fair and meaningful way to assess the impact of WTO membership on the Chinese legal system in relation to the rule of law is to proceed through the relevant principles prescribed by or further developed from the WTO system and China's accession commitments. These include the uniform administration of the Chinese legal system (due process and procedural fairness), transparency, equality (developed from the WTO principle of non-discrimination), and justiciability of government action (i.e., whether the government is bound by law, developed from WTO requirements related to judicial review procedures and an impartial judiciary). The WTO requirements on the Chinese legal system can be characterized as ends-based or purpose-driven, even though achieving these ends will inevitably have implications for the development of Chinese legal institutions.

Due process and fairness – that is, clearly prescribed and publicized procedures – must be followed in legal proceedings, and the same procedures must apply equally to all those in the same situation. It also entails procedural fairness, where everyone in the same legal system is entitled to the same procedural treatment and guarantees, such as the right to be heard by an independent and impartial tribunal or the right to appeal against administrative and/or judicial decisions. A transparent and predictable legal system means that laws are readily and publicly available and that they are not enforced retroactively. Barring exceptional circumstances, trials and judgments should be held and delivered in public session, and final decisions should be published.

Equality and non-discrimination are closely related.[32] Generally speaking, equality means the absence of discrimination. Whether in international trade law

31. See, for example, P. Sands, 'Treaty, Custom and the Cross-Fertilization of International Law', *Yale Human Rights and Development Law Journal* 1 (1998): 86–106, 5, and G. Gavinet, 'Les influences croisées entre juridictions nationales et internationales', *Revue de Science Criminelle et de droit pénal comparé* (Octobre/Décembre 2005): 799–817.

32. The conceptual complementarity and differences between non-discrimination in the WTO and the principle of equality in a legal system warrants further clarification. It is rather straightforward to make the conceptual linkages between the WTO's legal systemic requirements on China in relation to the principles of due process and procedural fairness, transparency, and justiciability of government action. Unlike the three principles, the WTO requirement of non-discrimination originates from the unique context of the GATT and manifests in the WTO bedrock principles of national and MFN treatments. The conceptual bridge from non-

or in public international law, '[e]quality, however, has never meant the same treatment for all; instead, equality consists in the like treatment of all similarly situated persons.'[33] In the context of a legal system, the principle of equality means that everyone is treated equally in the legal process, and that the law should not discriminate against any individual or entity. The notion of equal protection of the law implies that 'no person or class of persons shall be denied the same protection of the laws which is enjoyed by other persons or other classes in like circumstances in their lives, property, and in their pursuit of happiness'.[34] Similarly situated persons must receive similar treatment under the law. Lastly, justiciability of government action ensures that the government does not act above or outside the law. The availability of judicial review by an impartial tribunal provides an important avenue for the public to challenge the legality of government actions.

II ASSESSMENT OF FOUR RULE OF LAW PRINCIPLES IN CHINA

The four major areas of WTO systemic requirements on the Chinese legal system are interrelated, interdependent, and mutually reinforcing. They also can have a concurrent influence and nurture the growth of the above four rule of law principles in China. Uniformity in legislation and law implementation across the country, for example, undoubtedly has an impact on both the principles of due process and non-discrimination. Two main criteria are used to assess the status of these rule of law principles in China. First, the extent to which they have been incorporated into domestic laws, and whether the legislative contents reflect them; second, the emergence of these principles in administrative actions and jurisprudence.

A Due Process and Procedural Fairness

Due process is one of the WTO rules the Chinese government has invoked frequently to defend its interest. WTO members have devised a special product-specific safeguards mechanism to protect their domestic markets from disruption by the influx of Chinese goods.[35] Faced with this stringent mechanism against Chinese exports, the Chinese government invokes the principle of due process and urges WTO members to adhere to notions of procedural fairness when using safeguards mechanism.

---

discrimination in the WTO context to the general legal principle of equality will be discussed further in Part III, Ch. 7 Section II.C.

33. J.Y. Qin, 'Defining Nondiscrimination under the Law of the World Trade Organization', *Boston University International Law Journal* 23, no. 2 (2005): 215–297, 221, available at <ssrn.com/abstract=939432>, 7 Aug. 2007.
34. *Black's Law Dictionary*, 6th edn (St. Paul, MM: West Publishing Co., 1991), 573.
35. See Part II, Ch. 4.

The WTO accession Working Party Report recorded China's 'particular concern' about arbitrary implementation or abuse by WTO members of this special mechanism. The Chinese representative insisted that members should provide due process and use objective criteria in determining whether specific market conditions warrant the application of the mechanism.[36] As early as during the negotiations for accession, the Chinese government repeatedly invoked the due process principle to protect the interests of its domestic industries in the WTO. In turn, WTO members also requested that due process principles be respected in the administration of the Chinese trade and legal regime.

1 Legislative Changes

The concept of 'due process' is used frequently in Chinese legislation after China became a WTO member. For example, the notion of due process was incorporated into the state administration of taxation, which affects all taxpayers and encompasses all areas of the daily life of citizens. The *Provisional Rules for Taxation Administrative Reconsideration*[37] of 2004 stipulate that 'evidential materials shall not serve as the basis for making a decision about a case' if they are 'collected by violating due process' (Article 32(1)). The state organ responsible for reconsidering tax cases shall 'review the lawfulness … of all the factual evidence, *due process*, the legal basis and the legal rights and obligations' upon which an administrative act is based (Article 36). When reviewing the legality of an administrative act, it shall consider whether the specific act is based on 'correct applications of law, [and] due process' (Article 41(1)). Any administrative act 'violating due process' shall be determined unlawful and will be revoked (Article 41(3c)).

Never before in Chinese legal history has the principle of due process been given such a prominent place and played a decisive role in the review of administrative acts. More significantly, the rules and legislation concerned do not primarily concern foreign trade but cover all walks of life.

An increasing number of Chinese laws, while not specifically using the term 'due process', stipulate that legal procedures should be followed duly and applied equally to all individuals faced with a similar situation. For example, the ALL, discussed earlier[38] from the perspective of redefining the role between the market and the Chinese government, lays down specific obligations that licensing authorities must adhere to observe due process. It states that 'the establishment and grant of administrative license shall be in compliance with the principles of disclosure, equity and justice' (Article 5). It guarantees the citizens' and concerned parties' 'right to make a statement', their 'right to defend themselves', the 'right to apply for administrative review or institute administrative proceedings', and the 'right to

36. WTO China Working Party Report, para. 245, WT/MIN(01)/3.
37. *Provisional Rules for the Administrative Reconsideration of Taxation*, promulgated by the State Administration for Taxation on 24 Feb. 2004, effective 1 May 2004.
38. Part III, Ch. 6 Section I.B.

demand compensation according to law' if legitimate rights or interests have been breached (Article 7).

When government departments establish new categories of administrative licenses, the law requires that clear provisions are made with regard to which entities may grant licenses, as well as under which conditions and pursuant to which procedures and timelines this should be done (Article 17). Chapter IV of the ALL governs the procedure for granting licenses, and due process requirements are set out for the application, acceptance, review, decision, time limits, hearing, as well as renewal and extension of licenses. In sum, these new procedural requirements and the recent emphasis on the authorities' obligation (Chapter VII) to respect and follow due process requirements constitute a sharp contrast to the previous arbitrary practices prevalent throughout China in relation to administrative licensing.

2 Relevant Cases and Executive Action

More and more court cases and legal actions challenge the legality of government acts by invoking breaches of the principle of due process. Invoking the ALL, for example, ten lawyers from Henan province petitioned the NPC and the State Council with a request for repeal of 'licenses for temporary stay' issued by departments under the State Council and provincial governments. Relying on the procedural and due process requirements of the ALL, they argued that the law did not allow the aforementioned departments and governments to issue administrative licenses, and that the authorities concerned had not followed the legal procedures in issuing licenses that regulate the temporary stay of emigrants from other provinces. They therefore petitioned the NPC to declare the nationwide practice of issuing licenses for temporary stay null and void.[39] As of August 2007, no public information is available as to whether the NPC has decided on their petition. The petition itself, nevertheless, attracted a lot of media coverage, and some cities, such as Beijing, are considering the revocation of temporary stay license.[40]

Respect for the notion of due process and procedural fairness is also beginning to permeate judicial decisions. The *China Daily* published an editorial entitled 'Legal Procedure Counts',[41] which underlines the importance for government departments to follow legal procedures:

> [A]n investigative report by the People's Court of Chaoyang District in Beijing sheds light on some violations of legal procedure in the demolition of buildings at Xiushui Garment Market....

39. 律師上書指暫住證制度違法, 明报 ('Petition against Illegal Licenses on Temporary Stay', *Ming Pao* online edition, 26 Dec. 2006, <www.mingpaonews.com>).)
40. 北京調研是否取消暫住證 擬由居住證代替", 新華網 ('Beijing to Study Replacing Temporary Stay License', Xinhuanet, 11 Oct. 2006, <big5.xinhuanet.com/gate/big5/news.xinhuanet.com/politics/2006-10/11/content_5186992.htm>, 7 Aug. 2007).
41. 'Legal Procedure Counts', *China Daily*, Hong Kong edition, 18 Oct. 2006.

> In its first notice to evacuate the self-employed sellers from the market, the chengguan (urban management and supervision department) of the district labelled the market as a complex of illegal buildings by citing the municipal government regulations on urban planning. But the actual decision to tear down the market was made on the grounds that the market did not meet municipal environmental and sanitary standards.
>
> Such inconsistency damages the sanctity of the decision, and at the same time reveals the decision-makers' lack of respect for legal procedure….The food for thought in these cases is that government administrative departments must get to know their own jurisdictions, and their employees must be educated to observe proper legal procedures in the execution of administrative rules. Only by observing the right legal procedure can government departments be prevented from abusing their power and fairness be guaranteed for all involved.[42]

The court's report[43] followed a lawsuit filed by 150 stall-owners against the demolition of an outdoor market in East Beijing. While the court ruled that the demolition of illegal buildings was indeed legal, it at the same time criticized the government departments involved for not following the proper legal procedures. It added that the demolition order was based on inconsistent local government regulations, pointing out that various administrative departments frequently issue a joint notice for the coercive demolition of illegal constructions, even though some of the departments do not have jurisdiction over such matters.

B TRANSPARENCY

The transparency of the Chinese legal system has made significant process in recent years. A Chinese official has pointed out that as a result of implementing WTO commitments on legal transparency, many government departments unrelated to trade and commerce have now made their rules and regulations publicly available:

> In the past, many laws remained unknown to the public not because they were secret. It was just because transparency was not part of the work culture. No government department would take the initiative to make public their regulations because it was not a common practice. With WTO requirements nowadays, *transparency has replaced secrecy as the norm*.[44] It has become so common and normal that everyone is doing that.[45]

---

42. *Ibid.*
43. A term used by the *China Daily* article. It was not clear from the article whether the investigative report is part of the court's decision. The website of the Chaoyang District Court <cyfy.bjchy.gov.cn/chylaw/index.htm> only posted selected judgments until 2004; last visited 28 Apr. 2008.
44. Emphasis added.
45. Author's interview with a Chinese official who spoke on condition of anonymity, 19 Jul. 2005, Geneva.

To underline this move of bureaucratic culture towards increased transparency, the State Council, in January 2007, adopted a set of draft regulations that set out standards for both central and local governments on their 'governing transparency'.[46] The *China Daily* described the draft regulations as a 'fundamental change in the concept of the nature of government', adding that:

> [t]he rules tell government decision makers what the public is entitled to know about their work. Being informed is the precondition for citizens' participation in and supervision of the public affairs that affect their interests. From this perspective, the adoption of these draft regulations is of great significance in building an open, clean and honest government.[47]

1 Legislative Changes

The *Regulations on Open Government Information*[48] lays down detailed legal obligations for government departments to publicize information on a wide range of subjects, such as government procurement projects, land requisitions, relocation of residents and compensation, budgets and expenses, results of investigations into environmental protection issues, public health, food and drug safety, and administrative procedures.[49] The new law, the first of its kind in China, resembles access to information legislation in more sophisticated legal systems which provide legal guarantee and due process for citizens who request access to government information.

When explaining the legislative intent of the new law, *Zhang Qiong*, Deputy Director General of the State Council's Legislative Affairs Office, said that the underlining premises of the new law was 'the principle to make public all government information, and keeping information confidential should be treated as exceptional cases'.[50] The legislation aims to 'effectively ensure the people's right to know'

46. 'Right to be Informed', *China Daily*, Hong Kong edition, Editorial, 19 Jan. 2007.
47. *Ibid.* It is hard to imagine similar contents and choice of words in an editorial of the same *China Daily* five years ago. The editorial criticized many officials for assuming that they could make decisions on behalf of the public without letting them be informed. It states, for example, that 'with this frame of mind, what needs to be made public to the general public has become a matter of personal decision. The cover-up of the real situation of SARS (severe acute respiratory syndrome) by some government officials in 2003 was a typical example. A lack of transparency of government information can be disastrous'. The editorial cited further examples of the consequences of a non-transparent government, arguing 'who knows how many people would have fallen victim of SARS' without the dismissal of officials 'who lied to the public about what was really happening with SARS', and '[b]ehind the wall that separates the public from what they are entitled to know can be dirty tricks bringing illegal wealth to corrupt officials while causing harm to the interests of the public and the state.'
48. State Council decree 492, effective 1 May 2008, available in Chinese at <www.law-lib.com/law>.
49. *Regulations on Open Government Information*, Ch. 2.
50. '国务院法制办负责人就政府信息公开条例答记者问', 多维新闻网 ('State Council Legislative Affairs Office Answers Questions on Open Government Regulations', DWnews.

and it helps to 'contain and prevent corruption institutionally and at its roots'[51] he added. Among the exceptions are those involving 'state secrets, confidential commercial information and individual privacy' (Article 14). The new law also contains a clause to the effect that the release of official information 'should not harm state security, public safety, economic security and social stability' (Article 8).

The new law requires governments at various levels to compile directories for open information, which should include the name, address, telephone and fax numbers, and e-mail addresses of departments entrusted with the responsibility to release official information (Article 19). Individuals have the right to seek information from the government through a written inquiry (Article 20). Government departments should respond to public requests for information within fifteen days, or no more than thirty days in exceptional cases, upon receipt of such requests (Article 25).

The law became effective on 1 May 2008. It is too early to assess the impact of this new law of transparency. However, it is worth noting that the law provides for a mechanism through which individuals can appeal against any official refusal to release information and take officials to court if their legitimate requests for information are ignored (Article 33). It has become a common practice for new laws in post-WTO accession China to include a mechanism for recourse to administrative and judicial reviews. This phenomenon is partly due to the WTO's requirements on China to provide for judicial review of all trade-related official decisions. Underlying the requirement is the principle of justiciability of government action designed to ensure that government officials cannot behave above or outside the law.[52]

The legislative history of this new law on government transparency can be traced back to the initial efforts by the Chinese central government and some provincial authorities to fulfil the WTO's requirement on transparency of information. In China's WTO accession package, the Chinese government had made commitment that 'only those laws, regulations and other measures pertaining to or affecting trade in goods, services, TRIPS or the control of foreign exchange that are published and readily available to other WTO members, individuals and enterprises, shall be enforced'.[53] As a direct result of this commitment, a new *Ordinance on Procedural Rules for Formulating Administrative Regulations* and an *Ordinance on Procedural Rules for Formulating of Departmental Rules* came into effect on 1 January 2002. Both set out detailed transparency requirements and procedures for public consultations as well as for inputs into the Chinese rules and regulations making process.[54]

---

com, 24 Apr. 2007); see also 'Landmark decree to encourage gov't transparency', Xinhua News, 24 Apr. 2007, at <Xinhuanet.com>).

51. Benjamin Kang Lim & Guo Shipeng, 'China Vows Government Transparency, within limits', *Reuters*, 24 Apr. 2007.
52. More in part (D) of the current section.
53. Accession Protocol, 2 (C) 1; this allows for emergency situations to the effect that laws should be made available at the very latest at the time of implementation.
54. See also Part II, Ch. 5.

Law-makers are now legally obliged to follow these transparency and public consultation requirements, thereby complementing the due process requirements discussed earlier. It does not matter whether the subject matter is WTO-related or not, legislative processes incompatible with the new transparency procedures can be challenged – because of lack of transparency and/or incompatibility with due process requirements. The slogan 'published and readily available' has become a basic pre-requisite for all new Chinese laws, and this happens in less than six years after China's WTO accession.

On 1 January 2003, for example, Guangzhou City implemented new *Provisions on Publicizing Governmental Information.*[55] It states that '[i]ndividuals and organizations... shall have the right to obtain governmental information in accordance with the law' (Article 4). It adds that the basic principle and ground rule is to make public all government information, while retention of information can only be justified in exceptional cases, such as for the protection of state secrets or personal privacy (Articles 6 and 14). The Provisions set out mechanisms by which the public can apply for access to information, and binding procedures for the responses of government officials (Articles 15–19).

If public authorities do not comply, the requesting party 'shall have the right to apply for reconsideration, to bring a lawsuit or a claim for compensation in accordance with the law' (Article 29). The Provisions also contain a non-discrimination clause applying to foreigners, pursuant to which 'foreigners, stateless persons or foreign organizations [who] apply for the publicity of governmental information within the administrative area of Guangzhou City, ... shall have the same rights and obligations as those of the citizens and organizations of the People's Republic of China' (Article 33).

2 Relevant Cases and Executive Action

In the area of judicial administration, court hearings are becoming increasingly open to the public, even though some court hearings, especially those the Chinese government considers to be about 'sensitive cases', most of a political nature, such as trials of political dissidents, continue to be closed. Unlike in the past, judgments must be provided to the public unless exceptional circumstances demand otherwise. In the case of intellectual property rights litigations, discussed earlier, a government website, entitled *China Intellectual Property Rights Judgements*,[56] designed to improve transparency in the dissemination of court decisions, went

---

55. 'Provisions of Guangzhou City on Publicizing Governmental Information', promulgated by Guangdong Province on 6 Nov. 2002, effective 1 Jan. 2003, available in Chinese at <www.law-lib.com/law>; for other examples of transparency measures, see 'Administrative Measures for Government Procurement Information Announcements' on finance and banking, promulgated 19 Aug. 2004, effective 19 Sep. 2004; and 'Some Advice of the People's Government of Anhui Province on the Challenges after China's WTO Accession, Further Expanding the Open-up Policy, and Accelerating Economic Development', promulgated and effective 15 Mar. 2002, also available in Chinese at <www.law-lib.com/law>.
56. <ipr.chinacourt.org>.

online in March 2006. Some courts, mostly in large municipalities such as Beijing and Guangzhou, now publish their judgments online to improve accessibility.[57]

In what has become known as 'the right to know' case, *Ren Junjie*, a resident of Zhengzhou city in Henan province, sued the municipal zoning board for keeping local residents in the dark about the allocation of parking spaces. *Ren* discovered that many parking spaces in Zhengzhou streets were situated in pedestrian or slow lanes, and he unsuccessfully sought to examine the permits and other documents for these parking spaces from the municipal zoning board and records department of the municipal construction bureau. In February 2006, before the Zhongyuan first instance District Court, the municipal authorities argued that the plaintiff had no standing to examine the documents requested, as they were the property of the records department of the municipal construction bureau. The records department argued that the information requested remained classified. *Ren*'s legal action attracted some media coverage.[58] Courts in Zhengzhou post judgments on an official website.[59] As of 6 September 2007, the judgment in the case remained unavailable. The case signals an increased awareness among Chinese citizens of their right to know and legal avenues available to claim this right. With the entry into force of the new comprehensive law on government transparency, the growing awareness and the demand for open government will only grow stronger.

During the WTO accession negotiations, the Chinese government rejected a request from WTO members that it should undertake to make available information on judicial decisions and administrative rulings of both general application, as well as WTO-related decisions.[60] In 2001, the government was not yet prepared to accept to publicize judicial and administrative rulings. Five years later, several jurisdictions have created websites to publicize their judgments, which show how multi-faceted the WTO's impact on the development of rule of law principles in China can be.

The influence of the WTO, however, extends beyond the establishment of a basic WTO compatible legal structure. Improved transparency in judicial and administrative decisions, for example, became a fact five years after China's WTO accession, but this has not been the result of a legally binding WTO commitment. Rather, this was partly due to the continuous pressure from WTO members, especially in the area of intellectual property rights; more significantly, however, it was the result of an incremental change in the Chinese bureaucratic and legal culture. From the demand side, when both the public and private sectors may access information on all new legislation, they inevitably will come to expect similar levels of

57. China's answer to intellectual property rights questions raised by the European Union during the first WTO Trade Policy Review of China, Trade Policy Review Body, Minutes of Meeting 19–21 Apr. 2006, WTO Document: WT/TPR/M/161/Add.1, 15 Jun. 2006, 243–263.
58. See for example Zhang Shengli et al., 'Zhengzhou City Begins Citizen's Right to Know Case', 15 Mar. 2006, *Worker's Daily*, <www.grrb.com.cn>.
59. <zzfy.chinacourt.org>.
60. Working Party Report, para. 335; see also Part II, Ch. 5 Section II.C.

transparency for judicial rulings. Judicial officers requested to provide information have also become more receptive to the principle of transparency because they realize that their counterparts in the area of legislative activities do likewise.

Executive officials undergo a similar process of attitude change. In 2006, for example, the Beijing municipal government decided to publish information on key projects financed by the municipality to improve transparency. Its Development and Reform Commission issued guidelines which require that all key projects which have an impact on the ecology, environment, and utilization of resources, and those with an impact on the daily life of local residents are set out in detail for the public before they can be approved by the commission. The guidelines require a comprehensive overview of the nature, cost, scope, and plans for such projects, which will be posted on the commission's website for public comments. Residents have ten days to register suggestions, their opinions, or objections, and the commission directs the units and departments overseeing the projects in question to provide explanations and responses.[61] Transparency was used here as a tool to curb corruption and garner public support for the numerous construction projects associated with the hosting of the Beijing 2008 Summer Olympic Games.

Due to the combined effect of the principles of due process and transparency, the Chinese legal system, both in its legislative, judicial, and executive aspects, has clearly become more predictable when compared to the pre-WTO situation. On the whole, those affected by a new law will have few problems to find out about its contents, to ascertain whether the law is implemented in accordance with prescribed procedures, and to file a judicial or administrative challenge if its legality is in doubt.

C EQUALITY

The principles of equality and non-discrimination had some roots in the Chinese legal system before China's WTO accession. Equality figures prominently in the PRC Constitution, such as in the Preamble, in Article 4 on ethnic equality and in Article 33 on gender equality. However, there was no mechanism to invoke these constitutional provisions. Some indirect avenues for invoking constitutional provisions started to surface from 2002 onwards, when the Chinese government began to introduce measures to ensure uniformity of the administration of law as required by the WTO.[62] China has ratified a number of international human rights treaties in which the principles of non-discrimination and equality are fundamental to the State party's implementation of treaty obligations. For example, China is a state party to the *International Covenant on Economic, Social and Cultural Rights* (ICESCR), the *Convention on the Rights of the Child* (CRC), the *International Convention on the Elimination of All Forms of Racial Discrimination* (ICERD),

61. 'Add Project Transparency', *China Daily*, Hong Kong edition, 23 Aug. 2006.
62. See also Part II, Ch. 5 Sections II.B and II.E.

and the *Convention against Torture and Other Forms of Cruel, Inhuman and Degrading Treatment* (CAT).

However, it was not until China's WTO accession that the principle of non-discrimination began to be translated into a wide range of enforceable laws, primarily into trade and WTO-related laws, but also into other areas of laws. It must be noted that the non-discrimination principle, in its WTO context and international trade law, differs from the concept of non-discrimination as commonly understood and applied in public international law and non-WTO related domestic laws.[63] In the WTO, the principle of non-discrimination is translated into two fundamental principles that govern the multilateral trading system: MFN treatment and national treatment. They both mean trade without discrimination between trading partners. MFN treatment refers to non-discrimination among WTO members. The MFN principle is stipulated across all the subject-areas of the WTO.[64] National treatment refers to non-discrimination between WTO member's own nationals and those of all other WTO members.[65]

As the Chinese government seeks to comply with the non-discrimination principle, it is being written into trade-related Chinese laws and applied as MFN treatment and national treatment. However, as emphasized earlier, China's responses to WTO systemic requirements on the Chinese legal system often translate into the incorporation of WTO-induced measures and principles across the broad. This spill-over effect leads to increased system-wide awareness of these principles both within the government and in Chinese society. The same is true for the principle of non-discrimination in its wider application outside the realm of trade. It is applied in the sense that laws should be formulated without discrimination against certain groups or individuals and laws should be applied equally to all in similar circumstances. A key international provision on the principle of equality, Article 26 of the ICCPR, reads:

> All persons are equal before the law and are entitled without any discrimination to the equal protection of the law. In this respect, the law shall prohibit

---

63. The principles of non-discrimination in the two contexts do have some elements in common. For example, they both apply to de jure and de facto discrimination. See *Analytical Study of the High Commissioner for Human Rights on the Fundamental Principle of Non-discrimination in the Context of Globalization,* Report of the High Commissioner to the Sixtieth session of the United Nations Commission on Human Rights, E/CN.4/2004/40, 15 Jan. 2004, for more analysis on the differences and similarities of the principle of non-discrimination in the contexts of international human rights law and WTO law.
64. The WTO allows for exceptions to this principle when members form customs unions and/or enter into bilateral or regional free trade agreements for the purpose of advancing economic integration. These arrangements, however, should fulfil certain conditions, such as not making trade more restrictive or imposing higher tariffs on products from outsiders, in order to be WTO compatible.
65. National treatment takes effect once foreign goods, services and intellectual property items have entered the market. Therefore, charging customs duties on an imported product is not a violation of the principle of national treatment, even though locally produced goods are not subject to customs duties.

> any discrimination and guarantee to all persons equal and effective protection against discrimination on any ground such as race, colour, sex, language, religion political or other opinion, national or social origin, property, birth or other status.

Legal prohibition of and protection against discrimination are central to this provision.[66] Equality before the law 'essentially means that judges and administrative officials must not act arbitrarily in enforcing laws',[67] while equal protection of the law requires that 'the legislature must refrain from any discrimination when enacting laws; however, it must also prohibit discrimination by enacting special laws and afford effective protection against discrimination.'[68] Manfred Nowak concludes that the different dimensions of Article 26 ICCPR hinge on the meaning of discrimination[69] and form a single unit, which 'guarantees a general right to equality before the law and equal protection of the law, as well as a general prohibition of discrimination which is directed at the legislature'.[70] In other words, equality within the meaning of Article 26 ICCPR includes not only the right to be treated without discrimination in legal proceedings, but also the prohibition of discriminatory laws and the use of law to protect against discrimination. A report by the United Nations High Commissioner for Human Rights argues that the principle of equality complements the principle of non-discrimination, and that Article 26 of the ICCPR in fact 'creates a right to equality'.[71]

For purposes of the present analysis, the principle of equality goes beyond the question whether or not laws are enforced arbitrarily. In assessing the prevalence of the principle of equality in China, it is useful to focus on the extent to which non-discrimination has been invoked by citizens to protect their rights in the Chinese legal system. The increasing numbers of complaints and petitions filed by Chinese citizens against the authorities because of alleged discrimination suggest that the principle of equality is beginning to take root in the Chinese legal culture. The growing number of public interests cases indicates that the general public is gaining confidence in the Chinese legal system.

---

66. See also Art. 14 of the ICCPR, which stipulates that 'all persons shall be equal before the courts and tribunals'.
67. M. Nowak, *U.N. Covenant on Civil and Political Rights, CCPR Commentary*, 2nd rev. edn (Kehl: N.P. Engel Publisher, 2005), 606.
68. *Ibid.*, 607.
69. See Art. 2(1) of the Universal Declaration of Human Rights (UDHR) 1948, which serves a basis for provisions in subsequent international human rights instruments which stipulate prohibition against discrimination. It reads 'Everyone is entitled to all the rights and freedoms set forth in this Declaration, without distinction of any kind, such as race, colour, sex, language, religion, political or other opinion, national or social origin, property, birth or other status.'
70. M. Nowak, 600.
71. *Analytical Study of the High Commissioner for Human Rights on the Fundamental Principle of Non-discrimination in the Context of Globalization*, 5, para. 9.

1 Growing Disparities

Unlike in its response to the other three areas of legal systemic WTO accession commitments, the Chinese government has yet to introduce WTO-induced laws or new measures which are applicable generally throughout the Chinese legal system beyond trade-related areas. There was a system-wide review of laws to ensure their compliance with the WTO's non-discrimination principle, in terms of national treatment and MFN treatment. New mechanisms were put into place to ensure that relevant new laws are WTO compatible, and that commercial cases involving foreigners are adjudicated by middle-level courts or higher to reduce incidents of judicial local protectionism.[72]

The WTO's impact on the growing prevalence of the principle of equality in China is threefold. First, China's accession to the WTO has widely publicized the concept of non-discrimination. This has greatly increased public awareness of the notion of equality in Chinese society. Second, a number of WTO-induced system-wide measures, though not specific to non-discrimination, have enabled the public to invoke discrimination as a legal issue in administrative and judicial review cases. These measures are, for example, the introduction of the ALL, and the new mechanism allowing individuals to petition against legal provisions which are deemed incompatible with national laws and the PRC Constitution. Third, China's accelerated economic growth after its WTO accession has aggravated growing disparities in Chinese society and widened the inter-regional and the intra-city poverty gap, the latter referring to poor living standards of rural migrant workers in big cities. Despite China's economic growth, official statistics indicate that close to thirty million people in rural areas are still inadequately fed or clothed.[73]

The UN Committee on Economic, Social and Cultural Rights noted in 2005 that it was 'deeply concerned that despite the rapid economic development in recent years, poverty persists in the country, disproportionately affecting the rural population', and 'the disparity in income and in the enjoyment of an adequate standard of living continues to widen between the rich and the poor, in particular those in urban/rural areas, as well as those in coastal provinces/inland provinces'.[74] The Committee, for example, also noted 'with deep concern the de facto discrimination against internal migrants in the fields of employment, social security, health services, housing and education'.[75] The Committee was equally concerned about 'the persistence of gender inequalities in practice', about discrimination against persons with physical and mental disabilities, and ethnic minorities, especially in terms of employment and other socio-economic areas.[76]

72. See discussion in Part II, Ch. 5 Section II.D.
73. China's first report to the UN Committee on Economic, Social and Cultural Rights, 4 Mar. 2004, E/1990/5/Add.59, 49.
74. Concluding observations of the United Nations Committee on Economic, Social and Cultural Rights, People's Republic of China (including Hong Kong and Macau), 13 May 2005, E/C.12/1/Add.107, para. 30.
75. *Ibid.*, para. 15.
76. *Ibid.*, paras 16–17, 38.

Growing social disparities fuel social grievances. According to the Ministry of Public Security, in 2005 there were 87,000 incidents of disturbances of public order and social unrest in China, an increase of 6.6% compared to the previous year. Mass violent protests, riots, and petitions rose by 28% in 2004, to 74,000, compared to 58,000 in 2003 and only 10,000 a decade before.[77] Socio-economic disparities, together with the growing popularity of the concept of non-discrimination and increased availability of judicial avenues to redress inequalities, also prompted more individuals to seek legal redress of discriminatory treatments. This trend contributes to the incorporation of the principle of equality into the Chinese legal system.

2 Relevant Cases

In March 2006, the Legal Research and Service Center for Women at Beijing University Law School petitioned to the NPCSC that a State Council regulation,[78] which covered two sets of temporary measures governing retirement age, was discriminatory and should be subject to constitutional review. The first set, entitled *Temporary Measures Concerning the Placement of Aged, Physically Weak, Sick, and Disabled Cadres*, provides that male officials may retire at age 60, whereas female officials should retire at age 55. The second, *Temporary Measures Concerning Retirement and Resignation of Workers*, stipulates different retirement ages for men and women, to the effect that male workers may retire at age 60, whereas the retirement age for female workers is 50. The Centre's submission noted that the regulations, in setting out different retirement ages for men and women, violated the Constitution, which guarantees that 'Chinese citizens are equal under the law' (Article 33(2)) and 'Chinese female citizens shall enjoy political, economic, cultural, social, and family rights identical to those of male citizens' (Article 48(1)).[79] The regulations, and indeed the equality articles of the Constitution, had been in place since 1978, but their implementation had not been challenged legally for over twenty-seven years. While the result of the above petition is pending, that the discriminatory provisions were challenged in 2006 indicates a profound change of Chinese citizens' perception of law and the principle that everyone should be treated equally before the law.

Gender equality is not the only area where Chinese citizens seek to apply the principle of non-discrimination. Regionalism and local protectionism[80] are other areas where that the principle of equality is beginning to make a difference. In March 2006, the SPC agreed to revise a judicial interpretation entitled *Interpretation on Issues of Applying the Law to Cases of Personal Damages*. This followed a petition from two citizens to the effect that the Interpretation discriminated against

77. Irene Wang, 'Incidents of Social Unrest Hit 87,000', *South China Morning Post*, 20 Jan. 2006.
78. State Council Regulation No. 104, 1978.
79. Yu Huaiqing, 'Peking University Law School Suggests Subjecting Female Retirement Age to Constitutional Review', *China Women's Daily*, 8 Mar. 2006, <www.women.org.cn>.
80. See also Part I, Ch. 2 Section II.D.1.

the rural population.[81] In a letter to the SPC, Professor *Hu Xingdou* of Beijing Technology College and lawyer *Li Fangping* proposed an amendment to the Interpretation to achieve 'uniform standards' in the award of personal damages to plaintiffs from both rural and urban areas. According to the Interpretation, '[c]ompensation for deaths should be calculated based on the average annual disposable income of a city or county resident, or the average net annual income of a rural resident, under the jurisdiction of the court hearing the case. Damages should equal the value of twenty years of income (Article 29).' The complainants argued that the provision amounted to unlawful discrimination against citizens from rural areas, by calculating personal damages on the basis of their household registration (*hukou*) status. A SPC spokesperson said that an investigation would be conducted and suggested that the Interpretation would soon be revised.[82]

In another case involving discrimination based on regional considerations, the defendant, a local public security office, had to offer public apologies for 'regional discrimination'.[83] The dispute originated in March 2005 when the Shenzhen Longxin Police Station, in Guangdong province, posted street banners with slogans that targeted 'members of the Henan extortionist groups'. Two natives of Henan province filed a lawsuit against the police station in the Gaoxin District People's Court of Zhengzhou City, arguing that the posting of banners singling out people from a particular region violated the principle of equality. They complained that the posting had tainted the reputation of Henan province citizens and that they had the legal right to protect their reputation, and requested the court to order a formal apology. The parties eventually reached a friendly settlement, and the Longgang sub-bureau of the Shenzhen Public Security Bureau publicly apologized in May 2005 for the harm that the 'regional discrimination' posters had caused to citizens of Henan province.[84]

D JUSTICIABILITY OF GOVERNMENT ACTIONS

Judicial review and the opportunity to appeal administrative decisions or acts before impartial tribunals is explicitly required in China's WTO Accession Protocol and Working Party Report.[85] China's commitments in this respect have already led to changes in the traditional two-tier 'judicial supervision system', when a case involves foreigner litigants.[86] A series of judicial reform measures were referred to earlier, especially the introduction of a judicial examination system to improve the

81. Liao Weihua et al., 'Two Citizens Suggest that the Supreme Court Eliminate Urban-Rural Discrimination', 21 Mar. 2006, *China Law Digest*, <www.chinalawdigest.com/>.
82. *Ibid.*
83. Li Junde, 'Two Parties Settle in Unprecedented Case of Regional Discrimination', North News, <www.northnews.cn>, 9 Feb. 2006.
84. *Ibid.*
85. See, for example, China's WTO Accession Protocol 2(D)(1),Working Party Report, para. 76–79.
86. See Part II, Ch. 5 Section II.D.

professionalism and education level of Chinese judges, all prompted by WTO requirements.

The underlying assumption of judicial review is that a government is bound by law and should be subject to judicial scrutiny when private parties consider that governmental acts are beyond the power bestowed by law (*ultra vires*). The following court cases are testimony to the growing consciousness among Chinese citizens of that precept. More and more citizens take actions to challenge the legality of governmental acts and policies through judicial and other legal avenues. To sue government departments and officials is no longer exceptional but a common avenue of recourse for those who seek to address social injustice. This trend further suggests that legality is becoming an increasingly important factor in legitimizing Chinese government actions.

1 Legality Review Mechanisms in China

In systems governed by the principle of the separation of powers, the legal authority of the constitution is often and primarily invoked through the courts, where judges use constitutional provisions as benchmarks for their review of the legality of government actions or legislation. In China's case, where the model of separation of powers is not followed, the courts cannot review the legality of legislation. There are, however, indications that some forms of constitutional review of legislation may develop as a result of China's implementation of its WTO commitments.

Legislative review in a Chinese context, as distinct from judicial review of the legality of legislation common in Western legal tradition, refers to review of the legality of laws and regulations by the State Council, the NPC, its Standing Committee and its subsidiary organs. The *Law on Legislation* of 2000 for the first time in PRC history establishes a hierarchy among different laws, rules and regulations, and reaffirms the legal supremacy of the Constitution, and that laws inconsistent with the Constitution are illegal.[87] Before the end of 2001, however, no mechanism was in place to review the constitutionality of Chinese laws and regulations.

To fulfil WTO commitments in relation to the uniform administration of the Chinese legal regime, the *Ordinance on the Archives Filing of Regulations and Government Rules* came into effect on 1 January 2002. The new ordinance, together with the NPCSC's revision of the *Working Procedures for Filing and Reviewing Legislation* and the introduction of *Working Procedures for Filing and Reviewing Judicial Interpretations* of the end of 2005, have further revised the filing and review system, which allows citizens to petition the Legislative Affairs Commission of the NPCSC for review of the constitutionality and legality of State Council Regulations, as well as review of laws, regulations and rules at different

87. Article 78; Art. 90 of the 2000 Law on Legislation also states that citizens have the right to petition the NPC for review of the compatibility of rules and regulations with the constitution; but no operational mechanism for the filing of such petitions was established then.

levels.[88] This newly available petition mechanism allows individuals and private parties to invoke the legal authority of constitutional provisions.

Under the above review mechanism, the State Council, other departments, private organizations, or individuals can request an inquiry, conducted by a specialized committee and the Legislative Affairs Commission of the NPCSC, into regulations that conflict with the law or the Constitution. If a specialized committee believes a recorded piece of legislation contradicts the law or the constitution, it can either review this regulation on its own or request the departments concerned for discussion and correction. If the departments fail to take action, the NPCSC may revoke the conflicting legislation. These working procedures also apply to judicial interpretations issued by the SPC or the SPP. The new mechanism can still be improved, in particular the level of transparency of the deliberation process, but it represents a significant channel for invoking the authority of constitutional provisions.

Attitude change often precedes behavioural changes. In China's case, changes in the people's perception of the role of law in ensuring government accountability and resulting behavioural changes cannot yet be quantified and evaluated through neat statistics, such as by opinion polls or the overall number of cases of judicial and constitutional review. The following cases illustrate of these changes, regardless of whether or not the plaintiffs succeeded.

2 Relevant Cases

In March 2006, a popular website, Aiqinhai.org (Aegean Sea), was shut down by the Zhejiang authorities because it 'engaged in large-scale transmission of domestic and overseas current events reporting, but failed to declare proof of qualification as a news carrier to the corresponding department in charge'.[89] Constitutional scholar *Chen Yongmiao*, Aiqinhai's legal counsel *Sun Yueli*, and others petitioned the NPC to conduct a constitutional review of the case, arguing that the decision to shut down the website was against the ALL and the constitutional right to freedom of information and expression. The petitioners argued that Article 5 of the *Rules on the Administration of Internet News Information Services*, issued by the State Council Information Office and the Ministry of Information Industry, was incompatible with the ALL and could not justify shutting down the website. The provision in question stipulates that websites engaging in news information services are subject to examination and approval by the State Council Information Office before being granted an administrative license, although according to the

88. As discussed in Part II, Ch. 5 Sections II.B and II.E.

89. 'Delegation Requests Application of Constitutional Review regarding the Case Involving the Closing Down of the Aiqinhai.org Web Site', *China Law Digest*, <www.chinalawdigest.com>.

ALL, administrative licenses can only be established by law or administrative regulations, not issued by departmental rules.[90]

The case and other constitutional petitions demonstrate that Chinese citizens are now using this mechanism originally introduced as a result of WTO accession to seek constitutional review.[91] While the result of the petition remains unknown, *Zhang Jianhong*, the former editor of Aiqinhai.org, was detained on 6 September 2006, two days after he criticized China's human rights record in the context of its hosting the 2008 summer Olympic Games. *Zhang*, who wrote under an *alias* on another website, was accused of 'inciting subversion'.[92] This case indicates that while the Chinese government has become more open to allowing citizens to challenge the legality of official acts in general, it remains unprepared to tolerate dissenting views about politically sensitive matters.

The Aiqinhai petition followed the controversial closedown in January 2006 by the CPC's Central Propaganda Department of *Freezing Point*, a weekly supplement to the *China Youth Daily*. Jurist *Jiang Ping*, lawyer *Zhang Sizhi*, and other scholars published an open letter in February 2006, criticizing the Propaganda Department of the CPC Central Committee for the closing order. They accused the Propaganda Department of acting *ultra vires* and in violation of the Constitution. The letter drew approving comments from Chinese scholars, who wrote to CPC officials arguing that the Propaganda Department had no legal basis to bypass the Constitution and the law by exercising censorship of this sort. The controversy was widely covered by the media. The party organ had criticized an article, entitled *Modernization and Historical Textbooks* and published on 11 January 2006, which sought 'to reverse the verdict on crimes of the imperialist powers that invaded China'.[93] In response to this reaction, the CPC allowed *Freezing Point* to resume publication. However, the Propaganda Department did request the dismissal of the weekly's editor-in-chief and of his deputy, and a corrigendum to the impugned article in the first issue after resumption of publication.

---

90. See also China Human Rights and Rule of Law Update, United States Congressional-Executive Commission on China, July 2006, <www.cecc.gov>, where an English translation of the petition is available, 6 Mar. 2007.
91. A systemic record of petitions, if there is any, is not available in the public domain. Sporadic data indicates that the quantity of the Chinese people petitioning against the illegality of government actions is rising. According to media reports, Li Shuguang, Vice Dean of the Graduate School of the China University of Political Science and Law, revealed information disclosed to internal staff by Wang Mengkui, Director of the Development Research Center of the State Council, during an academic conference in Beijing on 4 Mar. 2005. Li cited figures that from 1979 to 1982, there were only 20,000 petitions by Chinese citizens complaining about various government actions. In 2005 alone, however, there were 30,000,000 such petitions. See for example, 'Petitions Exceed 30 Millions in 2005', *China Law Digest*, <www.chinalawdigest.com>, 7 Apr. 2006.
92. See 'China: Olympics Organizers Must Ensure Media Freedom', press release by The Committee to Protect Journalists, 22 Sep. 2006.
93. 'Central Committee of the Communist Youth League and the CCP Central Propaganda Department Accused of Constitutional Violations for the *Freezing Point* Incident', *China Law Digest*, <www.chinalawdigest>, 13 and 14 Feb. 2006.

In another case, Sichuan lawyers *Xing Lianchao* and *Sun Lei* argued that Article 5 of the March 2006 State Council *Regulations on the Management of Public Places of Entertainment* was unconstitutional. This provision prohibits four categories of citizens, including those who have been convicted of prostitution or smuggling; persons who have been stripped of their political rights; those who have received treatment for drug addiction; or those who have experienced administrative detention for engaging in prostitution, from operating or working in public places of entertainment. It was argued that such restrictions were discriminatory and violated the equality and labour rights provisions of the Constitution.[94]

Another constraint in the quest of independent adjudication in China is the regular practice of lower court judges to seek instructions from higher courts before deciding on sensitive or difficult cases. This practice effectively defeats the purpose of judicial supervision through the appeal and judicial review processes, and opens the door for other forms of interference, including those from party officials. However, there are signs that this practice is beginning to change. For example, the Shaanxi Provincial High Court passed a regulation in 2006 to the effect that lower-level courts would no longer be able to seek instructions from higher-level courts on matters related to the evaluation of facts or evidence in any given case. Under the regulation, higher courts may only give instructions on questions of the application of the law, and the trial committees of lower courts must determine whether to allow a request for instructions. If necessary, the final judgment of the court should be discussed by the trial committee, based on instructions from the higher court.[95]

III CONCLUDING REMARKS

The analysis of the latest developments in the Chinese legal system, matched against the four cross-cutting benchmark principles, suggests two important trends. First, China's WTO membership has served a catalyst for incorporating into Chinese laws four major legal principles in line with international standards. The process of incorporation takes place through legislative activities, court cases, and petitions to the NPCSC and the State Council, and in some instances a changing work culture of government officials. The examples cited to illustrate these changes are mostly in domains not directly governed by WTO rules. This supports a significant postulate of this study, namely that WTO-induced systemic legal principles are spilling over into aspects of Chinese laws beyond the realms of trade and economics.

---

94. Yao Shuoan, 'Regulations on the Management of Public Places of Entertainment Are Deemed Unconstitutional', <www.sohu.com>, 19 Mar. 2006.
95. Wang Ke, 'Shaanxi Provincial High Court Gradually Abolishes Traditional System of Seeking Instructions on Cases from Higher Levels', *People's Net*, <www.people.cn>, 19 May 2006.

These rule of law principles operate simultaneously to configure the ways and the extent to which the government may legally intervene with both the market and different aspects of the daily life of citizens. For example, the principle of transparency allows the public to know what is prescribed by law, what is legally permissible, and what is outside the government's legal authority. Pursuant to the principle of due process and procedural fairness, the government must implement these rules according to specified procedures. Under the principle of equality, every individual may demand that transparent rules are implemented under due process rules and applied equally to all.

These principles will continue to shape the Chinese legal system and its responses to challenges that confront both government and society. Taking one of the most pressing challenges – internal migration – as an example, we can identify an urgent need to regulate the increasing flow of rural residents towards the cities, in search of employment and better living standards. Yet the traditional household registration (*Hukou*), while valuable in that it keeps record of the vast population, has proven to be inadequate in coping with mass internal migration driven by the booming economy and the widening poverty gap between rural and urban areas.

Increasing incidents of discriminatory treatment between the new migrants and urban residents, unemployment, or black market job arrangements, and the lack of social security and benefits afforded to the newcomers cause tensions in different regions. With key rule of law principles taking hold in the Chinese legal system and the public expectation that these principles should be implemented, solutions to internal migration problems introduced by the government must respect these principles, in law and in public administration, if the citizens are expected to endorse the measures.

In March 2007, the NPCSC made public the full text of a draft employment promotion law, another important draft legislation which partly aims to deal with internal migration problems, and invited public comments.[96] Compare this to the moment when the draft Property Law was made public for comments in 2005. At that time, such a move was unprecedented, but in barely two years the principle of transparency has taken root to such an extent that the publication of draft laws and calls for comments has become a matter of routine. Nowadays, it is difficult to imagine that significant new Chinese laws could be passed without causing public discontent if the drafts did not go through public consultations.

Another important factor to be considered together with the above legal developments concerns the concept of legitimacy in China. There have been significant

---

96. See for example, Zhu Zhe, 'NPC Invites Public's Comments on New Employment Law', *China Daily*, Hong Kong edition, 27 Mar. 2007, and '就業促進法草案公布首日 社會各界提出意見1021件 反對就業歧視呼聲熱烈' ('Draft Employment Promotion Law Received 1021 Comments the First Day of Its Publication, Calling for a Stop to Employment Discrimination', *People's Daily*, 27 Mar. 2007.

attitude changes towards law in Chinese society where morality[97] used to be regarded as the principal basis of legitimacy. In traditional Chinese society, what was moral was considered legitimate and whatever was against the moral norms was considered illegitimate. In post-WTO accession China, law gradually assumes an important role of legitimization.

97. See Part I, Ch. 1 Section I.

Chapter 8

Challenges Ahead: Opportunities and Risks

'China is now in a critical period for reform and development, in which China's economic system and social structure, the interests of different sectors of society and people's thinking and concepts are all changing profoundly',[1] *Wu Bangguo*, Chairman of the Standing Committee of the Tenth NPC noted in March 2007. Suggesting that 'unprecedented social changes' provide ample opportunities but also 'inevitably create a wide variety of conflicts and problems', *Wu* emphasized the necessity for law to 'fully play its proper role in standardizing and guiding the functioning of society'.[2] Recent changes in the Chinese legal system may well provide rules-based solutions to these challenges which are crucial to sustain ruling legitimacy in China. Meanwhile, significant challenges remain ahead of Chinese legal development. Risks and opportunities abound, and depending on how the opportunities are seized and the risks are solved, the future will tell whether or not law can fulfil its important role in Chinese society, and indeed whether the rule of law can become a reality in China.

I OPPORTUNITIES FOR POSITIVE DEVELOPMENT

Despite risks and challenges, China now has a better chance to develop a stronger legal system crucial for its sustainable development. The WTO accession process and the stringent systemic requirements on the Chinese legal system produced a

1. Report of the Work of the NPCSC, presented to the annual session of the NPC, 11 Mar. 2007, English version available at the website of the Xinhua News Agency: <www.chinaview.cn/>, 12 Mar. 2007.
2. *Ibid.*

much clearer framework and orientation as China continues its legal reform. The CPC has great incentive to adhere to law-abiding behavioural standards and rules-based solutions to socio-economic and political challenges as legality will provide it with reinvigorated ruling legitimacy. With the four major rule of law principles taking root as a result of WTO-driven legal reform measures, law now plays a much stronger role in China and provides a clearer framework for future reforms. Departing from the traditionally non-litigious nature,[3] Chinese citizens nowadays are more prepared to defend their rights through lawsuits.

A CLEARER FRAMEWORK FOR REFORM: LESSONS FROM THE *PROPERTY LAW*

It has been said that China's accession to the WTO meant a no return of the country's economic reform and liberalization. Likewise, Chinese legal reform, in many key areas oriented towards meeting WTO requirements and convergence with international standards, has reached a stage where going back to the pre-WTO status quo is no longer an option. The final adoption of the controversial *Property Law* by the NPC during its 2007 annual session exemplifies the momentum of reform towards a model through which law has assumed the crucial role of providing a rules-based solution to social conflicts and other controversial issues. This draft law went through a record seven comprehensive reviews and over 100 NPCSC meetings before it was finally enacted on 16 March 2007.[4] The law, which consists of 247 articles, will enter into on 1 October 2007. It stipulates that 'the property of the state, the collective, the individual and other obliges is protected by law, and no units or individuals may infringe upon it' (Article 4).

The *Property Law* will have profound impact on China's economic and legal reforms, and it provides a good case study in the context of the present research. The new law, especially given the controversies surrounding its adoption, demonstrates that law is now playing a significant role in China to provide a long-term framework for continuous reform. The legislative process has also served as an important channel for debating controversial issues, which should be settled legally through legislative actions and mechanisms. The adoption of the *Property Law* was delayed for years partly because of strong opposition from some sectors, often referred to as leftist intellectuals and retired party officials, on primarily ideological grounds to the effect that as long as China remains a socialist country, public ownership should remain dominant and private property should not be afforded equal protection.[5]

---

3. See Part I, Ch. 1.
4. A total of 2,799 NPC delegates voted for the Property Law, 52 against, 37 abstained and one did not cast a vote. 'Top Legislature Adopts Landmark Property Law', *Xinhua*, 16 Mar. 2007. The law is available at <www.law-lib.com>, 6 Sep. 2007.
5. Their opposition to the *Property Law* centred on the contention that as a socialist country, China should maintain the supremacy of public ownership over private ownership, and that the two types of property should not receive equal protection.

China's pursuit of a 'socialist market economy' means that private ownership and market forces play an increasingly important role. The need for legal recognition and protection of private property rights preceded China's WTO accession. But the issue touches on the core of the ideological controversies that accompanied China's reform path, especially during the first fifteen years. The Chinese leadership was long reluctant to address the delicate issue of private property rights – even though this is crucial for the foundation and the sustainability of a market economy – for fear that it would spark off another wave of ideological debates.

With its WTO accession, extensive commitments and resulting legal and economic changes, the Chinese government decided to tackle the issue of legal protection of private property. This paved the way for the insertion of the phrase that the '[c]itizens' lawful private property is inviolable' into the Constitution (Article 13). This 2004 constitutional amendment was meant to prepare for the adoption of the landmark *Property Law*, which would provide guidance on a number of urgent issues, such as the controversies over management buyouts of SOEs and land requisitions which have triggered local riots. The draft *Property Law* prompted heated debates nationwide, which forced the NPC to postpone its scheduled adoption in March 2006.[6]

Chinese media[7] suggested that an open letter highly critical of the draft property law, which was published by Beijing University law professor *Gong Xiantian* in August 2005,[8] was a key reason for the postponement. The letter and reactions to it were particular illuminating, because the debates over private property rights encapsulated several aspects of mounting tensions between law and politics, as well as public and private ownerships, that had accumulated throughout the process of China's transformation. The letter, entitled *A Draft Property Law that Violates the Constitution and Departs from the Basic Principles of Socialism*, criticized that the draft law sought to legitimize the growing privatization of state assets in socialist China and argued that it would further weaken the putative dominant role of public ownership in socialist China and further widen social disparities. The letter asserted that the draft law violated the PRC Constitution by replacing the inviolability of public property with that of private property.

Supporters of the draft law replied that the letter's author confused constitutional authority with ideological and political theories. They argued that the draft law would consolidate the fruits of China's reform policy, and the draft law only

---

6. 'Patience Is a Virtue for Key Property Law', *China Daily*, Hong Kong edition, Editorial, 3 Mar. 2006.
7. See for example, 'Beijing Professor's Open Letter Challenges the Constitutionality of Draft Property Law, Stirring Debates over Capitalism and Socialism', <www.sina.com.cn>, reprinting an article published in *Southern Weekend*, 23 Feb. 2006 (in Chinese), and Jiang Ping, 'Formulating the Real Property Law Must Not Go Backwards', *China Industrial and Commercial Times*, 27 Feb. 2006.
8. China's Draft Property Law: Reaction and Counter-Reaction, 5 Mar. 2005, Chinese Law Prof Blog: <lawprofessors.typepad.com/china_law_prof_blog/2006/03/chinas_draft_pr.html#more>, 6 Mar. 2006.

dealt with the protection of property, whereas the question of the poverty gap was a matter of wealth distribution. The debate is symptomatic, in that it is fuelled by the daily reality of China which affects all strata of life, from the peasants whose lands are taken without adequate compensation, the fast growing number of city dwellers who have acquired properties in China's booming real estate market, and the *nouveaux riche* who have accumulated wealth through buying out SOEs and their assets.[9]

To many ordinary citizens, the draft *Property Law* would effectively legitimize the buyout of state assets by tycoons who accumulate impressive wealth through questionable means in the changing Chinese economy. The widening poverty gap made the draft *Property Law* particularly contentious, while simultaneously there was a compelling need for legal regulation of the burgeoning property market. The law should satisfy Chinese middle class property owners, who are keen to see their properties recognized and protected legally. Farmers in rural areas, however, obtain less than they had sought to get from the law. It fails to lift current legal restrictions on transfer and mortgage of agricultural lands, but delegated the matter to the State Council to legislate in due course. There is also no reference to loss of profit and relocation expenses in land requisition compensation.[10] Principal legal changes brought by the *Property Law* include:[11]

- greater protection of state-owned assets, including clauses specifying that illegal possession, looting, illegal sharing, withholding or destruction of state property by any unit or individual is prohibited;
- tightening up of conditions relating to the transfer of rights over contracted rural lands and land with existing homes;
- clear provisions specifying under what conditions homes and land can be acquired; and details about the land acquisition compensation scheme; and
- insertion of the word 'legal' in a protection clause to specify that legal private ownership should be protected.

Observers stated that '[t]he Party's decision to enact the law in spite of … resistance is a great symbolic victory for economic reform and the rule of law.'[12] To many, the law's enactment also reveals 'the dominant view at the very top towards reform'.[13] The debates over the *Property Law* once more underline the rising importance of law in harnessing legitimacy for policy and ideological changes, in addressing changing social and economic needs, and in providing legal authority and procedures to buttress sensitive political and policy decisions. Such issues

9. According to a survey by Euromoney China, five out of the country's fifty richest business leaders acquired their wealth through management buyouts, see 'China's 'Larry King' Has Talk Show Taken Off the Air', *Strait Times*, 16 Mar. 2006.
10. Rico Chan, 'New Law Aims to Better Protect Property Rights', *South China Morning Post*, 28 Mar. 2007.
11. Irene Wang, 'Property Law Finally Put to Congress', *South China Morning Post*, 9 Mar. 2007.
12. 'Property Rights in China: China's Next Revolution', *The Economist*, 8 Mar. 2007.
13. Steven Xu, 'China's Property Flaw', *South China Morning Post*, 27 Mar. 2007.

were in the past mostly dealt with through power politics, such as the CPC's internal directives, its propaganda machinery, or pronouncements by the Chinese leadership.

The law should not, however, be viewed in isolation. It is a continuation of the CPC's efforts to tackle the challenges confronting China by law, rather than resorting to power and might. In 2002, private entrepreneurs were allowed to join the CPC, followed by a constitutional amendment two years later to protect private property rights. The *Property Law* is necessary to legitimize and legally regulate a growing private sector, which now accounts for some two-thirds of China's GDP.[14] In major cities, home ownership has reached a level of some 70%,[15] while illegal land seizures continue to soar, rising 17.3% in 2006 to 131,000 cases, and becoming a major source of social unrest.[16]

To have pushed through the *Property Law* despite all the controversies underscores the central leadership's determination to use law and the legal system to provide a channel for citizens to voice their grievances and address divisive issues. It is also consistent with the latest policy of the Chinese leadership, which emphasizes importance of 'building a harmonious society', and that 'a harmonious society should be a rule of law society'.[17] The rationale behind this link, as explained by *Luo Guo*, CPC Secretary responsible for legal issues, is that the government needs to 'get better at using legal methods to harmonize economic relationships' and use the legal system to help citizens settle their problems. This would reduce social conflicts triggered by conflicts of interests, with the promise that the legal system must be fair if it is to encourage individuals to turn to law to resolve their disputes.[18]

B LEGALITY CRUCIAL FOR REGIME LEGITIMACY

There is a widespread conviction among Western China scholars that economic reforms in the PRC, over the past 25 years, have rendered ideology obsolete. According to conventional wisdom, economic performance is left as the only factor to bestow regime legitimacy to the Chinese party-state, implying that Communist one-party rule will immediately plunge into a serious legitimacy crisis should economic success falter one day.[19]

14. 'Property Rights in China: China's Next Revolution', *The Economist*, 8 Mar. 2007.
15. Steven Xu.
16. Jasmine Wang, 'Number of Illegal Land Grabs Soars', *South China Morning Post*, 22 Mar. 2007.
17. '16th CPC Central Committee: Building a Harmonious Society', CCTV Special, 21 Nov. 2006.
18. Andrew Batson, 'China Builds Commerce Codes', *Wall Street Journal*, 2 Mar. 2007.
19. H. Holbig, *Ideological Reform and Political Legitimacy in China: Challenges in the Post-Jiang Era*, German Institute of Global and Area Studies, Working Paper No. 18, 6 Mar. 2006.

Heike Holbig rightly questions whether economic growth alone is sufficient to sustain the ruling legitimacy of the CPC in China. She suggested that the 'Three Represents'[20] put forward by former PRC President *Jiang Zemin* and the slogan of 'Building a Harmonious Society'[21] introduced by current CPC leader *Hu Jintao* are evidence that despite remarkable economic achievements, the Chinese regime remains vulnerable to legitimacy crises and has sought to use these ideological innovations to prevent and overcome legitimacy crises.[22] One can agree with Holbig's observation that economic success does not immunize the CPC from legitimacy crises. On the contrary, the changing economic environment and widening Chinese income disparities have demonstrated that the CPC may well be going through a legitimacy crisis at the moment.[23]

However, this study argues that ideological innovations alone would not enable the CPC to weather the current social challenges and sustain its legitimacy. A closer look at the ideological discourses of *Jiang* and *Hu* suggests that the CPC is in fact using legality, or the notion of 'ruling the country according to law' or the rule of law, to regenerate and maintain regime legitimacy during times of profound changes in Chinese society. Recent evidence indicates that the CPC has realized the increasing role of law as source of legitimacy, and has used it to its advantage.[24] With mounting income discrepancies and more frequent incidents of

---

20. See Part I, Ch. 2, Section II.B and II.C.1 for the origin and meaning of the 'Three Represents'.
21. See for example, *Communiqué of the Sixth Plenum of the 16th CPC Central Committee*, Xinhua, 11 Oct. 2006, an English translation of the Communiqué of the Sixth Plenum of the 16th CPC Central Committee was published by Xinhua on 12 Oct. 2006, available at <www.china.org.cn/english/government/183627.htm>, 16 Aug. 2007; and 專題:中共十六屆六中全會 – 落實科學發展觀·構建和諧社會, 央視國際, <www.cctv.com> ('16th CPC Central Committee: Building a Harmonious Society', CCTV Special, 21 Nov. 2006).
22. H. Holbig, 3, and 19–29.
23. Modern Chinese history has witnessed several major disillusions on the part of the Chinese people. The fall of the *Qing* dynasty and the establishment of a new republic did not bring about a stronger country or better livelihood for the people. Instead, it was followed by a period of chaos during which warlords fought against each other in a divided country. The defence against the Japanese invasion in World War II and the triumph of the CPC over the Nationalist Party in the Civil War that ended in 1949 did not result in an equitable and stable society. Instead, the Great Leap Forward initiated by *Mao Zedong* left millions starving to death and the Cultural Revolution extinguished the little remaining hope the Chinese might have on communist ideology. The drive towards a socialist market economy under *Deng Xiaoping*'s rule has so far made only a portion of the population in excess of one billion richer, which also means the poverty gap growing wider. The June Fourth *Tiananmen* Square events in 1989 remain a taboo and still taint the ruling authorities today.
24. Before 2002, official statements, documents, and media reports used the phrase 'rule by law' or 'ruling the country according to law'. However, in recent years, official sources have been using the term 'rule of law'. The key difference between the two concepts arguably hinges on whether the ruling CPC is subject to the law, or simply using laws to achieving is ruling objectives. See Y. Zheng, 'From Rule by Law to Rule of Law? A Realistic View of China's Legal Development', *China Perspectives* 25 (1999): 31–43; and J. Li, 'Socialist Rule of Law with Chinese Characteristics', *Issues and Studies* 43, no. 1 (2007): 115–157, for the two concepts in the Chinese context and a discussion on the meaning of 'socialist rule of law'.

social unrest, the Chinese leadership increasingly uses law to hold the society together and to provide rules-based solutions to tensions triggered by social inequality. It does so by combating corruption with high profile prosecutions, by letting the citizens express their grievances and redress injustices through legal channels, such as suing local authorities. Last but not least, the leadership acknowledges that the government is bound by law and should govern according to law.

The CPC also uses judicial proceedings more frequently against corrupt party members, in addition to party disciplinary procedures. Its decision to prosecute nine Communist party members and high level officials in Shanghai, for instance, is one of many examples showing that the Chinese leadership is determined to maintain its ruling legitimacy and to fight corruption through law. Shortly before the start of the NPC annual session in March 2007, it was reported that the CPC decided to expel nine members, including the former chief of the Shanghai Labour and Social Security Bureau, and that it had referred the case known as the 'pension corruption scandal' to prosecutors for indictment. The scandal had already cost Shanghai's Communist Party Secretary *Chen Liangyu* his job. The Shanghai officials, all related to *Chen* in one way or the other, were accused of taking bribes and channelling contributions to the city's pension and housing fund, an amount to CNY 3.7 billion (USD 483 million), into risky real estate and other investments.[25] As the *China Daily* noted, '*Chen* was the first member of the CPC's Political Bureau to come under judicial investigation on corruption charges. His fall served as a powerful answer [retort] to the popular belief that the CPC's vows of iron fists were never meant for those in high positions.'[26]

Post-WTO accession legal developments have led to a re-distribution of influence between political power and legal authority. While China remains a one-party system and the political power of the CPC cannot be challenged through legal means, current trends indicate that the once lop-sided balance between politics and law is beginning to tip towards increased respect of legal authority. In recent years, the CPC has sought to buttress its legitimacy through internal reform, such as enlarging its membership by accepting private entrepreneurs as members, and broadening the basis for local party leadership elections. And above all, it stresses the importance of adherence to 'the rule of law'.[27]

Studies in political legitimacy point out that conformity to rules (legality) is one of the necessary criteria of regime legitimacy, while breach of rules and

25. 'Shanghai to Prosecute 9 Government, State Industry Officials over Pension Scandal', *Associated Press*, 2 Mar. 2007.
26. 'Our Corruption Busters', *China Daily*, 14 Feb. 2007; Zheng Xiaoyu, the former head of China's State Food and Drug Administration was sentenced to death and executed on 10 Jul. 2007, for a corruption conviction. It was the first time a death sentence was imposed on an Chinese official of his rank since 2000, see Chris Buckley & Ben Blanchard, 'China Executes Ex-drug Chief amid Health Scandals', *Reuters*, 10 Jul. 2007, at <www.reuters.com/article/worldNews/idUSPEK220682007071O>, 12 Jul. 2007, and David Barboza, 'A Chinese Reformer Betrays His Cause, and Pays', *International Herald Tribune*, 12 Jul. 2007.
27. *Communiqué of the Sixth Plenum of the 16th CPC Central Committee.*

legitimacy deficit (such as absence of shared beliefs) can lead to the breakdown of ruling legitimacy.[28] The inevitable nexus between respecting legal authority and the continuous rule of the CPC was explicit in the final report that *Zhang Zemin* presented to the 16th Congress of the CPC in 2002, entitled 'Improve the Socialist Legal System':

> We must see to it that there are laws to go by, the laws are observed and strictly enforced, and law-breakers are prosecuted. To adapt to the new situation characterized by the development of a socialist market economy, all-round social progress and China's accession to the WTO, we will strengthen legislation and improve its quality and will have formulated a socialist system of laws with Chinese characteristics by the year 2010. We must see to it that all people are equal before the law. We should tighten supervision over law enforcement, promote the exercise of administrative functions according to law, safeguard judicial justice and raise the level of law enforcement so that laws are strictly implemented. We must safeguard the uniformity and sanctity of the legal system and prevent or overcome local and departmental protectionism. We will extend and standardize legal services and provide effective legal aid. We should give more publicity to the legal system so that the people are better educated in law. In particular, we will enhance the public servants' awareness of law and their ability to perform their official duties according to law. Party members and cadres, especially leading cadres, should play an exemplary role in abiding by the Constitution and other laws.[29]

The principles cited in the 16th CPC Congress report, closely corresponding to the WTO's systemic requirements on Chinese law, have been further incorporated into the Chinese legal system since 2002. After *Hu Jintao* took over party leadership at the 16th CPC Congress in November 2002, he choose the occasion of the 20th anniversary of the promulgation and implementation of the PRC Constitution for his first landmark address on the CPC and legality.[30] Asserting that the PRC Constitution is 'the basic guideline for running the state and ensuring social stability', *Hu* said that the Constitution 'also provides the legal guarantee for the CPC to take the leadership of the country'.[31] He announced that '[r]unning the country by law is the basic strategy for the Party to lead the people in running the country', and that party officials at various levels should act in strict compliance with laws:[32]

---

28. H. Holbig, 10.
29. Full text of *Jiang Zemin*'s report at 16th Party congress, *China Daily*, <www.chinadaily.com.cn>, 16 Mar. 2007.
30. *Hu Jintao*, 'Honour Constitution's Guarantee for Citizens' Rights', speech at a rally marking the twentieth anniversary of the promulgation and implementation of the Constitution, 4 Dec. 2002, Beijing; unofficial English translation of the speech available at <www.humanrights.cn/zt/magazine/200402004823153254.htm>, 14 Aug. 2007.
31. While the substantive provisions of the PRC constitution do not mention the CPC at all, CPC leadership is affirmed as a fundamental principle in the Preamble.
32. In this speech, *Hu Jintao* also projected his reading of the Chinese legal system then: 'A socialist law system with Chinese characteristics centring on the Constitution has basically taken

'The Constitution is not only a norm every citizens should observe in behaviour, but also *a legal weapon* with which they can safeguard their citizens' rights.'[33]

Hu's remarks on the link between the CPC and the law can be seen as a precursor to the current CPC leadership's top priority encapsulated by the slogan 'Building a Harmonious Society.' The campaign to redirect the CPC ideology started with another important speech by *Hu* on 19 February 2005, on the occasion of a training course attended by major provincial and ministerial level party leaders at the Party School of the CPC Central Committee in Beijing, where *Hu*'s role as Secretary-General of the CPC was emphasized.[34] 'A harmonious society will feature democracy, the rule of law, equity, justice, sincerity, amity and vitality',[35] *Hu* said. He stated that '[t]he rule of law is important for the promotion, realization and safeguarding of a harmonious society. This principle should be rigorously implemented in all political, administrative and judicial sectors to ensure the powerful be checked and accountable for their misdeeds.'[36] In sum, this doctrine focuses on efficiency and justice based on the rule of law,[37] instilled with a touch of Confucian virtues of maintaining social stability and harmony.[38] The emphasis on social justice and the use of legal means to resolve socio-economic conflicts represents a shift of focus from economic growth, as in the past twenty-five years, to social issues and sustainable development. The premise of the harmonious society doctrine is the leadership of the CPC, while party leaders repeatedly stress that the party should lead according to the rule of law and that all party officials should act in strict compliance with the law.

A 2004 study *The Rule of Law and the Ruling Model of the Communist Party of China,*[39] initiated after the 16th CPC Congress, already stressed the subtle difference between the CPC's leadership, which remained unchallenged, and the *style* and the *modalities* by which the CPC rules. The study, conducted under the

---

shape. There are by and large laws to abide by in all aspects of the country's economic, political, cultural and social life. The administrative organs at different levels have set up and consolidated their law-enforcement mechanisms. By performing their administrative power in strict compliance with law, the way and procedures in which they exercise their power have been further standardized and legalized, and the legal system of administrative reviews, administrative procedures and state compensation has been established. We are actively carrying out reforms in the judicial system to promote and ensure judicial justice. We are also encouraging judicial and procuratorial organs at different levels to exercise their judicial and prosecution power independently and justly.'

33. Emphasis added.
34. Building a harmonious society was later formally adopted by the Sixth Plenum of the CPC's 16th Central Committee on 11 Oct. 2006; see for example, Maureen Fan, 'China's Party Leadership Declares New Priority: Harmonious Society', *Washington Post*, 12 Oct. 2006.
35. 'Building Harmonious Society CPC's TOP Task', *Xinhua*, 20 Feb. 2005.
36. 'Building Harmonious Society Crucial for China's progress: *Hu*', *China Daily*, 20 Feb. 2007.
37. Jiefen Li, 118.
38. See, for example, Shaohua Hu, 'Confucianism and Contemporary Chinese Politics', *Politics & Policy* 35, no. 1 (2007) 136–153.
39. 張恆山等, 法治與黨的執政方式研究, 北京, 法律出版社2004年; Zhang Hengshan et al., *A Study on the Rule of Law and the Ruling Model of the Communist Party of China* (Beijing: Law Press China, 2004).

auspices of the CPC by Professor *Zhang Hengshan*, Deputy Dean of the Department of Politics and Law, a party think tank, recommended to the CPC to lead according to rule of law principles. Some suggestions, especially those concerning the relationship between the CPC and the NPC and the judiciary, and constitutional rule, are taken seriously.

There is growing consensus among China scholars that the harmonious society doctrine represents an ideological adjustment of the CPC to use the rule of law discourse to consolidate its ruling legitimacy amidst mounting social tensions. Assessments differ, however, as to whether this can be effective and if the CPC's instrumental approach of using legality for its own legitimacy can lead to a genuine rule of law system.[40] This book argues that despite the uncertain status of the CPC in the Chinese legal system[41] and regardless of its motives, the CPC's recent focus on the rule of law has led to enhanced legal awareness within the party, the government, and Chinese society. The official endorsement, and indeed encouragement,[42] of the rule of law, and the use of law to resolve social conflicts and address injustice all have empowered Chinese citizens to use legality to hold party and government officials accountable. This trend, coupled with the growing popularity of some major rule of law principles in China, offers hope for the future of Chinese legal development.

C A Boost in Public Reliance on Law and the Legal System

As discussed, the change of the non-litigious tradition in Chinese society represents a significant development of China's legal reform. According to *Xiao Yang*, President of the SPC, the number of administrative lawsuits has dramatically increased, totalling 639,736 cases between 2000 and 2006. About 30% of the plaintiffs won their lawsuits.[43] Administrative lawsuits are commonly called '民告官

40. See, for example, J. Li; T. Heberer & G. Schubert, 'Political Reform and Regime Legitimacy in Contemporary China', *The German Journal on Contemporary Asia, ASIEN* 99 (2006): 9–28; C. Li, 'Hu's Policy Shift and the Tuanpai's Coming-of-Age', *China Leadership Monitor* 15 (2005): 1–16, <media.hoover.org/documents/clm15_lc.pdf>, 15 Aug. 2007, and W. Lam, 'Socialism with a Harmonious Face: Hu Jintao's Plan for Reform', *China Brief* 4, no. 20 (October 2004), The Jamestown Foundation, October 2004, <jamestown.org/china_brief/article.php?articleid=2372922>, 14 Aug. 2007.
41. See Part I, Ch. 2, Section II.B.1 and this chapter, Section II.
42. The Chinese government has been increasing its funding to provide legal aids to those who cannot afford the costs of legal proceedings. Procedures for access to courts and initialling a case have been simplified and the litigation fee reduced since 1 Apr. 2007. All are efforts to encourage and engage the people to channel their grievances and resolve social conflicts through legal means. See for example, 'China Establishes Legal Aid Fund for Senior Citizens', *Xinhua*, 8 Jun. 2006, 'China Launches Network to Provide Legal Aid for Migrant Workers', *Xinhua*, 26 Feb. 2007, *Xinhua* 11 Mar. 2006, 'Fairness, Justice Urged to Calm Social Conflicts', *Xinhua*, 31 Jan. 2007, and 'Judicial Reform to Ensure Justice', *Outlook Weekly*.
43. 'Serve Justly or be Sued', *China Daily*, Hong Kong edition, Editorial, 10 Apr. 2007.

Min Gao Guan'[44] in Chinese, and a literal translation refers to 'people suing government officials'.

Several reasons account for the trend of increased lawsuits against public authorities. As China moves towards a market economy, the traditionally predominant role of the government and an administrative-led system in Chinese society yield to market forces, regulated by transparent laws and rules. Such changes have prompted frequent conflicts between administrative power and the rights of individuals. A stronger role of law, the redefinition of the role between market and government, the availability of laws, mechanisms, and resources[45] for citizens to resolve disputes through legal channels, and the spill-over effects of the WTO-driven rule of law principles, as well as the necessity for the government and the CPC to rely on law to maintain both its legitimacy and social stability – all factors contribute to the Chinese society's increased emphasis on the law and the remarkable rise of litigation.[46] A *China Daily* editorial aptly sums up these attitude changes:

> Everybody is fallible, including government departments and officials. But never before in China's history of more than 2,000 years has there been a legal code allowing ordinary citizens to sue their government. Governments were supposed to manage public affairs in the best interests of the citizens. Citizens were never supposed to challenge the authority of the government. It is not easy for governments and their officials to change from ruling the citizens to serving the citizens.... It is no longer rare for individual citizens to bring a government department to court. These cases push governments at various levels to better use their power and integrate service to the public into their work.[47]

A well-publicized case in which twelve farmers successfully sued the provincial government of the eastern province of Zhejiang and its Governor further illustrates the citizens' changing attitude. The case concerned a land requisition project in Fenghua, Zhejiang. A decision by the local authorities in May 2004, approved by the provincial government, earmarked a three-acre plot of land for property development. Local peasants living there, dissatisfied with the compensation offered, took the local government to court arguing, inter alia, that the approval process had been illegal. After losing the administrative review against the local government in August 2005, the farmers unsuccessfully sought to persuade the provincial

---

44. A lawyer in Nanjing has established a website entitled '*Min Gao Guan*' ('people suing government officials'), which provides basic advice and collects jurisprudence of such cases from different parts of China, see <www.mingaoguan.com>.
45. For example, increased funding for legal aid; new projects launched to make legal aid more accessible to vulnerable groups such as migrant workers; simplified procedures for access to courts; and litigation fee reduced since 1 Apr. 2007.
46. According to the SPC's annual report to the NPC 2007, courts throughout China dealt with over 8 million cases in 2006.
47. 'Serve Justly or be Sued', *China Daily*, Hong Kong edition, Editorial, 10 Apr. 2007.

government to rescind its decision. *Zhang Zhaoliang* and eleven farmers appealed to a higher court, which ruled that the provincial government had acted illegally. The farmers won the case and the property development was brought to a halt.[48] In an interview,[49] the lead plaintiff later explained that the property development and the offer of inadequate compensation had prompted him to learn as much as possible about the available administrative and legal challenges.

Traditionally, local residents would travel to provincial capital or even to Beijing and complain to key officials to resolve their problems. This type of action is commonly called '上访 *San Fang*' in Chinese, literally translated as 'to visit those at a higher level'. Nowadays, taking the local authorities and officials to courts tends to become an alternative preferable for conflict resolution for many, such as *Zhang*.

Zhang's struggle is typical of the increasing number of Chinese who ponder whether to resort to legal tools to address their grievances. The positive outcome in his case, however, remains surprising to some, given that the institutional features in the Chinese court system that make it difficult for judges to discharge their duties impartially and independently. Many local courts still rely on local governments and parallel party organs for their funding and for judicial appointments, therefore making judges susceptible to executive and party interference. In some provinces, courts at the county level begin to transfer cases involving local authorities to the courts in other counties, to reduce the possibility of interference by local governments. In Taizhou, Zhejiang province, for example, some courts transfer such cases to other jurisdictions. According to news reports, during the first twelve months of this practice, government respondents lost forty-five out of seventy-two cases (about 63%), compared to the 13% who lost their case in the year preceding the new measure.[50] In an effort to increase transparency of legal proceedings, the High Court of Zhejiang, in April 2007, first authorized live webcast of proceedings in a civil case between two companies. It was announced that more courts would begin live webcast coverage of their proceedings.[51]

Given the above developments, the non-litigious mentality of Chinese citizens may soon belong to history. A Chinese social scientist has observed that in recent years, peasants in rural China are increasingly using the state's own laws to protect

---

48. The judgment, in Chinese ((2006) 浙行终字第11号张国其等12人诉浙江省人民政府土地行政复议案), is available at the official website of Zhejiang courts, <www.zjcourt.cn/portal/html/20060509000004/20060630000009.html>, 12 Apr. 2007. For news coverage of the case in English, see, for example, Wan Lixin, 'Government-Funded Courts Find Ways to Deliver Justice', *Shanghai Daily*, 13 Apr. 2007, available at <www.shanghaidaily.com/sp/article/2007/200704/20070413/article_312450.htm>, 13 Apr. 2007.
49. 'Zhang Zhaolian: I Use the Law to Correct the Government', CCTV, www.cctv.com, in Chinese (张召良: 我用法律为政府部门纠错), transcript available at *Xinhua*, <xinhuanet.com>.
50. L. Wan.
51. 'Public Welcome Live Web Cast of Proceedings by the High Court of Zhejiang', official website of Zhejiang courts, <www.zjcourt.cn>, 13 Apr. 2007.

their rights and engage in lawful resistance. 'The peasants use laws, regulations and orders by the central government as the standard by which to measure local governments' behavior.'[52] Peasants 'began to actively use the law itself to defend not only their own statutory rights but also those of others',[53] according to a study on social conflict in rural China published by *Yu Jianrong*. This development, coupled with the rule of law principles and the stronger role of law, contributes to enhancing a rule of law culture in China. Increased faith in the law and the citizens' frequent use of laws to fight for their rights are particularly important at this juncture of China's legal reform.[54] It is through such legal proceedings and the consistent use of law that the persistent problems of weak implementation of Chinese laws may be improved.

II RISKS AND CHALLENGES

Continued weak enforcement of laws and judicial decisions may still put achievements of the above at risk. If these weak links in China's legal reform are not addressed and solved, they may prompt general disillusion among the people, to the effect that no matter how impressive the legislative efforts are, they remain ineffective in daily reality. Another challenge to be surmounted concerns the uncertain status of the ruling CPC in Chinese law. While party influence is pervasive and party members are at all levels institutionally intertwined with the government structure, the status of the CPC is hardly addressed in Chinese laws, except the Preamble of the Constitution. If China wants to achieve what the Chinese leadership labels the 'running of the government according to the rule of law',[55] the issue of subjecting the CPC to the law must be addressed both de jure and de facto. China has enjoyed a fair degree of stability in the past quarter of the century, which allowed the government to focus on economic reform with remarkable success. However, some signs suggest that if pressing problems such as widening income and regional disparities, social inequality, and rapid marginalization of vulnerable groups continue to grow, an escalation of large-scale social conflicts is inevitable and the resulting instability may jeopardize the sustainability of continuous development.

---

52. J. Yu, 'Social Conflict in Rural China', *China Security* 3, no. 2 (Spring 2007): 2–17, 9.
53. *Ibid.*, 10.
54. Other cases suggest that it is no longer rare for ordinary people to sue the government and win. See, for example, Cai Li, 'Court Ruling a Win for Equal Rights', *China Daily*, Hong Kong edition, 27 Mar. 2007, in which seven women with rural residency successfully sued the local authorities for gender-discrimination concerning female residents' rights to build houses. The 'Min Gao Guan' (people suing government officials) website mentioned earlier also listed 37 successful cases in different parts of China, see <www.mingaoguan.com>, last visited 13 Jul. 2007.
55. J. Yu.

A WEAK IMPLEMENTATION RISKS DISILLUSION

Insufficient implementation of laws and weak enforcement of court rulings risk jeopardizing public confidence on the recently improved Chinese legal system. Various sections of this book have examined the problems of implementing laws and enforce judgments and their consequences.[56] It is important to point out here that the strengthened role of law in policy-making, the growing prevalence of rule of law principles in Chinese society, the enhanced legal awareness across all sectors, and the boosted public reliance on the legal system analysed earlier may well lead to gradual improvement in the implementation of laws in China. WTO-induced system-wide changes in laws, such as the ALL and the transparency ordinance, do afford individuals a new legal basis for challenging non-enforcement or improper application of laws. But for these legal challenges to produce meaningful results, the problems of persistent judicial irregularities and non-compliance with court rulings must be addressed. Below are some examples of latest efforts by the Chinese leadership to address these challenges.

The problems have become such that the official publication *China Daily* ran an editorial indicating that the CPC had decided to introduce a new mechanism to ensure enforcement of court rulings. 'We cannot afford to neglect legitimacy',[57] it said, and it applauded a decision by the CPC central authorities to tackle these deep-rooted enforcement problems. The editorial said the decision was 'a sensible starting point for consolidating the authority of the law'.[58] The emphasis here is on the CPC because the mechanism to improve the enforcement of court rulings and implementation of laws came as part of the decision of the Sixth Plenum of the sixteenth Central Committee of the CPC in 2006.[59] The rationale behind the mechanism, according to the CPC leadership, is that the absence of meaningful accountability mechanisms has led to what it called the 'rampant resistance to the enforcement of unfavourable court rulings'.[60]

As a result, the CPC Communiqué said:

> not only individuals and private enterprises, but State firms and government offices disregard court decisions without paying a price. One of the most annoying aspects of this phenomenon [is] barricades erected by local judicial or administrative authorities against court decisions considered to go against local interests.[61]

Details of the new measures are yet to emerge; even though available information suggests that there will be 'a nationwide information network on the implementation

56. See, for example, Part I, Ch. 2, Sections II.C and II.D and Part III, Ch. 6, Section II.C.
57. 'Ignored Court Rulings to be Legally Enforced', *China Daily*, Hong Kong edition, Editorial, 25 Jan. 2005.
58. *Ibid*.
59. 'Communiqué of the Sixth Plenum of the 16th CPC Central Committee', *Xinhua*, and 關於進–步加強人民法院, 人民檢察院工作的決定.
60. *Ibid*.
61. *Ibid*.

of court rulings and a database containing records of objections to court rulings'.[62] Part of the project would be to 'regulate enforcement and promote fairness' as well as to 'eradicate local and departmental protectionism', which made the 'talk of the rule of law previously sound hollow'.[63] The SPC is in the process of setting up the information network and database which would register enforcement information of millions of cases adjudicated by courts at different levels nationwide. The data would be used to track down and ultimately hold accountable those who ignore court rulings.[64]

According to SPC President *Xiao Yang*, in response to 'the people's strongly expressed view over the difficulties in enforcing court rulings',[65] a series of measures have been put in place. In the first half of 2006, the SPC and related authorities focused on clearing court judgments that still had to be enforced. The measures included investigations into the reasons for non-enforcement on 'a case by case basis', and prosecution of those who were legally responsible for non-compliance. *Xiao Yang* reported at the NPC 2007 annual session that some 78,000 judgments, involving an estimated total of CNY 216 billion (USD 30 billion), were enforced as a result. He added that in the last two months of 2006, the SPC, in follow-up actions designed to correct irregularities detected during the initial clearance process, referred eighty-five allegedly involved judicial and law-enforcement officials for prosecution. The SPC also reported that the newly developed information network and judgments enforcement database had been operational since 1 January 2007. The database would not only help monitor the situation of the implementation of court rulings and enhance judicial transparency, but also provide systematic information and evidence for holding accountable those who seek to obstruct compliance with the law.[66]

B UNCERTAIN LEGAL STATUS OF THE CPC

As reflected in the discussion about the Chinese leadership's determination to improve judicial enforcement, implementation of laws and govern the country in accordance with the rule of law, the CPC, as in all other major aspects of governance in China, plays a central role at both policy and operational levels. The uncertainty of legal status of the CPC goes beyond theoretical concerns and poses formidable challenges to the credibility of the Chinese legal system and its development towards the rule of law.

62. 司法体制改革强化公正, '瞭望', 2006年02月09日 ('Judicial Reform to Ensure Justice', *Outlook Weekly*, 9 Feb. 2006).
63. *Ibid.*
64. *Outlook Weekly*, 9 Feb. 2006.
65. Xiao Yang, President of the SPC, Report of the Work of Supreme People's Court, delivered at the Fifth Session of the Tenth National People's Congress, 13 Mar. 2007, available at Xinhuanet.
66. *Ibid.*

To take the anti-corruption campaign as an example, officials who have taken bribes or obstructed justice should be prosecuted through the criminal justice system. However, one can observe that most, if not all, individuals who hold government positions are at the same time CPC members. In these cases, holding government officials legally accountable for their crimes is primarily treated as an issue of party discipline, and only secondarily as an issue to be handled by the Chinese legal system.

All instances of prosecution of officials discussed in previous parts went through a dual-track process. This means that the law breaking officials are first investigated by the CCDI of the CPC and then, if appropriate, referred for prosecution. Unlike in the Chinese legal system, continuous efforts to improve transparency and due process of legal proceedings do not apply to CPC disciplinary procedures. Investigations and disciplinary proceedings under the CPC are governed by party rules. They are not open to the public and the announcement of the results of such investigations remains at the discretion of the party leadership. According to the anti-corruption body of the CPC, in 2006 'nearly 100,000 members of the Communist Party were penalized for corruption, and 3,530 were handed over to prosecutors'.[67] It remains unknown to the general public why over 96,000 party officials, though sanctioned for corruption under party disciplinary procedures, did not face legal prosecution. Does it mean that in those cases, party discipline alone was sufficient to punish corrupt officials and to exempt them from the criminal justice system? According to the state news agency *Xinhua*, '[c]orruption and commercial bribery have become a social problem in China, arousing public anger. The fight against corruption and building a clean government is seen as an urgent issue for the Communist Party of China.'[68] As long as party officials are treated differently in the Chinese legal system, the CPC's fight against corruption and, indeed, for securing its legitimacy, will remain a thorn in the Chinese legal system.

The CPC uncertain legal status also poses significant challenges to the daily operation of the Chinese legal system. As the infamous 'seed case' reveals, the parallel party supervision of judicial activities alongside the state structure is a major obstacle to judicial autonomy in the administration of justice. Judicial appointments and the budgets of local courts largely continue to be controlled by the corresponding local governments and people's congresses, which in turn are under the supervision of local CPC leaders.

At the centre of the seed case is Judge *Li Huijuan* of Luoyang Middle Court, Henan province, who is also a CPC member. In 2003, Judge *Li* presided over a civil case which involved a dispute concerning the prices of seeds. A provincial law stipulated that seed prices should be set by the state while a national law, as a result of relinquishing price control after China's WTO accession, favoured

---

67. Ng Tze Wei, 'Anti-graft Fight to Remain Centred on Corrupt Officials', *South China Morning Post*, 13 Mar. 2007.
68. 'Chief Justice: 9 Provincial-Level Officials Convicted for Corruption in 2006', *Xinhua*, 13 Mar. 2007.

prevailing market rates. Judge *Li* declared the provincial law invalid because it contradicted the national law, in accordance with the provisions of the *Law on Legislation*. She ruled against the interests of the local government and party officials in the local people's congress. Henan Province officials angrily complained that the ruling was politically flawed, and the Luoyang Middle Court's Discipline Committee suspended her.[69]

Li left for Beijing to seek help from an association of female judges, which promised to contact the SPC on her behalf. Her case soon attracted the attention of Chinese media and legal reform scholars. Several lawyers formally requested that the NPC review the situation. A conference was organized at Tsinghua University to debate the case and other issues about judicial autonomy. Ultimately, media attention and intervention by legal scholars saved *Li*'s job. She returned to her work in mid-2004, and the NPCSC announced the establishment of a review panel to mediate conflicts of law. The same year, Henan province's High Court reheard the seed case and ruled exactly as *Li* had done, though it criticized her for invalidating the provincial law.[70]

In another case, judges in Hunan were sanctioned by the CPC's Discipline Inspection Commission for exposing the chief judge's corruption.[71] In May 2004, *Wang Guofeng* and other judges accused the chief judge of Hunan of unlawful misconduct during a political study session of the Court of Shuanfeng County, Hunan. Although the chief judge was later dismissed and transferred to another post, the Discipline Inspection Commission punished the three informers for violating party and administrative discipline. A team of the local party committee investigated the allegations and found that the incident had disrupted the court's work. According to news report, a judge involved in exposing the corruption said that punishing them in the name of party and administrative discipline amounted to contempt of law, while another judge argued that the rule of law should be above any organization, or group rules or discipline.[72]

Abuse of power by party officials increasingly triggers resentment among local citizens. Hundreds of policemen stormed and blocked off a village in Human province after fighting erupted between villagers and local party officials accused of illegally seizing public property. The clash occurred during a meeting in which locals accused the village party secretary of illegal sale of a large plot of land and trees, which belonged to the whole village.[73] Undoubtedly, unequivocal statements from the CPC leadership requesting party officials to behave in strict compliance with laws under the latest doctrine of 'building a harmonious society' represent a positive move. However, the current approach of guaranteeing CPC

---

69. Jim Yardley, 'A Young Judge Tests China's Legal System', *The New York Times*, 28 Nov. 2005.
70. *Ibid.*
71. Zhang Huayong, 'Hunan Judge is Punished for Exposing Corrupt Chief Judge', *Sina Net*, 22 Jan. 2005, at <www.sina.com>.
72. *Ibid.*
73. He Huifeng, 'Man Dies in Skirmish with Enraged Villagers', *South China Morning Post*, 29 Mar. 2007.

leadership in the Preamble of the Constitution but leaving the CPC out of the substantive constitutional provisions and Chinese law is flawed. It is hardly conducive to better compliance with the law by the CPC itself and by those with senior party positions.

The dual-track approach to punishing corrupt party officials – party disciplinary procedures first and possibly criminal procedures – shows that there can be two sets of rules in achieving justice. One applies to common people while the other serves as a cushion between CPC officials and the legal system. The healthy development of the Chinese legal system, the authority of law, and, indeed, the ruling legitimacy of the CPC leadership requires further clarifications of the CPC's status in Chinese law. Rhetoric about legality is insufficient. Such clarifications should ultimately subject the CPC to the law through appropriate legislation and institutional arrangements.

C Response to Social Conflicts: Rules-Based Approach or Power Politics?

The Chinese leadership has recently officially acknowledged that 'there exist many contradictions and problems, which affect social harmony'.[74] To address these problems, it has set the year 2020 as a deadline for achieving the following:

> [T]he socialist democratic and legal system is further improved; the fundamental principle of administering the country according to law is implemented in an all-around way; people's rights and interests enjoy concrete respect and guarantee; [the] widening of gap between urban and rural development and development between different regions is gradually reversed; a reasonable and orderly income distribution pattern takes shape in general; [the] wealth of households increase universally and people lead more affluent lives; [the] employment rate is relatively high and a social security system covering both urban and rural residents is established in general.[75]

These objectives exemplify what the Chinese leadership considers to be the most pressing issues threatening social stability and its ruling legitimacy. They are insufficient concrete guarantees of the people's rights and interests, growing disparities in rural-urban and regional developments, uneven income distribution and a widening poverty gap,[76] worsening unemployment and underemployment, and

---

74. 'Communiqué of the Sixth Plenum of the 16th CPC Central Committee', *Xinhua.*
75. *Ibid.*
76. *Key Indicators 2007: Inequality in Asia*, Asian Development Bank (ADB), August 2007; <www.adb.org/Documents/Books/Key_Indicators/2007/default.asp>, 17 Aug. 2007. The report found that relative inequality had widened more substantially in China than any other Asian country except for Nepal. China's Gini coefficient, designed to measure wealth inequality, increased from 40.7 in 1993 to 47.3 in 2004 (a zero coefficient means perfect wealth equality, a 100 coefficient means extreme unequal wealth distribution, with one person owning everything). The ABD pointed out that while increased income disparities were not unusual in

inadequate social security protection for vulnerable groups such as laid-off workers of SOEs and migrant workers. A scholar from the Chinese Academy of Social Sciences, an official think tank, suggests that fair constitutionalism is required in China to avert a revolution:

> In Chinese society today, large-scale conflicts are most likely to erupt in rural versus urban areas. This is primarily due to a combination of the central government's inability to control the vast and remote areas of China, and the lack of a clear set of common interests among the highly diverse populations of rural China. In the past ten years, China has experienced a rapid period of transition from a planned to a market economy. In the process, farmers' economic interests have grown far more slowly than the national average. This widening 'wealth gap' has made social justice a focal issue for disgruntled peasants. Peasant interests have also been gravely impacted by the huge tide of land appropriation in recent years.
>
> In the next decade or two, China will likely enter a period of frequent social conflict. Peasants are likely to join hands with workers and members of the lower intellectual class and confront the elitist alliance that dominates society, creating political, economic, and social upheaval in China. *To prevent social unrest from triggering a revolution, it is imperative to address issues of social injustice as well as create the effective channels for their expression. Such a mechanism must be built upon fair constitutionalism* and reform of the core values in Chinese society.[77]

Social unrest is not necessarily harmful for development and can have positive implications for policy changes and systemic improvements. However, if social conflicts remain unaddressed and are left to escalate, they can lead to large-scale riots and disruption of ongoing reforms. The Chinese leadership's approach in dealing with social unrest arguably is the most important factor affecting the country's future. In this regard, the focus of concern of this study is whether the Chinese government, when faced with these mounting challenges, can persist in addressing them according to and through the law.

It is suggested that a rules-based approach to resolving conflicts within Chinese society is the only viable and sustainable approach for the Chinese leadership. Such an approach will help generate social consensus, offer transparent and legally entrenched policies to redressing injustices, enhance the authority of law, and strengthen the legal system's capacity to deal with new challenges. Judging from the official discourse over the doctrine of harmonious society and adherence

---

countries such as China experiencing rapid economic growth, such extreme differences were socially harmful. The report also added that widening inequality can also threaten growth if it results in social unrest. See, for example, 'Wealth Gap Spreads Across Asia', *BBC News* online, 8 Aug. 2007, <news.bbc.co.uk/2/hi/business/6936525.stm>, and 'Asia's Rich and Poor: For Whosoever Hath, to Him Shall Be Given, and He Shall Have More', *The Economist*, 9 Aug. 2007, <www.economist.com/world/asia/displaystory.cfm?story_id=9616888>, 17 Aug. 2007.

77. J. Yu, 3; emphasis added.

to legality, it is legitimate to argue that strengthening the rule of law constitutes a fundamental pillar of the leadership's approach to alleviate social conflicts. But, if large-scale upheavals threaten the regime, ample historic precedents show that misjudgment or insecurity can trigger brutal suppression by resorting to crude political power or military might. A power politics approach may well suppress social unrest in the short run, but it would only further undermine the regime's legitimacy without addressing the root causes of conflicts. This approach would be detrimental to Chinese legal development, undermine the authority of law, destroy people's confidence in the legal system, and jeopardize the hard-earned achievements from over two decades of legal reform. The signs are that the Chinese leadership has realized the cost of resorting to a power politics path, and, however cautiously and circumspectly, that it will favour adherence to legality and continuous legal reform.

III CONCLUSION: CHINA'S LONG MARCH FORWARD

Eight years after joining the world trading system, China still feel the WTO's significant influence on its economic development and continuous reform. Equally significant is the impact of the WTO rules-based system on the Chinese legal system. The scope of this study is wide because it has assessed the implications of WTO membership for the Chinese legal order from a holistic perspective, and the much stronger role that law plays in Chinese society nowadays. The period covered in the research is long because it began with the salient features in traditional Chinese legal heritage during its dynastic period; continued to lessons learned from pre-WTO legal reforms; detailed a fifteen-year long process of accession negotiations; and examined legal developments in post-WTO accession China until early 2009.

This study set out to verify two hypotheses. Firstly, joining the WTO has enabled China to reform its legal order towards a system that incorporates major rule of law principles. Secondly, the WTO has provided an external impetus that guides Chinese legal reform in a way that domestic forces alone could neither achieve nor sustain. Without the external WTO requirements and post-accession scrutiny, as well as China's interaction with other WTO members, it would be more difficult for these rule of law principles to become institutionalized and entrenched in China.

The examples studied support the postulate that four key rule of law principles have made significant advances in China as a result of WTO membership. In some cases, this study has clearly established a correlation between China's WTO accession and subsequent changes in the Chinese legal system. The most conspicuous examples are new legislation and judicial interpretations introduced by the Chinese government in response to WTO accession commitments.[78]

---

78. See Part II, Ch. 5 Section II.

Most of the new laws introduced by the Chinese government to fulfil its WTO systemic commitments are applicable beyond trade-related matters. This supports the principal postulate of this study that the Chinese government used the WTO accession as an external push to overcome reform bottlenecks.[79] It is not surprising that, for example, a bolstered 'central archiving and review' system[80] to ensure the uniformity in both the contents and the implementation of local and national laws, is applied to all Chinese laws without being restricted to WTO-related laws only. In its efforts to fulfil WTO requirements on the uniform administration of trade-related legal regimes, the government seeks to regain control through measures that enable it to strengthen its influence on the administration of laws nationwide. Initial measures to clear up existing WTO-incompatible local rules and directives have allowed the central government to ensure that local authorities can no longer issue and enforce laws out of line with central policies.

The 2004 ALL[81] and the 2007 *Regulations on Open Government Information*[82] are other examples of 'across the board' efforts which, apart from fulfilling WTO accession commitments, prompt systemic changes by harnessing administrative power to due process of law and better public access to information. Arbitrary administrative power, weak due process, and lack of transparency all acted as constraints for legal reform in pre-WTO China.

Perhaps the most far-reaching significance of WTO-induced systemic measures is that they provide legally prescribed solutions to overcome reform constraints. The solutions are definite policy decisions entrenched in transparent laws, which can be invoked by citizens to assert their rights and to monitor public authorities. Problems of secrecy and arbitrary administrative actions remain, but they are no longer the systemic constraints that hold back China's legal reform.

The impact of the WTO on other areas is less direct but no less significant. The growing acceptance of the principle of non-discrimination in Chinese society is a case in point. The WTO principle of non-discrimination acquired prominence in China during the final accession negotiations and has been invoked frequently in Chinese courts as a general principle of equality. For China, to join the WTO was not purely an exercise in legal procedure of accession to an international treaty. Partly because of the length of the negotiations and partly because of the Chinese government's publicity campaign, Chinese media intensively covered the WTO and its key principles for at least six months before and after accession.[83] The non-discrimination principle has become so entrenched that it is widely cited and applied by Chinese citizens beyond trade issues, and it is often used

79. See Part II, Ch. 3 Section II.
80. Introduced through the 2002 *Ordinance on the Archivist Filing of Regulations and Government Rules*, *Working Procedures for Filing and Reviewing Legislation* and *Working Procedures for Filing and Reviewing Judicial Interpretations*, which together provide a stronger mechanism to implement the 2000 *Law on Legislation*, see Part II, Ch. 5 for details.
81. See analysis in Part III, Ch. 6 Section I.B.
82. See Part III, Ch. 7 Section II.B.
83. For example, a daily Internet search using the key word 'WTO' yielded over 1,000 articles in Chinese print media alone for the period of September 2001 to February 2002.

interchangeably with the notion of equality for all and legal protection of equality.[84] The popularity of the principle is significant, considering that under the traditional Chinese legal system, to treat people differently according to their social stratus was long a dominant element in Chinese legal culture.[85]

China's WTO membership initiated a process which changes the perception of law in Chinese culture, both from the perspective of the government and of the people. This study has examined how the Chinese government increasingly uses law as a policy-making tool, and how law is used to redefine the role between market forces and the government.[86] More increased reliance on law by the government runs parallel with a growing confidence in and more frequent use of the Chinese legal system by individuals and private entities. The new mechanisms established to fulfil China's WTO-related judicial review requirements and the growing public awareness of legality have triggered many cases in which individuals took government authorities to court.[87] This trend signals enhanced justiciability of government action, a factor conducive to a more law-based society as a result of increased legal checks on government power. It also reflects a change of the traditional non-litigious attitude of Chinese citizens.

These attitude changes are fundamental to the continuous development of Chinese legal reform. Since joining the WTO, the Chinese government has been strong in legislative compliance but less so when it comes to the implementation of WTO-inspired new laws, and the enforcement of administrative and judicial decisions arising from them.[88] On strictly WTO-related areas, except the seven cases referred to the WTO dispute settlement level discussed earlier,[89] foreign enterprises remain reluctant to resort to Chinese courts to resolve commercial disputes. The external push from WTO members and foreign investors remains strong in pressing for legislation and policy changes at the WTO and international levels. However, the domestic dynamics arising from legal proceedings initiated by Chinese citizens are the main force for subjecting the new laws and principles to judicial scrutiny. While domestic actors more often go to courts, they are more likely to do so in non-foreign trade-related cases but invoke legislation with those WTO-induced principles such as due process, transparency and equality. By virtue of this continuous process, the four rule of law principles examined in the present study[90] will continue to spill over to other areas of Chinese law.

Finally, the significance of legal authority as an emerging new source of legitimacy in China cannot be overstated. The CPC has realized that law is becoming an option of legitimacy that can cement the nation. The government also uses

---

84. See examples and court cases discussed in Part III, Ch. 7 Sections II.C and II.D.
85. See discussion in Part I, Ch. 1 Sections I.C and Section II.C.
86. See Part III, Ch. 6 Sections I and II.
87. See Part II, Ch. 5 Section II.E and Part III, Ch. 7 Section II.D.
88. See Part III, Ch. 6 Section II, in particular, Section II.C on intellectual property rights laws.
89. The semi-conductor, tax refund, the auto parts, and the enforcement of TRIPS, distribution services, financial information services and export tax breaks cases, see Part II, Ch. 5 Section II.D; and Part III, Ch. 6 Section II.C, respectively.
90. See Part III, Ch. 7 Section II.

law as a means to resolve peacefully growing social conflicts. The efforts put into the *Property Law* and the lengthy public consultation process[91] best reflect the growing importance of law as a kind of social contract.[92] Some studies suggested that 'high rate of unemployment and the risk of social tension' as a result of China's WTO membership may lead to the slowing down of its reform and transformation to market economy.[93] Marginalized groups such as migrant workers and peasants, losers of Chinese economic reform, are increasingly using the law to protect their rights.[94] The changing Chinese perception of law and the enhanced rights awareness in Chinese society will play a crucial role in shaping the future of China.

Lessons learned from contemporary Chinese history bear witness to the importance of law. Challenges confronting Chinese society today are no less formidable than those during the years of the late *Qing* dynasty rulers, *Mao* and *Deng*. Late *Qing* legal reform exemplified a 'copycat approach', whereby a few ruling elites superficially imported foreign laws and models, which however would not lead to lasting changes in Chinese society.[95] These reforms did not involve the general public and made no impact on people's daily lives. *Mao* tried to do away with law and used politics and Communist ideology to mobilize the people,[96] and Chinese citizens suffered dire consequences from years of lawlessness.[97] *Deng* pragmatically used laws whenever deemed convenient for his economic reform policy.[98] Legal reform measures were driven by practical economic needs but not governed by cross-cutting principles; nor were there sincere efforts to make the government itself law-abiding. These measures, therefore, only had a limited impact and did not generate systemic changes, nor did they enhance public confidence in the legal system.[99]

There are clear signs that Chinese society is better equipped *after* WTO accession and more inclined to allow law to play its crucial role. Never before have the major principles of the rule of law been so prominent with the public and government officials. For the first time in PRC history, law, as in the case of the *Property*

---

91. See Part III, Ch. 8 Section I.A.
92. The term used here refers to laws as contractual arrangements binding both the government and private actors, without implying that the current situation in China fully contains the democratic and participatory elements as suggested in Rousseau's Social Contract theory; Jean-Jacques Rousseau, *The Social Contract* (Harmondsworth: Penguin, 1968).
93. S.M. Shafaeddin, 'Some Implications of Accession to WTO for China's Economy', *International Journal of Development Issues* 1, no. 2 (2002): 93–128, 118.
94. For a survey of rights awareness in Chinese society, see夏勇編, 走向權利的時代 – 中國公民權利發展研究, 北京, 中國政法大學出版社, 1999年; X. Yong (ed.), *Towards an Age of Rights – A Perspective of the Civil Rights Development in China* (China University of Politics and Law Press, 1999).
95. See Part I, Ch. 1 Section III.
96. See Part I, Ch. 2 Section I.
97. See, for example, Jung Chang & Jon Halliday, *Mao: The Unknown Story* (Random House, 2005), especially Parts Five and Six.
98. See Part I, Ch. 2 Sections II.A and II.B.
99. See Part I, Ch. 2 Sections II.C and II.D.

Law, has been called upon as a key tool to help address crucial social, economic, and political issues. With growing social inequalities, corruption, and continued structural changes in the Chinese economy, and other pressing issues, it is hoped that China will continue to rely upon and adhere to the law in surmounting these challenges. A rules-based approach offers the best prospects for China to weather the storms ahead and develop towards a rule of law society.

Appendix
WTO China Accession Protocol
(Without annexes)

WORLD TRADE ORGANIZATION

WT/L/432
23 November 2001
(01-5996)

ACCESSION OF THE PEOPLE'S REPUBLIC OF CHINA

Decision of 10 November 2001

The Ministerial Conference,

Having regard to paragraph 2 of Article XII and paragraph 1 of Article IX of the Marrakesh Agreement Establishing the World Trade Organization, and the Decision-Making Procedures under Articles IX and XII of the Marrakesh Agreement Establishing the World Trade Organization agreed by the General Council (WT/L/93),

Taking note of the application of the People's Republic of China for accession to the Marrakesh Agreement Establishing the World Trade Organization dated 7 December 1995,

Noting the results of the negotiations directed toward the establishment of the terms of accession of the People's Republic of China to the Marrakesh Agreement Establishing the World Trade Organization and having prepared a Protocol on the Accession of the People's Republic of China,

Decides as follows:

The People's Republic of China may accede to the Marrakesh Agreement Establishing the World Trade Organization on the terms and conditions set out in the Protocol annexed to this decision.

PROTOCOL ON THE ACCESSION OF THE PEOPLE'S REPUBLIC OF CHINA

Preamble

The World Trade Organization ('WTO'), pursuant to the approval of the Ministerial Conference of the WTO accorded under Article XII of the Marrakesh Agreement Establishing the World Trade Organization ('WTO Agreement'), and the People's Republic of China ('China'),

Recalling that China was an original contracting party to the General Agreement on Tariffs and Trade 1947,

Taking note that China is a signatory to the Final Act Embodying the Results of the Uruguay Round of Multilateral Trade Negotiations,

Taking note of the Report of the Working Party on the Accession of China in document WT/ACC/CHN/49 ('Working Party Report'),

Having regard to the results of the negotiations concerning China's membership in the WTO,

Agree as follows:

Part I – General Provisions

1. General

1. Upon accession, China accedes to the WTO Agreement pursuant to Article XII of that Agreement and thereby becomes a Member of the WTO.

2. The WTO Agreement to which China accedes shall be the WTO Agreement as rectified, amended or otherwise modified by such legal instruments as may have entered into force before the date of accession. This Protocol, which shall include the commitments referred to in paragraph 342 of the Working Party Report, shall be an integral part of the WTO Agreement.

3. Except as otherwise provided for in this Protocol, those obligations in the Multilateral Trade Agreements annexed to the WTO Agreement that are to be implemented over a period of time starting with entry into force of that Agreement shall be implemented by China as if it had accepted that Agreement on the date of its entry into force.

4. China may maintain a measure inconsistent with paragraph 1 of Article II of the General Agreement on Trade in Services ('GATS') provided that such a measure is recorded in the List of Article II Exemptions annexed to this Protocol and meets the conditions of the Annex to the GATS on Article II Exemptions.

2. Administration of the Trade Regime

(A) Uniform Administration

1. The provisions of the WTO Agreement and this Protocol shall apply to the entire customs territory of China, including border trade regions and minority autonomous

areas, Special Economic Zones, open coastal cities, economic and technical development zones and other areas where special regimes for tariffs, taxes and regulations are established (collectively referred to as 'special economic areas').

2. China shall apply and administer in a uniform, impartial and reasonable manner all its laws, regulations and other measures of the central government as well as local regulations, rules and other measures issued or applied at the sub-national level (collectively referred to as 'laws, regulations and other measures') pertaining to or affecting trade in goods, services, trade-related aspects of intellectual property rights ('TRIPS') or the control of foreign exchange.

3. China's local regulations, rules and other measures of local governments at the sub-national level shall conform to the obligations undertaken in the WTO Agreement and this Protocol.

4. China shall establish a mechanism under which individuals and enterprises can bring to the attention of the national authorities cases of non-uniform application of the trade regime.

(B) Special Economic Areas

1. China shall notify to the WTO all the relevant laws, regulations and other measures relating to its special economic areas, listing these areas by name and indicating the geographic boundaries that define them. China shall notify the WTO promptly, but in any case within 60 days, of any additions or modifications to its special economic areas, including notification of the laws, regulations and other measures relating thereto.

2. China shall apply to imported products, including physically incorporated components, introduced into the other parts of China's customs territory from the special economic areas, all taxes, charges and measures affecting imports, including import restrictions and customs and tariff charges, that are normally applied to imports into the other parts of China's customs territory.

3. Except as otherwise provided for in this Protocol, in providing preferential arrangements for enterprises within such special economic areas, WTO provisions on non-discrimination and national treatment shall be fully observed.

(C) Transparency

1. China undertakes that only those laws, regulations and other measures pertaining to or affecting trade in goods, services, TRIPS or the control of foreign exchange that are published and readily available to other WTO Members, individuals and enterprises, shall be enforced. In addition, China shall make available to WTO Members, upon request, all laws, regulations and other measures pertaining to or affecting trade in goods, services, TRIPS or the control of foreign exchange before such measures are implemented or enforced. In emergency situations, laws, regulations and other measures shall be made available at the latest when they are implemented or enforced.

2. China shall establish or designate an official journal dedicated to the publication of all laws, regulations and other measures pertaining to or affecting trade in goods, services, TRIPS or the control of foreign exchange and, after publication of its laws, regulations or other measures in such journal, shall provide a reasonable period for comment to the appropriate authorities before such measures are implemented, except for those laws, regulations and other measures involving national security, specific measures setting foreign exchange rates or monetary policy and other measures the publication of which would impede law enforcement. China shall publish this journal on a regular basis and make copies of all issues of this journal readily available to individuals and enterprises.

3. China shall establish or designate an enquiry point where, upon request of any individual, enterprise or WTO Member all information relating to the measures required to be published under paragraph 2(C)1 of this Protocol may be obtained. Replies to requests for information shall generally be provided within 30 days after receipt of a request. In exceptional cases, replies may be provided within 45 days after receipt of a request. Notice of the delay and the reasons therefor shall be provided in writing to the interested party. Replies to WTO Members shall be complete and shall represent the authoritative view of the Chinese government. Accurate and reliable information shall be provided to individuals and enterprises.

(D) Judicial Review

1. China shall establish, or designate, and maintain tribunals, contact points and procedures for the prompt review of all administrative actions relating to the implementation of laws, regulations, judicial decisions and administrative rulings of general application referred to in Article X:1 of the GATT 1994, Article VI of the GATS and the relevant provisions of the TRIPS Agreement. Such tribunals shall be impartial and independent of the agency entrusted with administrative enforcement and shall not have any substantial interest in the outcome of the matter.

2. Review procedures shall include the opportunity for appeal, without penalty, by individuals or enterprises affected by any administrative action subject to review. If the initial right of appeal is to an administrative body, there shall in all cases be the opportunity to choose to appeal the decision to a judicial body. Notice of the decision on appeal shall be given to the appellant and the reasons for such decision shall be provided in writing. The appellant shall also be informed of any right to further appeal.

3. Non-discrimination

Except as otherwise provided for in this Protocol, foreign individuals and enterprises and foreign-funded enterprises shall be accorded treatment no less favourable than that accorded to other individuals and enterprises in respect of:

(a) the procurement of inputs and goods and services necessary for production and the conditions under which their goods are produced, marketed or sold, in the domestic market and for export; and
(b) the prices and availability of goods and services supplied by national and sub-national authorities and public or state enterprises, in areas including transportation, energy, basic telecommunications, other utilities and factors of production.

4. Special Trade Arrangements

Upon accession, China shall eliminate or bring into conformity with the WTO Agreement all special trade arrangements, including barter trade arrangements, with third countries and separate customs territories, which are not in conformity with the WTO Agreement.

5. Right to Trade

1. Without prejudice to China's right to regulate trade in a manner consistent with the WTO Agreement, China shall progressively liberalize the availability and scope of the right to trade, so that, within three years after accession, all enterprises in China shall have the right to trade in all goods throughout the customs territory of China, except for those goods listed in Annex 2A which continue to be subject to state trading in accordance with this Protocol. Such right to trade shall be the right to import and export goods. All such goods shall be accorded national treatment under Article III of the GATT 1994, especially paragraph 4 thereof, in respect of their internal sale, offering for sale, purchase, transportation, distribution or use, including their direct access to end-users. For those goods listed in Annex 2B, China shall phase out limitation on the grant of trading rights pursuant to the schedule in that Annex. China shall complete all necessary legislative procedures to implement these provisions during the transition period.

2. Except as otherwise provided for in this Protocol, all foreign individuals and enterprises, including those not invested or registered in China, shall be accorded treatment no less favourable than that accorded to enterprises in China with respect to the right to trade.

6. State Trading

1. China shall ensure that import purchasing procedures of state trading enterprises are fully transparent, and in compliance with the WTO Agreement, and shall refrain from taking any measure to influence or direct state trading enterprises as to the quantity, value, or country of origin of goods purchased or sold, except in accordance with the WTO Agreement.

2. As part of China's notification under the GATT 1994 and the Understanding on the Interpretation of Article XVII of the GATT 1994, China shall also provide

full information on the pricing mechanisms of its state trading enterprises for exported goods.

7. Non-Tariff Measures

1. China shall implement the schedule for phased elimination of the measures contained in Annex 3. During the periods specified in Annex 3, the protection afforded by the measures listed in that Annex shall not be increased or expanded in size, scope or duration, nor shall any new measures be applied, unless in conformity with the provisions of the WTO Agreement.

2. In implementing the provisions of Articles III and XI of the GATT 1994 and the Agreement on Agriculture, China shall eliminate and shall not introduce, re-introduce or apply non-tariff measures that cannot be justified under the provisions of the WTO Agreement. For all non-tariff measures, whether or not referred to in Annex 3, that are applied after the date of accession, consistent with the WTO Agreement or this Protocol, China shall allocate and otherwise administer such measures in strict conformity with the provisions of the WTO Agreement, including GATT 1994 and Article XIII thereof, and the Agreement on Import Licensing Procedures, including notification requirements.

3. China shall, upon accession, comply with the TRIMs Agreement, without recourse to the provisions of Article 5 of the TRIMs Agreement. China shall eliminate and cease to enforce trade and foreign exchange balancing requirements, local content and export or performance requirements made effective through laws, regulations or other measures. Moreover, China will not enforce provisions of contracts imposing such requirements. Without prejudice to the relevant provisions of this Protocol, China shall ensure that the distribution of import licences, quotas, tariff-rate quotas, or any other means of approval for importation, the right of importation or investment by national and sub-national authorities, is not conditioned on: whether competing domestic suppliers of such products exist; or performance requirements of any kind, such as local content, offsets, the transfer of technology, export performance or the conduct of research and development in China.

4. Import and export prohibitions and restrictions, and licensing requirements affecting imports and exports shall only be imposed and enforced by the national authorities or by sub-national authorities with authorization from the national authorities. Such measures which are not imposed by the national authorities or by sub-national authorities with authorization from the national authorities, shall not be implemented or enforced.

8. Import and Export Licensing

1. In implementing the WTO Agreement and provisions of the Agreement on Import Licensing Procedures, China shall undertake the following measures to facilitate compliance with these agreements:

(a) China shall publish on a regular basis the following in the official journal referred to in paragraph 2(C)2 of this Protocol:

- by product, the list of all organizations, including those organizations delegated such authority by the national authorities, that are responsible for authorizing or approving imports or exports, whether through grant of licence or other approval;
- procedures and criteria for obtaining such import or export licences or other approvals, and the conditions for deciding whether they should be granted;
- a list of all products, by tariff number, that are subject to tendering requirements, including information on products subject to such tendering requirements and any changes, pursuant to the Agreement on Import Licensing Procedures;
- a list of all goods and technologies whose import or export are restricted or prohibited; these goods shall also be notified to the Committee on Import Licensing;
- any changes to the list of goods and technologies whose import and export are restricted or prohibited.

Copies of these submissions in one or more official languages of the WTO shall be forwarded to the WTO for circulation to WTO Members and for submission to the Committee on Import Licensing within 75 days of each publication.

(b) China shall notify the WTO of all licensing and quota requirements remaining in effect after accession, listed separately by HS tariff line and with the quantities associated with the restriction, if any, and the justification for maintaining the restriction or its scheduled date of termination.

(c) China shall submit the notification of its import licensing procedures to the Committee on Import Licensing. China shall report annually to the Committee on Import Licensing on its automatic import licensing procedures, explaining the circumstances which give rise to these requirements and justifying the need for their continuation. This report shall also provide the information listed in Article 3 of the Agreement on Import Licensing Procedures.

(d) China shall issue import licences for a minimum duration of validity of six months, except where exceptional circumstances make this impossible. In such cases, China shall promptly notify the Committee on Import Licensing of the exceptional circumstances requiring the shorter period of licence validity.

2. Except as otherwise provided for in this Protocol, foreign individuals and enterprises and foreign-funded enterprises shall be accorded treatment no less favourable than that accorded to other individuals and enterprises in respect of the distribution of import and export licences and quotas.

9. Price Controls

1. China shall, subject to paragraph 2 below, allow prices for traded goods and services in every sector to be determined by market forces, and multi-tier pricing practices for such goods and services shall be eliminated.

2. The goods and services listed in Annex 4 may be subject to price controls, consistent with the WTO Agreement, in particular Article III of the GATT 1994 and Annex 2, paragraphs 3 and 4 of the Agreement on Agriculture. Except in exceptional circumstances, and subject to notification to the WTO, price controls shall not be extended to goods or services beyond those listed in Annex 4, and China shall make best efforts to reduce and eliminate these controls.

3. China shall publish in the official journal the list of goods and services subject to state pricing and changes thereto.

10. Subsidies

1. China shall notify the WTO of any subsidy within the meaning of Article 1 of the Agreement on Subsidies and Countervailing Measures ('SCM Agreement'), granted or maintained in its territory, organized by specific product, including those subsidies defined in Article 3 of the SCM Agreement. The information provided should be as specific as possible, following the requirements of the questionnaire on subsidies as noted in Article 25 of the SCM Agreement.

2. For purposes of applying Articles 1.2 and 2 of the SCM Agreement, subsidies provided to state-owned enterprises will be viewed as specific if, inter alia, state-owned enterprises are the predominant recipients of such subsidies or state-owned enterprises receive disproportionately large amounts of such subsidies.

3. China shall eliminate all subsidy programmes falling within the scope of Article 3 of the SCM Agreement upon accession.

11. Taxes and Charges Levied on Imports and Exports

1. China shall ensure that customs fees or charges applied or administered by national or sub-national authorities, shall be in conformity with the GATT 1994.

2. China shall ensure that internal taxes and charges, including value-added taxes, applied or administered by national or sub-national authorities shall be in conformity with the GATT 1994.

3. China shall eliminate all taxes and charges applied to exports unless specifically provided for in Annex 6 of this Protocol or applied in conformity with the provisions of Article VIII of the GATT 1994.

4. Foreign individuals and enterprises and foreign-funded enterprises shall, upon accession, be accorded treatment no less favourable than that accorded to other individuals and enterprises in respect of the provision of border tax adjustments.

12. Agriculture

1. China shall implement the provisions contained in China's Schedule of Concessions and Commitments on Goods and, as specifically provided in this Protocol, those of the Agreement on Agriculture. In this context, China shall not maintain or introduce any export subsidies on agricultural products.

2. China shall, under the Transitional Review Mechanism, notify fiscal and other transfers between or among state-owned enterprises in the agricultural sector (whether national or sub-national) and other enterprises that operate as state trading enterprises in the agricultural sector.

13. Technical Barriers to Trade

1. China shall publish in the official journal all criteria, whether formal or informal, that are the basis for a technical regulation, standard or conformity assessment procedure.

2. China shall, upon accession, bring into conformity with the TBT Agreement all technical regulations, standards and conformity assessment procedures.

3. China shall apply conformity assessment procedures to imported products only to determine compliance with technical regulations and standards that are consistent with the provisions of this Protocol and the WTO Agreement. Conformity assessment bodies will determine the conformity of imported products with commercial terms of contracts only if authorized by the parties to such contract. China shall ensure that such inspection of products for compliance with the commercial terms of contracts does not affect customs clearance or the granting of import licences for such products.

4. (a) Upon accession, China shall ensure that the same technical regulations, standards and conformity assessment procedures are applied to both imported and domestic products. In order to ensure a smooth transition from the current system, China shall ensure that, upon accession, all certification, safety licensing, and quality licensing bodies and agencies are authorized to undertake these activities for both imported and domestic products, and that, one year after accession, all conformity assessment bodies and agencies are authorized to undertake conformity assessment for both imported and domestic products. The choice of body or agency shall be at the discretion of the applicant. For imported and domestic products, all bodies and agencies shall issue the same mark and charge the same fee. They shall also provide the same processing periods and complaint procedures. Imported products shall not be subject to more than one conformity assessment.

China shall publish and make readily available to other WTO Members, individuals, and enterprises full information on the respective responsibilities of its conformity assessment bodies and agencies.

(b) No later than 18 months after accession, China shall assign the respective responsibilities of its conformity assessment bodies solely on the basis of the scope of work and type of product without any consideration of the origin of a product. The respective responsibilities that will be assigned to China's conformity assessment bodies will be notified to the TBT Committee 12 months after accession.

14. Sanitary and Phytosanitary Measures

China shall notify to the WTO all laws, regulations and other measures relating to its sanitary and phytosanitary measures, including product coverage and relevant international standards, guidelines and recommendations, within 30 days after accession.

15. Price Comparability in Determining Subsidies and Dumping

Article VI of the GATT 1994, the Agreement on Implementation of Article VI of the General Agreement on Tariffs and Trade 1994 ('Anti-Dumping Agreement') and the SCM Agreement shall apply in proceedings involving imports of Chinese origin into a WTO Member consistent with the following:

(a) In determining price comparability under Article VI of the GATT 1994 and the Anti-Dumping Agreement, the importing WTO Member shall use either Chinese prices or costs for the industry under investigation or a methodology that is not based on a strict comparison with domestic prices or costs in China based on the following rules:
   (i) If the producers under investigation can clearly show that market economy conditions prevail in the industry producing the like product with regard to the manufacture, production and sale of that product, the importing WTO Member shall use Chinese prices or costs for the industry under investigation in determining price comparability;
   (ii) The importing WTO Member may use a methodology that is not based on a strict comparison with domestic prices or costs in China if the producers under investigation cannot clearly show that market economy conditions prevail in the industry producing the like product with regard to manufacture, production and sale of that product.

(b) In proceedings under Parts II, III and V of the SCM Agreement, when addressing subsidies described in Articles 14(a), 14(b), 14(c) and 14(d), relevant provisions of the SCM Agreement shall apply; however, if there are special difficulties in that application, the importing WTO Member may then use methodologies for identifying and measuring the subsidy benefit which take into account the possibility that prevailing terms and conditions in China may not always be available as appropriate benchmarks. In applying such methodologies, where practicable, the importing WTO Member should adjust such prevailing terms and conditions before considering the use of terms and conditions prevailing outside China.

(c) The importing WTO Member shall notify methodologies used in accordance with subparagraph (a) to the Committee on Anti-Dumping Practices and shall notify methodologies used in accordance with subparagraph (b) to the Committee on Subsidies and Countervailing Measures.

(d) Once China has established, under the national law of the importing WTO Member, that it is a market economy, the provisions of subparagraph (a) shall be terminated provided that the importing Member's national law contains market economy criteria as of the date of accession. In any event, the provisions of subparagraph (a)(ii) shall expire 15 years after the date of accession. In addition, should China establish, pursuant to the national law of the importing WTO Member, that market economy conditions prevail in a particular industry or sector, the non-market economy provisions of subparagraph (a) shall no longer apply to that industry or sector.

16. Transitional Product-Specific Safeguard Mechanism

1. In cases where products of Chinese origin are being imported into the territory of any WTO Member in such increased quantities or under such conditions as to cause or threaten to cause market disruption to the domestic producers of like or directly competitive products, the WTO Member so affected may request consultations with China with a view to seeking a mutually satisfactory solution, including whether the affected WTO Member should pursue application of a measure under the Agreement on Safeguards. Any such request shall be notified immediately to the Committee on Safeguards.

2. If, in the course of these bilateral consultations, it is agreed that imports of Chinese origin are such a cause and that action is necessary, China shall take such action as to prevent or remedy the market disruption. Any such action shall be notified immediately to the Committee on Safeguards.

3. If consultations do not lead to an agreement between China and the WTO Member concerned within 60 days of the receipt of a request for consultations, the WTO Member affected shall be free, in respect of such products, to withdraw concessions or otherwise to limit imports only to the extent necessary to prevent or remedy such market disruption. Any such action shall be notified immediately to the Committee on Safeguards.

4. Market disruption shall exist whenever imports of an article, like or directly competitive with an article produced by the domestic industry, are increasing rapidly, either absolutely or relatively, so as to be a significant cause of material injury, or threat of material injury to the domestic industry. In determining if

market disruption exists, the affected WTO Member shall consider objective factors, including the volume of imports, the effect of imports on prices for like or directly competitive articles, and the effect of such imports on the domestic industry producing like or directly competitive products.

5. Prior to application of a measure pursuant to paragraph 3, the WTO Member taking such action shall provide reasonable public notice to all interested parties and provide adequate opportunity for importers, exporters and other interested parties to submit their views and evidence on the appropriateness of the proposed measure and whether it would be in the public interest. The WTO Member shall provide written notice of the decision to apply a measure, including the reasons for such measure and its scope and duration.

6. A WTO Member shall apply a measure pursuant to this Section only for such period of time as may be necessary to prevent or remedy the market disruption. If a measure is taken as a result of a relative increase in the level of imports, China has the right to suspend the application of substantially equivalent concessions or obligations under the GATT 1994 to the trade of the WTO Member applying the measure, if such measure remains in effect more than two years. However, if a measure is taken as a result of an absolute increase in imports, China has a right to suspend the application of substantially equivalent concessions or obligations under the GATT 1994 to the trade of the WTO Member applying the measure, if such measure remains in effect more than three years. Any such action by China shall be notified immediately to the Committee on Safeguards.

7. In critical circumstances, where delay would cause damage which it would be difficult to repair, the WTO Member so affected may take a provisional safeguard measure pursuant to a preliminary determination that imports have caused or threatened to cause market disruption. In this case, notification of the measures taken to the Committee on Safeguards and a request for bilateral consultations shall be effected immediately thereafter. The duration of the provisional measure shall not exceed 200 days during which the pertinent requirements of paragraphs 1, 2 and 5 shall be met. The duration of any provisional measure shall be counted toward the period provided for under paragraph 6.

8. If a WTO Member considers that an action taken under paragraphs 2, 3 or 7 causes or threatens to cause significant diversions of trade into its market, it may request consultations with China and/or the WTO Member concerned. Such consultations shall be held within 30 days after the request is notified to the Committee on Safeguards. If such consultations fail to lead to an agreement between China and the WTO Member or Members concerned within 60 days after the notification, the requesting WTO Member shall be free, in respect of such product, to withdraw concessions accorded to or otherwise limit imports from China, to the extent necessary to prevent or remedy such diversions. Such action shall be notified immediately to the Committee on Safeguards.

9. Application of this Section shall be terminated 12 years after the date of accession.

17. Reservations by WTO Members

All prohibitions, quantitative restrictions and other measures maintained by WTO Members against imports from China in a manner inconsistent with the WTO Agreement are listed in Annex 7. All such prohibitions, quantitative restrictions and other measures shall be phased out or dealt with in accordance with mutually agreed terms and timetables as specified in the said Annex.

18. Transitional Review Mechanism

1. Those subsidiary bodies[1] of the WTO which have a mandate covering China's commitments under the WTO Agreement or this Protocol shall, within one year after accession and in accordance with paragraph 4 below, review, as appropriate to their mandate, the implementation by China of the WTO Agreement and of the related provisions of this Protocol. China shall provide relevant information, including information specified in Annex 1A, to each subsidiary body in advance of the review. China can also raise issues relating to any reservations under Section 17 or to any other specific commitments made by other Members in this Protocol, in those subsidiary bodies which have a relevant mandate. Each subsidiary body shall report the results of such review promptly to the relevant Council established by paragraph 5 of Article IV of the WTO Agreement, if applicable, which shall in turn report promptly to the General Council.

2. The General Council shall, within one year after accession, and in accordance with paragraph 4 below, review the implementation by China of the WTO Agreement and the provisions of this Protocol. The General Council shall conduct such review in accordance with the framework set out in Annex 1B and in the light of the results of any reviews held pursuant to paragraph 1. China also can raise issues relating to any reservations under Section 17 or to any other specific commitments made by other Members in this Protocol. The General Council may make recommendations to China and to other Members in these respects.

3. Consideration of issues pursuant to this Section shall be without prejudice to the rights and obligations of any Member, including China, under the WTO Agreement or any Plurilateral Trade Agreement, and shall not preclude or be a precondition to recourse to consultation or other provisions of the WTO Agreement or this Protocol.

4. The review provided for in paragraphs 1 and 2 will take place after accession in each year for eight years. Thereafter there will be a final review in year 10 or at an earlier date decided by the General Council.

---

1. Council for Trade in Goods, Council for Trade-Related Aspects of Intellectual Property Rights, Council for Trade in Services, Committees on Balance-of-Payments Restrictions, Market Access (covering also ITA), Agriculture, Sanitary and Phytosanitary Measures, Technical Barriers to Trade, Subsidies and Countervailing Measures, Anti-Dumping Measures, Customs Valuation, Rules of Origin, Import Licensing, Trade-Related Investment Measures, Safeguards, Trade in Financial Services.

Part II – Schedules

1. The Schedules annexed to this Protocol shall become the Schedule of Concessions and Commitments annexed to the GATT 1994 and the Schedule of Specific Commitments annexed to the GATS relating to China. The staging of concessions and commitments listed in the Schedules shall be implemented as specified in the relevant parts of the relevant Schedules.

2. For the purpose of the reference in paragraph 6(a) of Article II of the GATT 1994 to the date of that Agreement, the applicable date in respect of the Schedules of Concessions and Commitments annexed to this Protocol shall be the date of accession.

Part III – Final Provisions

1. This Protocol shall be open for acceptance, by signature or otherwise, by China until 1 January 2002.

2. This Protocol shall enter into force on the thirtieth day following the day of its acceptance.

3. This Protocol shall be deposited with the Director-General of the WTO. The Director-General shall promptly furnish a certified copy of this Protocol and a notification of acceptance by China thereof, pursuant to paragraph 1 of Part III of this Protocol, to each WTO Member and to China.

4. This Protocol shall be registered in accordance with the provisions of Article 102 of the Charter of the United Nations.

Done at Doha this tenth day of November two thousand and one, in a single copy, in the English, French and Spanish languages, each text being authentic, except that a Schedule annexed hereto may specify that it is authentic in only one or more of these languages.

Bibliography

References in English

Primary Sources

GATT and WTO Documents

Cambodia Accession Protocol. World Trade Organization, WT/MIN(03)/18, 2003.

China – Request for Observer Status. General Agreement on Tariffs and Trade, L/5712, 26 October 1984.

China Accession to the General Agreement. General Agreement on Tariffs and Trade, GATT/TN.1/38 and GATT/CP.3/92, 5 September 1949.

China's Accession Protocol. World Trade Organization, WT/L/432, 2001.

China – Measures Affecting the Protection and Enforcement of Intellectual Property Rights: Request for the Establishment of a Panel by the United States. World Trade Organization, WT/DS362/7, 22 August 2007.

China's Schedule of Concessions and Commitments on Trade in Goods. World Trade Organization, WT/ACC/CHN/49/Add.1 and WT/MIN(01)/3/Add.1, 2001.

China's Schedule of Commitments on Trade in Services. World Trade Organization, WT/ACC/CHN/49/Add.2 WT/MIN(01)/3/Add.2, 2001.

China's Status as A Contracting Party, Communication from the People's Republic of China. General Agreement on Tariffs and Trade, L/6017, 14 July 1986.

China Working Party Report. World Trade Organization, WT/ACC/CHN/49, 2001.

Chinese Taipei Accession Protocol. World Trade Organization, WT/L/433, 2001.

Chinese Taipei Working Party Report. World Trade Organization, WT/ACC/TPKM/18, 2001.

Communication from the Secretary-General of the United Nations regarding China. General Agreement on Tariffs and Trade. GATT/CP/54, 6 March 1950.

Communication Received from the Permanent Mission of the People's Republic of China. General Agreement on Tariffs and Trade, COM.TEX/W/92, 28 April 1981.

First Trade Policy Review of China, Report by the Government. World Trade Organization, WT/TPR/G/161, 17 March 2006.

First Trade Policy Review of China, Report by the WTO Secretariat. WT/TPR/S/161, 28 February 2006.

First Trade Policy Review of China, Trade Policy Review Body, Minutes of Meeting 19–21 April 2006. World Trade Organization, WT/TPR/S/161 and WT/TPR/M/161/Add.1.

Minutes of General Council Meeting on 9-11 and 18 December 1998. World Trade Organization, WT/GC/M/32.

Minutes of Council Meeting on 14 May 1987. General Agreement on Tariffs and Trade, C/M209.

Minutes of Council Meetings Held on 15 July 1986 and 4 August 1986. General Agreement on Tariffs and Trade, C/M/201.

Minutes of Council Meeting 29 September – 1 October 1992. General Agreement on Tariffs and Trade, C/M/259.

Report of the Committee Meeting on 19–20 January 1984 and 2 March 1984. General Agreement on Tariffs and Trade, COM.TEX/36.

Request for Consultations by China: United States – Preliminary Anti-dumping and Countervailing Duty Determinations on Coated Free Sheet Paper from China. World Trade Organization, WT/DS368/1, 14 September 2007.

Request for Consultations by the United States. World Trade Organization, WT/DS362/1, 16 April 2007.

Request for Information pursuant to Article 63.3 of the TRIPS Agreement. Communication from Japan. World Trade Organization, IP/C/W/463, 14 November 2005.

Request for Information pursuant to Article 63.3 of the TRIPS Agreement. Communication from the Switzerland. World Trade Organization, IP/C/W/462, 14 November 2005.

Request for Information pursuant to Article 63.3 of the TRIPS Agreement. Communication from the United States. World Trade Organization, IP/C/W/461, 14 November 2005.

Saudi Arabia's Accession Protocol. World Trade Organization, WT/L/627, 2005.

Summary Record of the First Meeting. General Agreement on Tariffs and Trade, SR/27.1, 19 November 1971.

Summary Record of the Sixth Meeting. General Agreement on Tariffs and Trade, GATT/CP.5/SR.6, 9 November 1950.

Summary Record of the Third Meeting. General Agreement on Tariffs and Trade, SR.22/3, 8 March 1965.

Working Party on China's Status as a Contracting Party. General Agreement on Tariffs and Trade, L/6191, 19 June 1987.

Selected Laws and Regulations

Administrative Measures for Government Procurement Information Announcements, 19 September 2004.

Administrative Procedure Law of the People's Republic of China. Law Press China, 2004.

Arbitration Law of the People's Republic of China. Law Press China, 2004.

Catalogue for the Guidance of Foreign Investment Industries. 2005.

Constitution of the People's Republic of China. 1982, amended in 1988, 1993, 1999, 2004, and 2007.

Copyright Law of the People's Republic of China. Law Press China, 2004.

Foreign Trade Law of the People's Republic of China, 1994 and 2004 versions. Law Press China, 2004.

General Principles of the Civil Law of the People's Republic of China. Law Press China, 2002.

Guidelines on Encouraging and Supporting the Development of the Non-Public Sector including Individual and Private Enterprises. The PRC State Council, 2005.

Law of the People's Republic of China on Administrative Licensing. Law Press China, 2004.

Law of the People's Republic of China on Administrative Penalty. Law Press China, 2004.

Law of the People's Republic of China on Administrative Supervision. Law Press China, 2004.

Law of the People's Republic of China on Administrative Reconsideration. Law Press China, 2004.

Law of the People's Republic of China on Lawyers. Law Press China, 2004.

Law of the People's Republic of China on State Compensation. Law Press China, 2004.

Law on Legislation, the People's Republic of China. Law Press China, 2003.

Litigation and Non-litigation Procedure, Civil Procedure Law of the People's Republic of China. Law Press China, 2002.

Measures for the Administration of Foreign Investment in the Commercial Sector. The PRC Ministry of Commerce, 2004.

Measures on China WTO Enquiry Offices. China's Ministry of Foreign Trade and Economic Cooperation, 2002.

Ordinance on Procedural Rules for Formulating Administrative Regulations. The PRC State Council, 2002.

Ordinance on Procedural Rules for Formulating Departmental Rules. The PRC State Council, 2002.

Ordinance on the Archives Filing of Regulations and Government Rules. The PRC State Council, 2002.

Patent Law of the People's Republic of China. Law Press China, 2004.

Provisions of Guangzhou City on Publicizing Governmental Information. Guangdong Province, 2003.

Provisions on Guiding Foreign Investment Direction. The PRC State Council, 2002.
Provisions of the Supreme People's Court on Certain Issues Concerning the Applicability of Laws in the Hearing and Handling of Anti-Dumping Administrative Cases. 2003.
Provisions of the Supreme People's Court on Some Issues Concerning the Jurisdiction of Civil and Commercial Cases Involving Foreign Elements, No. 5 of the Interpretations of the Supreme People's Court. 2002.
Regulations of the People's Republic of China on Anti-Dumping. 2001.
*Regulations of the People's Republic of China on Countervailing Measure*s. 2001.
Regulations of the People's Republic of China on Safeguards. 2002.
Regulations on Information Accession and Information Disclosure in Industry Injury Investigations. 2003.
Rules on the Archives Filing of Legislations and Government Rules. 1990.
Several Issues of Concrete Application of Laws in Handling Criminal Cases of Infringing Intellectual Property. 2004.
*Several Issues of Concrete Application of Laws in Handling Civil Cases Concerning Dissension on Internet Domain Nam*e. 2004.
Several Issues of Concrete Application of Laws in Handling Civil Cases Concerning Dissension on Trademark Rights. 2004.
Some Advice of the People's Government of Anhui Province on the Challenges after China's WTO Accession, Further Expanding the Open-up Policy, and Accelerating Economic Development, Anhui Province. 2002.
The Legal Texts: The Results of the Uruguay Round of Multilateral Trade Negotiations. World Trade Organization, Cambridge University Press, 1999.
Trademark of the People's Republic of China. Law Press China, 2004.
Working Procedures for Filing and Reviewing Administrative Rules and Regulations, Local Regulations, Autonomous Regulations and Specific Regulations, and Special Economic Zone Regulations. 2005.
Working Procedures for Filing and Reviewing Judicial Interpretations. 2005.
Working Procedures for Filing and Reviewing Legislation. 2002.

Official Speeches, Statements and Documents

Analytical Study of the High Commissioner for Human Rights on the Fundamental Principle of Non-discrimination in the Context of Globalization. Report of the High Commissioner to the Sixtieth session of the United Nations Commission on Human Rights, E/CN.4/2004/40, 15 January 2004.
Annual Reports of US Congressional-Executive Commission on China. Year 2002 to 2006.
China's first report to the United Nations Committee on Economic, Social and Cultural Rights, E/1990/5/Add.59, 4 March 2004.
Concluding observations of the United Nations Committee on Economic, Social and Cultural Rights. People's Republic of China (including Hong Kong and Macau), E/C.12/1/Add.107, 13 May 2005.

Déclaration de Bamako. Organisation de la Francophonie, adopted at Bamako, Mali, 3 November 2000.

Honour Constitution's Guarantee for Citizens' Rights. Speech by *Hu Jintao* on the occasion of the 20th anniversary of the promulgation and implementation of the Constitution, 4 December 2002.

Letter on TRIPS Information Request by U.S. Ambassador to the WTO, Peter Allgeier, to Chinese Ambassador to the WTO. *Sun Zhenyu,* 20 January 2006.

New Progress in China's Protection of Intellectual Property Rights. Information Office of the State Council of the People's Republic of China, April 2005.

Report to Congress on China's WTO Compliance. United States Trade Representative, 11 December 2004.

Report to the United Nations Commission on Human Rights. The Right of Everyone to the Enjoyment of the Highest Attainable Standard of Physical and Mental Health – Special Rapporteur on the Right to Health, Paul Hunt, Mission to the World Trade Organization, E/CN.4/2004/49/Add.1, March 2004.

Statement by *Long Yongtu*, Head of the Chinese Delegation, to the China WTO Working Party meeting, 22 March 1996.

Statement by *Long Yongtu*, Head of the Chinese Delegation, to the China WTO Working Party meeting on the completion of China's accession negotiations, 17 September 2001.

Statement by *Shen Jueren*, Head of the Chinese Delegation at the 3rd session of GATT's Working Party on China, 26 April 1988.

Statement of the Representative of the International Monetary Fund to the China WTO Working Party meeting, 22 March 1996.

Statement by W. Douglas Newkirk, Assistant U.S. Trade Representative for GATT Affairs, to the 2nd meeting of GATT's Working Party on China, 23 February 1988.

Books and Journal Articles

Abbott, F.M. (ed.). *China in the World Trading System: Defining the Principles of Engagement.* Cambridge: Kluwer Law International, 1998.

Albrow, M. & E. King (eds), *Globalization, Knowledge and Society: Readings from International Sociology.* London: Sage, 1990.

Alston, P. 'The Myopia of the Handmaidens: International Lawyers and Globalization'. *European Journal of International Law* 8, no. 3 (1997): 435–448.

Arup, C. 'Lawyers for China: The Impact of Membership of the World Trade Organization on Legal Services and Law in China'. *Journal of World Intellectual Property* 4, no. 5 (2001): 741–766.

Arup, C. *The New World Trade Organization Agreements – Globalizing Law through Services and Intellectual Property.* Cambridge: Cambridge University Press, 2000.

Barfield, C.E. *Free Trade, Sovereignty, Democracy: The Future of the World Trade Organization*. Washington, DC: AEI Press, 2001.

Bath, V. *Changes to China's Foreign Investment Regime following China's Accession to the World Trade Organisation and the Implications for Australian Investors*. Conference paper given at the 26th International Trade Law Conference, Sydney, Australia, 23 September 2004.

Belton, R.K. *Competing Definitions of the Rule of Law, Implications for Practitioners*. Rule of Law Series, Democracy and Rule of Law Project, Carnegie Endowment for International Peace, no. 55, 2005.

Bernhardt, R. (ed.). *Encyclopaedia of Public International Law*, vol. 1. North-Holland: Elsevier, 1992.

Bhattasali, D., S. Li & W.J. Martin (eds). *China and the WTO: Accession, Policy Reform, and Poverty Reduction Strategies*. Washington, DC: World Bank, 2004.

Black's Law Dictionary. 6th edn, St. Paul, MM: West Publishing Co., 1991.

Breslin, S. *Capitalism with Chinese Characteristics: The Public, the Private and the International*. Working Paper no. 104, Asia Research Centre, Murdoch University, 2004.

Broadfoot, R. *Survey on Investors rate Asian Legal Systems*. Political and Economic Risk Consultancy, Coudert Brothers' In-House Briefing Asia-Pacific, July–August 2001.

Cass, D.Z., B.G. Williams & G. Barker (eds). *China and the World Trading System: Entering the New Millennium*. Cambridge: Cambridge University Press, 2003.

Cassese, A. 'On the Current Trends towards Criminal Prosecution and Punishment of Breaches of International Humanitarian Law'. *European Journal of International Law* (1998): 2–17.

Chang, G. *The Coming Collapse of China*. New York: Random House, 2001.

Chang, J. & J. Halliday. *Mao: The Unknown Story*. New York: Random House, 2005.

Chen, A. *An Introduction to the Legal System of the People's Republic of China*. Hong Kong: LexisNexis Butterworths, 2004.

Chen, D. *Reasonable Government or Limited Government in Licensing? A Critical Survey of the Draft Administrative Licensing Law of P.R.C.* Paper given at Asian Law Centre, the University of Melbourne, 6 August 2002.

Chi, F. (ed.). *China's Economic Reform at the Turn of the Century*. Beijing: Foreign Languages Press, 2000.

'China in the World Economy – the Domestic Policy Challenges', *Synthesis Report*. Paris: Organization for Economic Cooperation and Development (OECD), 2002.

Ching, C. & H.Y. Ching. *Handbook on China's WTO Accession and Its Impacts*. London: World Scientific Publishing, 2003.

Chou, B.K.P. *Downsizing Administrative Licensing System and Private Sector Development in the PRC, A Preliminary Assessment*. Asia Development Bank Institute, Discussion Paper no. 52 (2006): 1–30.

Choukrounen, L. 'Rule of Law through Internationalisation: The Objective of the Reforms?'. *China Perspectives*, Special Edition, *China and WTO*, French Centre for Research on Contemporary China, Issue 40 (2002): 7–20.

Clark, D. 'The Many Meanings of the Rule of Law'. In *Law, Capitalism and Power in Asia: The Rule of Law and Legal Institutions*, edited by K. Jayasuriya. London: Routledge, 1999.

Clarke, D.C. 'China's Legal System and the WTO: Prospect for Compliance'. *Global Studies Law Review* 2 (2003): 97–120.

Clarke, D.C. 'Empirical Research into the Chinese Judicial System'. *Beyond Common Knowledge: Empirical Approaches to the Rule of Law*, edited by G.E. Jensen & T.C. Heller. Stanford: Stanford University Press, 2003.

Cohen, J.A. 'Reforming China's Civil Procedure: Judging the Courts'. *American Journal of Comparative Law* 45 (1997):793–801.

Compilation of Laws and Regulations concerning Foreign Investment in China. Beijing: China International Press, 2001.

Cottier, T. & K.N. Schefer. 'The Relationship of WTO Law, National and Regional Law'. *Journal of International Economic Law* (1993): 83–117.

Cottier, T. & P.C. Mavroidis (eds). 'The Role of the Judge in International Trade Regulation: Experience and Lessons for the WTO'. *World Trade Forum* 4 (2002): 212–217.

Cottier, T. 'Emerging Doctrines of Good Governance: The Impact of the WTO and China's Accession'. In *China in the World Trading System: Defining the Principles of Engagement*, edited by F. Abbott. Cambridge: Kluwer Law International, 1998.

Ding, X.L. 'The Illicit Asset Stripping of Chinese State Firms'. *China Journal* 43 (2000): 1–28.

Dittmer, L. & G. Liu. *China's Deep Reform: Domestic Politics in Transition*. Lanham, Md: Rowman & Littlefield Publishers, 2006.

Duncan, C. 'Out of Conformity: China's Capacity to Implement World Trade Organization Dispute Settlement Body Decisions after Accession'. *American University International Law Review* 18 (2002): 399–477.

Fang, S. 'Are You Prepared for This Legal Maze? How to Serve Legal Documents, Obtain Evidence and Enforce Judgments in China'. *University of Missouri at Kansas City Law Review* 72 (2003): 215–240.

Garcia-Rubio, M. *On the Application of Customary Rules of State Responsibility by the WTO Dispute Settlement Organs: A General International Law Perspective*. Geneva: Graduate Institute of International Studies, 2001.

Garnaut, R. & L. Song (eds). *China 2002: WTO Entry and World Recession*. Canberra: Asia Pacific Press, 2002.

Gavinet, G. 'Les influences croisées entre juridictions nationales et internationales'. Revue de Science Criminelle et de droit pénal comparé, Octobre/Décembre 2005, 799–817.

Gertler, J.L. *The Process of China's Accession to the World Trade Organization*. Speech given at the Third Annual Conference of the Library of International Relations, Chicago-Kent College of Law, 6–7 November 1997.

Gervais, D. *The TRIPS Agreement – Drafting History and Analysis*. London: Sweet and Maxwell, 2003.

Giddens, A. *Runaway World: How Globalization Is Reshaping Our Lives*. London: Profile Books, 1999.

Gray, J. *Hayek on Liberty*. New York: Basil Blackwell, 1984.

Greenwood, J. 'The Impact of China's WTO Accession on Capital Freedom'. *Cato Journal* 21, no. 1 (2001): 91–100.

Groombridge, M.A. & C.E. Barfield. *Tiger by the Tail: China and the World Trade Organization*. Washington, DC: AEI Press, 1999.

Grynberg, R., Vi. Ognivtsev & M.A. Razzaque. *Paying the Price for Joining the WTO: A Comparative Assessment of Services Sector Commitments by WTO Members and Acceding Countries*. London: Commonwealth Secretariat, 2002.

Gu, Y. 'Entering the Chinese Legal Market: A Guide for American Lawyers Interested in Practicing Law in China'. *Drake Law Review*, Issue 48 (1999): 173–211.

Guo, L. 'What Makes a Lawyer in China? The Chinese Legal Education System after China's Entry into the WTO'. *Willamette Journal of International Law and Dispute Resolution* 10 (2002): 197–229.

Halverson, K. *China's WTO Accession: Economic, Legal and Political Implications*. Paper given at the Conference of the International Economic Law Group, American Society of International Law, Georgetown University Law Center, October 2002.

Hart, H.L.A. *The Concept of Law*. Oxford: Clarendon Press, 1961.

Hayek, F.A. *Law, Legislation, and Liberty. Vol. I: Rules and Order*. Chicago, IL: University of Chicago Press, 1973.

Heberer, T. & G. Schubert. 'Political Reform and Regime Legitimacy in Contemporary China'. *ASIEN* 99, *The German Journal on Contemporary Asia* (2006): 9–28.

Henkin, L. *How Nations Behave*. New York: Colombia University Press, 1979.

Higgins, R. *Problems & Process, International Law and How We Use It*. Oxford: Clarendon Press, 1998.

Hoeckman, B., A. Matoo & P. English (eds). *Development, Trade, and the WTO, A Handbook*. Washington, DC: The World Bank, 2002.

Hoekman, B. & M. Kostecki. *The Political Economy of the World Trading System – from GATT to WTO*. Oxford: Oxford University Press, 1997.

Holbig, H. & R. Ash (eds). *China's Accession to the World Trade Organization: National and International Perspectives*. London: RoutledgeCurzon, 2002.

Holbig, H. *Ideological Reform and Political Legitimacy in China: Challenges in the Post-Jiang Era*. German Institute of Global and Area Studies, Working Paper no. 18 (2006): 1–36.

Holton, R.J. *Globalization and the Nation-State*. London: Macmillan Press, 1998.

Hormats, R.D. *Beginning the Journey, China, the United States, and the WTO*. Report of an Independent Task Force, Council on Foreign Relations, 2001.

Horsley, J.P. 'Rule of Law in China: Incremental Progress'. In *China: The Balance Sheet*, edited by C.F. Bergsten, B. Gill, N.R. Lardy & D. Mitchell. New York: Public Affairs Press, 2006.

Hsu, Berry Fong-Chung, et al. '*Banking Liberalization and Restructuring in Post-WTO China*'. *Banking & Finance Law Review* (2005): 23–59.

Hu, S. 'Confucianism and Contemporary Chinese Politics'. *Politics & Policy* 35, no. 1 (2007): 136–153.

Huang, R. *How Has Accession to the WTO Changed Trade Policy Making in China?* Paper given at the Workshop on Trade Policy Making in Developing Countries, London School of Economics and Political Science, 25 May 2005.

Huang, T.W. 'One Treaty, Two Members: China and Taiwan within the Context of WTO'. *Journal of World Investment* 1, no. 2 (2000): 261–292.

Hung, V.M.Y. 'China's WTO Commitment on Independent Judicial Review: Impact on Legal and Political Reform'. *The American Journal of Comparative Law* 52 (2004): 77–132.

Ianchovichina, E. & W. Martin. 'Trade Liberalization in China's Accession to WTO'. *Journal of Economic Integration* 16, no. 4 (2001): 421–445.

Jackson, J.H. & J.V. Feinerman. 'China's WTO Accession: Survey of Material'. *Journal of International Economic Law* 4, no. 2 (2001): 329–336.

Jackson, J.H. 'The WTO Dispute Settlement Understanding: Misunderstandings on the Nature of Legal Obligation'. *The American Journal of International Law* 91, no. 1 (1997): 60–64.

Jensen, E.G. & T.C. Heller (eds). *Beyond Common Knowledge: Empirical Approaches to the Rule of Law*. Stanfrod: Stanford University Press, 2003.

Killion, M.U. 'Western Institution Building: The War, Hayek's Cosmos and the WTO'. *The Berkley Electronic Press* (2005): 454–500.

Kong, Q. *China and the World Trade Organization: A Legal Perspective*. Singapore: World Scientific Publishing, 2002.

Kueh, Y.Y. 'Coping with Globalization in China: Strategic Implications of WTO Accession'. *Journal of World Investment* 3, no. 1 (2002): 37–64.

Lam, Esther, et al. *A Practical Guide to the WTO for Human Rights Advocates*. Bangkok and Geneva: 3D: Trade-Human Rights-Equitable Economy and Asian Forum for Human Rights and Development, 2004.

Lam, W. 'Socialism with a Harmonious Face: Hu Jintao's Plan for Reform'. *China Brief*, The Jamestown Foundation 4, no. 20 (2004).

Lan Chuan-pu (ed.). *Survey of 30 Years' Development of Laws and Regulations in our Country*. Beijing, 1980.

Langlois Jr., J.D., 'The WTO and China's Financial System'. *The China Quarterly* 167 (2001): 610–629.

Lardy, N.R. *Integrating China into the Global Economy*. Washington, DC: Brookings Institution Press, 2002.

Lee, K.T., J.Y. Lin & S.J. Kim (eds). *China's Integration with the World Economy: Repercussions of China's Accession to the WTO*. Seoul: KIEP, 2001.

Lee, Y. 'The Specific Safeguard Mechanism in the Protocol on China's Accession to the WTO: A Serious Step Backward from the Achievement of the Uruguay Round'. *Journal of World Intellectual Property* 5, no. 2 (2002): 219–232.

Li, C. 'Hu's Policy Shift and the Tuanpai's Coming-of-Age'. *China Leadership Monitor* 15 (2005): 1–16.

Li, J. 'Socialist Rule of Law with Chinese Characteristics'. *Issues and Studies* 43, no. 1 (2007): 115–157.

Li, Y. *China's Accession to the WTO: Exaggerated Fears?* Geneva: United Nations Conference on Trade and Development, November 2002.

Liang, Z. 'Explicating Law: A Comparative Perspective of Chinese and Western Legal Culture'. *Journal of Chinese Law* 3 (1989): 55–91.

Lubman, S. 'Bird in a Cage: Chinese Law Reform after Twenty Years'. *Journal of International Law and Business* 20 (2000): 383–413.

Lubman, S. *Bird in a Cage: Legal Reform in China after Mao*. Stanford: Stanford University Press, 1999.

Ma, X. 'China's Commitment to Transparency under WTO – Concepts of China's Law and Administrative Regulations'. *Legal Updates and News*. Morrison & Foerster, 2001.

MacCormick, N. 'Institutional Normative Order: A Conception of Law'. *Cornell Law Review* 82 (1997): 1051–1070.

MacCormick, N. 'Norms, Institutions and Institutional Fact'. *Law and Philosophy* 17 (1998): 301–345.

MacCormick, N. 'Sovereignty: Myth and Reality'. In *Towards Universal Law: Trends in National European and International Law Making*, ed. N. Jareborg (Uppsala: Justus Forlag, 1995), 227–248.

Mastel, G. 'China and the World Trade Organization: Moving Forward without Sliding Backward'. *Law and Policy in International Business* 31, no. 3 (2000): 981–1002.

Matthews, D. *Globalizing Intellectual Property Rights – The TRIPS Agreement*. London: Routledge, 2002.

Mo, J. 'Reform of the Patent System of the People's Republic of China after WTO'. *Journal of World Intellectual Property* 4, no. 1 (2002): 33–90.

Norton, P.M. & W.A. Kermit. 'China's New Anti-Dumping Rules: Battleground for New Protectionism'. *China Law & Practice* 16, no. 1 (2002): 79–83.

Nowak, M. *U.N. Covenant on Civil and Political Rights, CCPR Commentary*. 2nd rev. edn. Kehl: N.P. Engel Publisher, 2005.

Orts, Eric W. 'The Rule of Law in China'. *Vanderbilt Journal of International Law* 34 (2001): 43–107.

Palmeter, D. *The WTO as a Legal System – Essays on International Trade Law Policy*. London: Cameron May, 2003.

Pattison, P. & D. Herron. 'The Mountains Are High and the Emperor Is Far Away: Sanctity of Contract in China'. *American business Law Journal* 40 (2003): 459–487.

Peerenboom, R. 'Globalization, Path Dependency and the Limits of Law: Administrative Law Reform and Rule of Law in the People's Republic of China'. *Berkeley Journal of International Law* 19 (2001): 61–255.

Peerenboom, R. 'Let One Hundred Flowers Bloom, One Hundred Schools Contend: Debating Rule of Law in China'. *Michigan Journal of International Law* 23 (2002): 471–519.

Peerenboom, R. 'Ruling the Country in Accordance with Law: Reflections on the Rule and Role of Law in Contemporary China'. *Cultural Dynamics* 11 (1999): 315–316.

Peerenboom, R. 'The New Foreign Investment Guidelines'. *China Law & Practice* (2002): 19–22.

Peerenboom, R. *China's Long March toward Rule of Law*. Cambridge: Cambridge University Press, 2002.

Petersmann, E.U. & M.A.Pollack (eds). *Transatlantic Economic Disputes: The EU, the US and the WTO*. Oxford: Oxford University Press, 2003.

Petersmann, E.U. *Constitutional Functions and Constitutional Problems of International Economic Law*. Beijing: Higher Education Press, 2004.

Petersmann, E.U. *Implementation of WTO Rulings: The Role of Courts and Legislatures in the US and Other Jurisdictions (EC, China)*. Draft discussion paper for the Columbia University Conference on the WTO, April 2006.

Petersmann, E.U. *The GATT/WTO Dispute Settlement System*. London: Kluwer Law International, 1997.

Qian, Y. & J. Wu. *China's Transition to a Market Economy: How Far Across the River.* Paper given at the Conference on Policy Reform in China at the Center for Research on Economic Development and Policy Reform (CEDPR), Stanford University, 18–20 November 1999.

Qian, Y. 'Symposium on China and the World Economy'. *The Economics of Transition* 9, no. 3 (2001): 675–677.

Qin, J.Y. 'Defining Nondiscrimination under the Law of the World Trade Organization'. *Boston University International Law Journal* 23 (2005): 215–297.

Qureshi, A.H. *The World Trade Organization: Implementing International Trade Norms*, Manchester: Manchester University Press, 1996.

Rawls, J. *A Theory of Justice*. Oxford: Oxford University Press, 1977.

Rodrik, D. *Has Globalization Gone Too Far?* Washington, DC: Institute for International Economics, 1997.

Roessler, F. 'Competition and Trade Policies: The Constitutional Function of International Economic Law'. *Aussenwirtschaft* 41 Jahrgang, Heft II/III, Grusch: Ruegger (1986): 467–474.

Roessler, F. *Essays on the Legal Structure, Functions & Limits of the World Trade Order*. London: Cameron May, 2000.

Rousseau, J.J. *The Social Contract.* Harmondsworth: Penguin, 1968.

Rugman, A. *The End of Globalization, Why Global Strategy Is a Myth & How to Profit from the Realities of Regional Markets*. New York: Amacom, 2001.

Sands, P. 'Treaty, Custom and the Cross-Fertilization of International Law'. *Yale Human Rights and Development Law Journal* 1 (1998): 86–106.

Schermers, H.G. & N.M. Blokker. *International Institutional Law – Unity within Diversity*. The Hague: Kluwer Law International, Martinus Nijhoff Publishers, 1995.

Shafaeddin, S.M. 'Some Implications of Accession to WTO for China's Economy'. *International Journal of Development Issues* 1, no. 2 (2002): 93–128.

Shestack, J.J. *The Rule of Law and Human Rights*. Remarks to the Institute for Korean-American Studies, Spring Symposium, 2000.

Shukla, S.P. 'From the GATT to the WTO and Beyond'. In *Governing Globalization: Issues and Institution*, edited by Deepak Nayyar. Oxford: Oxford University Press, 2002.

Smith, D. & G. Zhu. *China and the WTO: Going West*. London: Sweet and Maxwell, 2002.

Srinivasan, T.N. *Trade and Human Rights*. Discussion Paper no. 765, Economic Growth Center, Yale University, 1996, 1–40.

Stiglitz, J. *Globalization and its Discontents*. New York: Norton, 2003.

Supachai, P. & M. Clifford. *China and the WTO: Changing China, Changing World Trade*. Singapore: J. Wiley & Sons, 2002.

Sur, S. 'The State between Fragmentation and Globalization'. *European Journal of International Law* 8, no. 3 (1997): 421–434.

Trebilcock, M.J. & R. Howse. *The Regulation of International Trade*. London and New York: Routledge, 1999.

Turner, K.G., J.V. Feinerman & R.K. Guy (eds). *The Limits of the Rule of Law in China*. Seattle: University of Washington Press, 1999.

van der Geest, W. 'Bringing China into the Concert of Nations: An Analysis of Its Accession to the WTO'. *Journal of World Trade* 32 (1998): 99–114.

Voitovich, S.A. *International Economic Organizations in the International Legal Process*. The Hague: Martinus Nijhoff Publishers, 1995.

Wang, C. & X. Zhang (eds). *Introduction to Chinese Law*. Hong Kong: Sweet and Maxwell Asia, 1997.

Wang, Y. 'China's Stakes in WTO Accession: The Internal Decision-making Process'. In *China's Accession to the World Trade Organization, National and International Perspectives*, edited by H. Holbig & R. Ash. London: RoutledgeCurzon, 2002.

Wang, Z. 'The Developing Rule of Law in China'. *Harvard Asia Quarterly* 4 (2000): 1–15.

Watal, J. *Intellectual Property Rights in the WTO and Developing Countries*. The Hague: Kluwer Law International, 2001.

Weiss, F., Erik D. & P. de Waart (eds). *International Law with a Human Face*. The Hague: Kluwer Law International, 1998.

'WTO: The Real Work Begins'. *China Business Review* 27, no. 1, Special Issue, US-China Business Council, (2000): 20–41.

Yang, G. & J. Cheng 'The Process of China's Accession to the WTO'. *Journal of International Economic Law* 4, no. 2 (2001): 297–328.

Yang, Y. 'China's WTO Accession – The Economics and Politics'. *Journal of World Trade* 34 (2002): 77–94.

Young & Alwyn. 'The Razor's Edge: Distortions and Incremental Reform in the People's Republic of China'. *Quarterly Journal of Economics* 115, no. 4 (2000): 1091–1135.

Yu, J. 'Social Conflict in Rural China'. *China Security* 3, no. 2 (2007): 2–17.
Zhang, J.J. 'Arbitration, China Style: Negotiating a Changing Legal Landscape'. *International Law News* 32, no. 2, American Bar Association (2003): 1–3.
Zheng, Y. 'From Rule by Law to Rule of Law? A Realistic View of China's Legal Development'. *China Perspectives* 25 (1999): 31–43.

References in Chinese

Primary Sources

Annual Reports of the Supreme People's Court to the National People's Congress. The People's Republic of China, 2002 to 2007.
人民法院提交全国人民代表大会报告, 2002–2007.
Communiqué of the Sixth Plenum of the 16th Communist Party of China Central Committee, 11 October 2006.
關於進一步加強人民法院、人民檢察院工作的決定, 第十六届中共中央委员会公告， 2006.
Five-Year Reform Plan, 1999–2003. The Supreme People's Court, 22 October 1999.
人民法院五年改革纲要 (1999–2003).
Judgment of the *Zhang Zhaolian case*. 2006.
浙行终字第11号张国其等12人诉浙江省人民政府土地行政复议案， 2006年.
Law of the People's Republic of China on Government Procurement. 2003.
中華人民共和國政府採購法， 2003.
Law of the People's Republic of China on Chinese-Foreign Cooperative Joint-Ventures. 1988, amended in 2000.
中外合作经营企业法， 2000.
Law of the People's Republic of China on Chinese-Foreign Equity Joint-Venture. 1979, amended in 1990 and 2001.
中外合资经营企业法， 2001.
Law of the People's Republic of China on Foreign-Capital Enterprises. 1986, amended in 2000.
外资企业法, 2000.
Program for Comprehensively Implementing Government Administration in Accordance with the Law. 2004.
全面推进依法行政实施纲要， 2004.
Regulations on Open Government Information. Promulgated 17 January 2007, effective 1 May 2008.
政府信息公开条例, 2008.
Second Five-Year Reform Plan, 2004–2008. The Supreme People's Court, 26 October 2005.
人民法院第二个五年改革纲要 (2004–2008).
Speech by *Deng Xiaoping* in 1985 and 1992.
鄧小平講話，1985及1992.
Speech by *Jiang Zemin* in the 14th CPC General Assembly, 1992.
江澤民講話，中共全體大會，1992.

Speech by *Jiang Zemin* in a meeting for the 80th anniversary of the CPC, 1 July 2001.
江澤民講話，中共全體大會, 2001.
State Council's Decision on Administration in accordance with Law. 1999.
国务院关于全面推进依法行政的决定, 1999.

Books and Journal Articles

Chang, H. *The Chinese Legal System Explained*. Hong Kong: The Chinese University of Hong Kong, 1994.
張鍌，中國法律，中文大學出版社，1994年.
Gao Jiang, et al. *History of the Chinese Legal System*. Shanghai: The People's Publishing, 2000.
郭建、姚榮濤、王志強，中國法制史，上海人民出版社，2000年.
Ge, Y. *Employment Tension after WTO Accession: Prevention and Solution*. Beijing: State Council Development Research Center, 7 August 2001.
葛延风, 防范和化解加入WTO后的就业矛盾, 国务院发展研究中心, 2001年8月7日.
He, M. (ed.). *China's White Paper on Foreign Trade and Economic Cooperation Year 2002*. Beijing: Ministry of Foreign Trade and Economic Cooperation, 2002.
何茂春編，中國對外經濟貿易白皮書2002, 中國對外貿易經濟合作部, 2002年.
He, M. *China's WTO Commitments and its Adjustments in Policies and Law*. China Wuzhi Publishing, 2002.
何茂春，中國對入世承諾要點及政策法律的調整，中國物資出版社，2002年.
Huang, R. *1587 – A Year of No Significance*. New Haven: Yale University, 1981.
黄仁宇，萬歷十五年，北京，三聯書店，2002年11月第12版.
Huang, R. *Yellow River and Blue Mountains – Memoir*. Taiwan: Linking Publishing, 2001.
黄仁宇，黄河青山－黄仁宇回憶錄，台灣，聯經出版，2001年.
Jiang, B. *WTO and Judicial Review*. Beijing: The People's Court Press, 2002.
江必新，WTO與司法審查，北京，人民法院出版社，2002年.
Ji, W. *Constitutionalism– Law and Social Changes in an Era of Globalization*. Beijing: Beijing University Press, 2002.
季衛東，憲政新論 – 全球化時代的法與社會變遷，北京大學出版社，2002年.
Ji, W. *A Review of China's Changing Foreign-Related Laws: Breakthrough under WTO Pressure*. Unpublished paper.
季文华, 中国涉外法律体系的变革回顾：WTO压力下的突破.
Ju, T. *Law and Society in Traditional China*. Beijing: Zhonghua Bookstore, 2003.
瞿同祖，中國法律與中國社會，北京，中华書局，2003年.

Kim, H.I. Chen Guangping translated, *Fundamental Legal Concepts of China and the West.* Shenyang: Liaoning People's Publishing, 1989.
金勇義，中國與西方的法律觀念，瀋陽，遼寧人民出版社，1989年.
Lin, D. *Confucian Ethic and Legal Culture – A Sociological Analysis*. Taiwan: Ju Liu Publishing, 1994.
林端，儒家理論與法律文化 – 社會學觀點的探索，台灣，巨流圖書公司，1994年.
Li, G. *Bibliography of Shen Jiaben*. China, Beijing: Law Press, 2000.
李贵连，沈家本传，北京，法律出版社，2000年.
Ma, W. *WTO and the Legal System of Financial Supervision in China*. Beijing: The People's University Press, 2002.
馬衛華，WTO與中國金融監管法律制度研究，北京，中國人民大學出版社，2002年.
Wang, Y. *A Comparative Study on Legal Reforms in Asia*. Beijing: The People's University Press of China, 2002.
王雲霞，東方法律改革比較研究，北京，中國人民大學出版社，2002年.
Xia, Y. (ed.). *Towards An Age of Rights – A Perspective of the Civil Rights Development in China*. Beijing: China University of Politics and Law Press, 1999.
夏勇編，走向權利的時代 – 中國公民權利發展研究，北京，中國政法大學出版社，1999年.
Yuan, S. *WTO and Administrative Law*. Beijing: Beijing University Press, 2002.
袁曙宏、宋功德，WTO 與行政法，北京大學出版社2002年.
Zhang, Hengshan, et al. *A Study on the Rule of Law and the Ruling Model of the Communist Party of China.* Beijing: Law Press China, 2004.
張恆山等，法治與黨的執政方式研究，北京，法律出版社2004年.
Zhang, J. *A Brief Review of Chinese Legal History*. Beijing: Qun Zhong Press, 1988.
張晉藩，法史鑑略，北京，群眾出版社，1988年.

Index

GLOBAL TRADE LAW SERIES

1. Emmanuel T. Laryea, *Paperless Trade: Opportunities, Challenges and Solutions*, 2002 (ISBN 90-411-9897-0).
2. Xiang Gao, *The Fraud Rule in the Law of Letters of Credit: A Comparative Study*, 2002 (ISBN 90-411-9898-9).
3. Yuwa Wei, *Comparative Corporate Governance: A Chinese Perspective*, 2003 (ISBN 90-411-9908-X).
4. Ross P. Buckley (ed.), *The WTO and the Doha Round: The changing Face of World Trade*, 2003 (ISBN 90-411-9947-0).
5. Bradley J. Condon, Joyce C. Sadka, Tapen Sinha (eds), *Insurance Regulation in North America: Integrating American, Canadian and Mexican Markets*, 2003 (ISBN 90-411-2301-6).
6. Jan Hoogmartens, *EC Trade Law Following China's Accession to the WTO*, 2004 (ISBN 90-411-2301-6).
7. Yang Guohua, Bryan Mercurio, Li Yongjie, *WTO Dispute Settlement Understanding: A Detailed Interpretation*, 2005 (ISBN 90-411-2361-X).
8. Jan Job de Vries Robbé, Paul U. Ali, *Securitisation of Derivatives and Alternative Asset Classes, Yearbook*, 2005 (ISBN 90-411-2375-X).
9. Markus W. Gehring, Marie-Claire Cordonier Segger, *Sustainable Develop ment in World Trade Law*, 2005 (ISBN 90-411-2366-0).
10. Yann Aubin, Arnaud Idiart. *Export Control Law and Regulations Handbook: A Practical Guide to Military and Dual-Use Goods Trade Restrictions and Compliance*, 2007 (ISBN 90-411-2601-5).
11. Henry Kibet Mutai, *Compliance with International Trade Obligations: The Common Market for Eastern and Southern Africa*, 2007 (ISBN 978-90-411-2664-1).
12. Yong-Shik Lee, *Economic Development through World Trade: A Developing World Perspective*, 2007 (ISBN 978-90-411-2681-8).
13. Yanning Yu, *Circumvention and Anti-Circumvention Measures: The Impact on Anti-Dumping Practice in International Trade*, 2007 (ISBN 978-90-411-2686-3).
14. Ross Buckley, Vai Io Lo, Laurence Boulle, *Challenges to Multilateral Trade: The Impact of Bilateral, Preferential and Regional Agreements*, 2008 (ISBN 978-90-411-2711-2).
15. K.D. Raju, *World Trade Organization Agreement on Anti-dumping: A GATT/ WTO and Indian Jurisprudence*, 2008 (ISBN 978-90-411-2780-8).
16. Xiaochen Wu, *Anti-dumping Law and Practice in China*, 2008 (ISBN 978-90-411-2790-7).
17. Amin Alavi, *Legalization of Development in the WTO: Between Law and Politics*, 2008 (ISBN 978-90-411-2795-2).
18. Henrik Andersen, *EU Dumping Determinations and WTO Law*, 2009 (ISBN 978-90-411-2827-0).

19. Sherzod Shadikhodjaev, *Retaliation in the WTO Dispute Settlement System*, 2009 (ISBN 978-90-411-2811-9).
20. Yi Shin Tang, *The International Trade Policy for Technology Transfers: Legal and Economic Dilemmas on Multilateralism versus Bilateralism*, 2009 (ISBN 978-90-411-2825-6).
21. Reem Anwar Ahmed Raslan, *Antidumping: A Developing Country Perspective*, 2009 (ISBN 978-90-411-3128-7).
22. Pietro Poretti, *The Regulation of Subsidies within the General Agreement on Trade in Services of the WTO: Problems and Prospects*, 2009 (ISBN 978-90-411-3162-1).
23. Esther Lam, *China and the WTO: A Long March towards the Rule of Law*, 2009 (ISBN 978-90-411-3144-7).